# STRONG WORDS

## modern poets on modern poetry

*edited by*

**W.N. HERBERT
& MATTHEW HOLLIS**

# BLOODAXE BOOKS

Selection, introduction and notes copyright © 2000
W.N. Herbert & Matthew Hollis.

Copyright of manifestos rests with authors and other rights
holders as cited in the acknowledgements on pages 289-96,
which constitute an extension of this copyright page.

ISBN: 1 85224 515 8

First published 2000 by
Bloodaxe Books Ltd,
Highgreen,
Tarset,
Northumberland NE48 1RP.

Reprinted 2002, 2006

**www.bloodaxebooks.com**
For further information about Bloodaxe titles
please visit our website or write to
the above address for a catalogue.

Bloodaxe Books Ltd acknowledges
the financial assistance of Arts Council England.

The publication of this book forms part of an
education project supported by the National Lottery
through Arts Council England

**1005917321**

Cover printing by J. Thomson Colour Printers Ltd, Glasgow.

Printed in Great Britain by
Bell & Bain Limited, Glasgow, Scotland.

# CONTENTS

# A NOTE ON THE TEXT

Dates given for statements are those of first publication; where this differs considerably from the time of writing, both dates are given, divided by an oblique stroke (writing/publication). Editorial omissions are indicated by square-bracketed ellipsis; all other ellipses are the authors' own. The endnotes in Larkin, Maguire and Pound are the authors' own. In Bloodaxe's house style, single inverted commas denote quotation (direct or implied) while double are used for "qualification", irrespective of usage in previously published texts.

# INTRODUCTION

# Writing into the Dark

You would think that anyone wanting to know about poetry [...] would go to someone who KNEW something about it.
                    EZRA POUND, *ABC of Reading*[1]

All writers, all artists of any kind [...] have had some philosophy, some criticism of their art; and it has often been this philosophy, or this criticism, that has evoked their most startling inspiration.
                    W.B. YEATS, 'The Symbolism of Poetry'[2]

*Strong Words* is a collection of short statements by poets about poetry. It begins with Pound, Yeats and Eliot, moves through the key figures of the 20th century, and concludes with pieces commissioned from some of the best contemporary poets. We have attempted in each case to find the illuminating moment in a poet's prose, the point at which they reveal something of their own process, or something of their general philosophy toward the medium of poetry. We have sought out both the explicit manifesto and the more unguarded moment, the point at which both writer and reader discover something new – whether it sits within a canonical essay, or comes in a deliberately off-the-cuff remark. This anthology, then, tracks our search for the unmissable comment, the revelatory statement, and hopefully marks the emergence of this kind of statement as a new form, living at the heart of essay, manifesto, letter and interview.

'When you're actually engaged in the process of writing,' James Fenton once remarked, 'you must always be writing into the dark.'[3] There are two kinds of darkness that surround the modern poem – one of which is necessary, one of which is not. The first consists of the complexity that a poem generates; the second, of the layers of obscurity our culture kicks up when confronted by a poem.

The first kind of darkness is a necessary space in which a poem can do its work – with form, or with the levels of symbols and sounds that reinforce and sometimes trouble its surface meaning. No good poem ever steps fully into the light or becomes completely accessible, but remains, instead, almost infinitely approachable. This dark is nurturing: belief in it results in the uncomfortable conviction that it is not the poem's job to explain itself. Rather, the poem is there to affect the reader, to mean something to them that is immediate and powerful, however complex that encounter may prove to be.

The most problematic emotion caused by this first darkness, however, is fear: fear of the poem, and fear of what we suppose the poem to be doing. And this is what causes the second type of darkness, which is brought about by the effort to explain away ambiguity, to reduce the poem to a statement like any other. Poems can seem governed by mysterious rules, accessible only to members of an exclusive club. Poetry itself is regarded with some suspicion as a refuge for the pretentious and wilfully obscure. Yet at the same time it is acknowledged as the mode to which we all turn at moments of bereavement or joy; and it remains the standard by which we describe the admirable in other media: sport, cinema, even cookery are all occasionally graced by the apparently untroubled epithet, "poetic". Poetry, you could be forgiven for thinking, is perfectly all right until it is being written by poets.

Education attempts to redress this fear by formalising the way we read: we are encouraged to understand the 'rules' of reading (or 'codes' as Tom Leonard dubs them, p.196) over and above responding pleasurably to any given poem. And so reading a poem, often a distinctively private experience, may become in the classroom something more like a points-scoring exercise, mapping the mechanics of the act. People can leave school with a sense that reading or writing poetry is like checking off a list of techniques: an intricate hobby rather than something which could be part of their daily experience.

Print and broadcasting media add their own shade to the darkness. In their attempts to represent the public's need for clarity, the media often appear to question the very relevance of poetry to the way we live. Most simply, they do this through the modest space they devote to it; more crucially, they marginalise poetry by discussing it only on their own terms: when an award is being offered, or when a well-known poet comments on something beyond the perceived field of poetry's interests. Rarely is poetry broached on *its* terms: as a commonplace, everyday medium – 'the stuff of ordinary lives' (David Constantine, p.226) – that remakes the way we look at the world by drawing attention to the language with which we depict it. Anxious to convey realities, the media sometimes assume their methods to be transparent, and do not always sympathise with a form which celebrates the opacity of words. Ever keen to present themselves as the principal arbiters of contemporary culture, they intervene on behalf of the reader, often replacing what they judge to be the overly-complicated work of appreciation with details of the poet's biography, which tends to be a more newsworthy subject than those solitary and subjective acts, reading and writing poems. The result, again, is to encourage the reader to shy away from a difficult, fearful encounter.

In addition, poets' own attempts to explain their (to them entirely natural) processes of composition can sometimes further complicate matters. The essay, the interview, the lecture, can appear as esoteric and mandarin as the poem sometimes does. To fear of the poem, then, we must add fear of the statement about poetry. Reader, if you feel this, you're not alone: many poets share your fear. Some are reluctant to make any pronouncement about poetry for this reason. We know, we asked them. Yet many poets *are* prepared to risk a degree of compromise to burn off some of the unnecessary obscurities surrounding their craft. In these statements they share our intention as editors and hopefully yours as readers: to pursue what is truly accessible. This anthology is their tinder, their book of matches – we believe it can provide the means to shed some light on the act of writing.

Shouldn't poetry be able to stand on its own? Obviously it can, and has done so for thousands of years, from Homer to Heaney, from Sappho to Stevenson, reaching people with little knowledge of the poet or how the poem came to be formed. But this is a time in which we have seen poets move on to the television and popular radio, and into the pages of the glossies; where residencies have sprung up on trains, in prisons, supermarkets and zoos; where sales, sponsorship, and prize-money are soaring; where poets are becoming personalised and packaged, and poetry more engaged with and more diverse than ever before. This is a time of tags and accolades: the 'new Rock 'n' Roll', National Poetry Day, *The Nation's Favourite*, *Poems on the Underground*. It is a period which has seen four Nobel Prizes and four Whitbreads awarded to poetry; poetry bestsellers like *Birthday Letters* and *Beowulf*; a new Poet Laureate together with a heightened social profile for the Laureateship. With all this in mind, this seems a good moment to look back and offer another angle – not biography or criticism, but the poets' own comments, their statement, their poetics.

When poets publish their poems, they abandon them to their own devices: the poem becomes another object in the world to be experienced or overlooked. The creative act is essentially complete. But the statement, we believe, reconnects the writer with that act. Eric Satie's famous composition *Trois Gymnopédies* has been likened to three walks around a statue, in which the central object does not change, but the perspective does. *Strong Words*, we hope, offers just such a view: that of the poet walking around his or her own creation. Not the only perspective perhaps, but it is an insightful one.

A word about the ordering of this book. A good poem will always transcend and transgress whatever boundaries are set for it, whether they are those of a school of writing or of a school of criticism. Equally, a good poetics will address itself to these moments of transgression first, and to the critical idiom of the day second. So rather than reinforce the usual boundaries – Modernism, the Movement, the Beats, Black Mountain, Confessional, etc – *Strong Words* attempts to chart a flow of transgression from poet to poet. We take this flow to be as important as the groupings it moves between. In place of a chronology by birth or publication dates, in place of a chart of movements, our principle of organisation has been: school's out. We hope you will go with the flow.

This approach is not intended to dismiss but to augment conventional ordering and academic protocol. Our universities have shown us how writing any poem occurs within an infectious social and cultural context. They have offered invaluable perspectives on the limitations of biography, the relevance of literary models, and the primacy of theories of language, gender and race. But just as they describe ideologies, they simultaneously impose their own. The poem, as a result, becomes less necessary, more an adjunct to theory's exploration of the limitless dimensions of text. Meanwhile the historic death of the author has seen the poet become little more than the ghost at the academic feast. Once again, we might be forgiven for believing that only someone else, this time the academic, is really qualified to comment on the poem's procedures.

Yet the poetic statement, as presented here, demonstrates that poets have always been intensely conscious of the self-reflexive nature of language *and* its cultural role. Their commentaries offer the invaluable insights of those who are accustomed to working at the typeface. They are, after all, Pound's 'experts'; well versed in the anarchic energies of poetic language, well used to negotiating the tides of influence. For if the academy, in Harold Bloom's phrase, views influence as an 'anxiety' to be overcome, poets conversely regard it as an enabling and pleasurable force.[4] It is the means by which we communicate with each other, with our contemporaries, our immediate predecessors, and our poetic ancestors.

When anthologies profess an 'identity' there is usually trouble. *The Penguin Book of Contemporary British Poetry* (1982) unified Irish and Scots writers under the banner of 'British' – and Heaney, for one, protested.[5] A decade later, *The New Poetry* (1993) approached this same problem by emphasising the plurality of 'British poetry'.

But this pluralism, the editors argued, actually marked 'a new cohesiveness': a poetry unified in its disunity. By naming what they had suggested was unnameable – 'British poetry' – they distended the term almost to the point of indeterminacy.[6] We want to suggest instead that there is, in Creeley's phrase, 'no country' (p.101): not a disparate state that is somehow "British" poetry (which includes Irish, Afro-Caribbean and Antipodean writing) but something more open-ended still. Not British but here. Sometimes not even here, but read here: a living influence. So that one of the things that *Strong Words* records is the remarkable impact of American poets and their particular engagement with the manifesto. Another is the way the work of, say, Les Murray or Derek Walcott has helped to reshape our notions of centrality and the margins. A third is the impression of Europe with its vigorous tradition of manifesto-making – a presence you may feel in Elaine Feinstein or David Constantine (although for reasons of space we have been unable to represent the continent's original writings).[7] This transgressive flow of influence means that today we are increasingly able to read across borders.

One of the more contentious borders crossed in this book is between those statements already written (by poets whose historic role would appear to be secure), and those commissioned from living writers. It might be assumed that these two parts more readily demand two separate books, each with its own specialist audience. But where the canonical meets the contemporary is where we live. After all, reader, this juxtaposition of the great and the less well-known, this collision of the familiar and the new, constitutes your present moment. In these most relative of times perhaps we should admit, given the increasing remoteness in language and attitude of those great poets of the past century, and given our contrasting relative fluency in the idioms of the present, that the past can only be as revelatory as the contemporary, and not more so.

Clearly, it is also the case that, at the time of composition, the poets of the first half of *Strong Words* were often the less well-known figures of their day. And similarly, there are poets writing now who will be seen as just as important in fifty or a hundred years as Pounds, Yeats and Eliot are now. We just hope we've got the right ones. Instead of exclusively focusing on the established greats, then, we have attempted to shift the emphasis, so that where the two halves of our book meet it is possible to hear dialogue rather than instruction, conversation rather than perceived wisdom. There are some surprising exchanges between the pages of this book. The words may not always be polite but they are strong.

The poets may not all be grand but we believe them to be important.

Those contemporary poets we invited had all published two or more collections. There are undoubtedly poets writing now who, although they didn't meet this criterion, will contribute to the next generation of statements, further illuminating what it means to write (and read) a poem. Equally, there were many figures we should have invited and failed to. Nonetheless, we believe that the pieces gathered here are indispensable in clearing that fog of fear and misinterpretation, of raising a lantern to the dark. In this sense, finally, *Strong Words* is part of a continuing process: that the statement about poetry has only fully done its work when it returns the reader to the poem.

## NOTES

1. Ezra Pound, *ABC of Reading* (New York: New Directions, 1960), 30.

2. W.B. Yeats, 'The Symbolism of Poetry', *Essays and Introductions* (New York: Macmillan, 1961), 154.

3. 'An Interview with James Fenton', *Poetry Review*, 72/2, June 1982, 21.

4. Harold Bloom, *The Anxiety of Influence: A Theory of Poetry* (New York: Oxford University Press, 1973).

5. Blake Morrison & Andrew Motion (eds.), *The Penguin Book of Contemporary British Poetry* (Harmondsworth: Penguin, 1982), 13: Seamus Heaney, 'very deliberately put first' in the anthology, replied in *An Open Letter* (Derry: Field Day Theatre Company, 1983), 7: 'This "British" word / Sticks deep in native and *colon* / Like Arthur's sword'.

6. Michael Hulse, David Kennedy & David Morley (eds.), *The New Poetry* (Newcastle upon Tyne: Bloodaxe, 1993), 16.

7. For a selection of statements by Russian poets see Carl R. Proffer (ed.), *Modern Russian Poets on Poetry* (Ann Arbor: Ardis, 1976).

# EZRA POUND

Ezra Pound was born in 1885, in Hailey, Idaho. He emigrated to London in 1909 with a project to reinvent poetry from the 'doughy mess' of Romanticism; famously, to 'make it new'. More than anyone, he defined the spirit of Modernism, demanding of English poetry that it became 'news that STAYS news.' A propagandist of many forms, Pound was the founding father of Imagism and, with Wyndham Lewis, the chief figure of the Vorticist movement (an English relation of Italian Futurism). Infamously, Pound spent the Second World War in Rome, broadcasting pro-fascist addresses, until his arrest and deportation back to the United States in 1945. Pleading insanity, he was declared unfit to stand trial for treason and committed to an asylum for 12 years. In 1958 he was released and moved back to Italy, where he died in 1972. The first draft of his *Cantos* appeared in 1925, the last in 1969, to be collected the following year.

It was over tea in Kensington, in 1912, that Pound informed H.D. (Hilda Doolittle) and Richard Aldington that they were Imagistes. And this, to him, entailed three things: direct treatment, an economy of words, and the sequence of the musical phrase (free verse). Pound sought a poetic form to reflect the 'absolute rhythm' of an individual's life, not merely the copy-cat iambics of tradition. And he sought a language 'made out of concrete things', a granite-hard tongue that was 'austere, direct, free from emotional slither'. First published in 1913, and expanded in 1918, 'A Retrospect' announces the birth of Modernism in poetry, and signposts the century to come.

# *from* A Retrospect [1]
## (1918)

There has been so much scribbling about a new fashion in poetry, that I may perhaps be pardoned this brief recapitulation and retrospect.

In the spring or early summer of 1912, 'H.D.', Richard Aldington and myself decided that we were agreed upon the three principles following:

1. Direct treatment of the "thing" whether subjective or objective.

2. To use absolutely no word that does not contribute to the presentation.

3. As regarding rhythm: to compose in the sequence of the musical phrase, not in sequence of a metronome.

Upon many points of taste and of predilection we differed, but agreeing upon these three positions we thought we had as much right to a group name, at least as much right, as a number of French "schools" proclaimed by Mr Flint in the August number of Harold Monro's magazine for 1911.

This school has since been "joined" or "followed" by numerous people who, whatever their merits, do not show any signs of agreeing with the second specification. Indeed *vers libre* has become as prolix and as verbose as any of the flaccid varieties that preceded it. It has brought faults of its own. The actual language and phrasing is often as bad as that of our elders without even the excuse that the words are shovelled in to fill a metric pattern or to complete the noise of a rhyme-sound. Whether or no the phrases followed by the followers are musical must be left to the reader's decision. At times I can find a marked metre in "vers libres", as stale and hackneyed as any pseudo-Swinburnian, at times the writers seem to follow no musical structure whatever. But it is, on the whole, good that the field should be ploughed. Perhaps a few good poems have come from the new method, and if so it is justified.

Criticism is not a circumscription or a set of prohibitions. It provides fixed points of departure. It may startle a dull reader into alertness. That little of it which is good is mostly in stray phrases; or if it be an older artist helping a younger it is in great measure but rules of thumb, cautions gained by experience.

I set together a few phrases on practical working about the time the first remarks on imagisme were published. The first use of the word 'Imagiste' was in my note to T.E. Hulme's five poems, printed at the end of my 'Ripostes' in the autumn of 1912. I reprint my cautions from *Poetry* for March, 1913.

### A FEW DON'TS

An 'Image' is that which presents an intellectual and emotional complex in an instant of time. I use the term 'complex' rather in the technical sense employed by the newer psychologists, such as Hart, though we might not agree absolutely in our application.

It is the presentation of such a 'complex' instantaneously which gives that sense of sudden liberation; that sense of freedom from time limits and space limits; that sense of sudden growth, which we experience in the presence of the greatest works of art.

It is better to present one Image in a lifetime than to produce voluminous works.

All this, however, some may consider open to debate. The immediate necessity is to tabulate A LIST OF DON'TS for those beginning to write verses. I can not put all of them into Mosaic negative.

To begin with, consider the three propositions (demanding direct treatment, economy of words, and the sequence of the musical phrase), not as dogma – never consider anything as dogma – but as the result of long contemplation, which, even if it is some one else's contemplation, may be worth consideration.

Pay no attention to the criticism of men who have never themselves written a notable work. Consider the discrepancies between the actual writing of the Greek poets and dramatists, and the theories of the Graeco-Roman grammarians, concocted to explain their metres.

## LANGUAGE

Use no superfluous word, no adjective which does not reveal something.

Don't use such an expression as 'dim lands *of peace*'. It dulls the image. It mixes an abstraction with the concrete. It comes from the writer's not realising that the natural object is always the *adequate* symbol.

Go in fear of abstractions. Do not retell in mediocre verse what has already been done in good prose. Don't think any intelligent person is going to be deceived when you try to shirk all the difficulties of the unspeakably difficult art of good prose by chopping your composition into line lengths.

What the expert is tired of today the public will be tired of tomorrow.

Don't imagine that the art of poetry is any simpler than the art of music, or that you can please the expert before you have spent at least as much effort on the art of verse as the average piano teacher spends on the art of music.

Be influenced by as many great artists as you can, but have the decency either to acknowledge the debt outright, or to try to conceal it.

Don't allow "influence" to mean merely that you mop up the particular decorative vocabulary of some one or two poets whom you happen to admire. A Turkish war correspondent was recently caught red-handed babbling in his despatches of 'dove-grey' hills, or else it was 'pearl-pale', I cannot remember.

Use either no ornament or good ornament.

## RHYTHM AND RHYME

Let the candidate fill his mind with the finest cadences he can discover, preferably in a foreign language,[2] so that the meaning of the words may be less likely to divert his attention from the movement; e.g. Saxon charms, Hebridean Folk Songs, the verse of

Dante, and the lyrics of Shakespeare – if he can dissociate the vocabulary from the cadence. Let him dissect the lyrics of Goethe coldly into their component sound values, syllables long and short, stressed and unstressed, into vowels and consonants.

It is not necessary that a poem should rely on its music, but if it does rely on its music that music must be such as will delight the expert.

Let the neophyte know assonance and alliteration, rhyme immediate and delayed, simple and polyphonic, as a musician would expect to know harmony and counterpoint and all the minutiae of his craft. No time is too great to give to these matters or to any one of them, even if the artist seldom have need of them.

Don't imagine that a thing will "go" in verse just because it's too dull to go in prose.

Don't be "viewy" – leave that to the writers of pretty little philosophic essays. Don't be descriptive; remember that the painter can describe a landscape much better than you can, and that he has to know a deal more about it.

When Shakespeare talks of the 'Dawn in russet mantle clad' he presents something which the painter does not present. There is in this line of his nothing that one can call description; he presents.

Consider the way of the scientists rather than the way of an advertising agent for a new soap.

The scientist does not expect to be acclaimed as a great scientist until he has *discovered* something. He begins by learning what has been discovered already. He goes from that point onward. He does not bank on being a charming fellow personally. He does not expect his friends to applaud the results of his freshman class work. Freshmen in poetry are unfortunately not confined to a definite and recognisable class room. They are 'all over the shop'. Is it any wonder 'the public is indifferent to poetry?'

Don't chop your stuff into separate *iambs*. Don't make each line stop dead at the end, and then begin every next line with a heave. Let the beginning of the next line catch the rise of the rhythm wave, unless you want a definite longish pause.

In short, behave as a musician, a good musician, when dealing with that phase of your art which has exact parallels in music. The same laws govern, and you are bound by no others.

Naturally, your rhythmic structure should not destroy the shape of your words, or their natural sound, or their meaning. It is improbable that, at the start, you will be able to get a rhythm-structure strong enough to affect them very much, though you may fall a victim to all sorts of false stopping due to line ends and cæsurae.

The Musician can rely on pitch and the volume of the orchestra. You can not. The term harmony is misapplied in poetry; it refers to simultaneous sounds of different pitch. There is, however, in the best verse a sort of residue of sound which remains in the ear of the hearer and acts more or less as an organ-base.

A rhyme must have in it some slight element of surprise if it is to give pleasure; it need not be bizarre or curious, but it must be well used if used at all.

*Vide* further Vildrac and Duhamel's notes on rhyme in '*Technique Poétique*'.

That part of your poetry which strikes upon the imaginative *eye* of the reader will lose nothing by translation into a foreign tongue; that which appeals to the ear can reach only those who take it in the original.

Consider the definiteness of Dante's presentation, as compared with Milton's rhetoric. Read as much of Wordsworth as does not seem too unutterably dull.[3]

If you want the gist of the matter go to Sappho, Catullus, Villon, Heine when he is in the vein, Gautier when he is not too frigid; or, if you have not the tongues, seek out the leisurely Chaucer. Good prose will to you no harm, and there is good discipline to be had by trying to write it.

Translation is likewise good training, if you find that your original matter "wobbles" when you try to rewrite it. The meaning of the poem to be translated can not "wobble".

If you are using a symmetrical form, don't put in what you want to say and then fill up the remaining vacuums with slush.

Don't mess up the perception of one sense by trying to define it in terms of another. This is usually only the result of being too lazy to find the exact word. To this clause there are possibly exceptions.

The first three simple prescriptions will throw out nine-tenths of all the bad poetry now accepted as standard and classic; and will prevent you from many a crime of production.

'...*Mais d'abord il faut être un poète*,' as MM. Duhamel and Vildrac have said at the end of their little book, '*Notes sur la Technique Poétique*'.

Since March 1913, Ford Madox Hueffer has pointed out that Wordsworth was so intent on the ordinary or plain word that he never thought of hunting for *le mot juste*.

John Butler Yeats has handled or man-handled Wordsworth and the Victorians, and his criticism, contained in letters to his son, is now printed and available.

I do not like writing *about* art, my first, at least I think it was my first essay on the subject, was a protest against it. [...]

## CREDO

*Rhythm.* – I believe in an "absolute rhythm", a rhythm, that is, in poetry which corresponds exactly to the emotion or shade of emotion to be expressed. A man's rhythm must be interpretative, it will be, therefore, in the end, his own, uncounterfeiting, uncounterfeitable.

*Symbols.* – I believe that the proper and perfect symbol is the natural object, that if a man use "symbols" he must so use them that their symbolic function does not obtrude; so that a sense, and the poetic quality of the passage, is not lost to those who do not understand the symbol as such, to whom, for instance, a hawk is a hawk.

*Technique.* – I believe in technique as the test of a man's sincerity; in law when it is ascertainable; in the trampling down of every convention that impedes or obscures the determination of the law, or the precise rendering of the impulse.

*Form.* – I think there is a "fluid" as well as a "solid" content, that some poems may have form as a tree has form, some as water poured into a vase. That most symmetrical forms have certain uses. That a vast number of subjects cannot be precisely, and therefore not properly rendered in symmetrical forms.

'Thinking that alone worthy wherein the whole art is employed.'[4] I think the artist should master all known forms and systems of metric, and I have with some persistence set about doing this, searching particularly into those periods wherein the systems came to birth or attained their maturity. It has been complained, with some justice, that I dump my note-books on the public. I think that only after a long struggle will poetry attain such a degree of development, or, if you will, modernity, that it will vitally concern people who are accustomed, in prose, to Henry James and Anatole France, in music to Debussy. I am constantly contending that it took two centuries of Provence and one of Tuscany to develop the media of Dante's masterwork, that it took the latinists of the Renaissance, and the Pleiade, and his own age of painted speech to prepare Shakespeare his tools. It is tremendously important that great poetry be written, it makes no jot of difference who writes it. The experimental demonstrations of one man may save the time of many – hence my furore over Arnaut Daniel – if a man's experiments try out one new rime, or dispense conclusively with one iota of currently accepted nonsense, he is merely playing fair with his colleagues when he chalks up his result.

No man ever writes very much poetry that "matters". In bulk, that is, no one produces much that is final, and when a man is not doing this highest thing, this saying the thing once for all and perfectly; when he is not matching 'Immortal Aphrodite, on your patterned throne' or 'Hist – said Kate the Queen', he had much better be making the sorts of experiment which may be of use to him in his later work, or to his successors.

'The lyf so short, the craft so long to lerne.' It is a foolish thing for a man to begin his work on a too narrow foundation, it is a disgraceful thing for a man's work not to show steady growth and increasing fineness from first to last.

As for "adaptations"; one finds that all the old masters of painting recommend to their pupils that they begin by copying masterwork, and proceed to their own composition.

As for 'Every man his own poet', the more every man knows about poetry the better. I believe in every one writing poetry who wants to; most do. I believe in every man knowing enough of music to play 'God bless our home' on the harmonium, but I do not believe in every man giving concerts and printing his sin.

The mastery of any art is the work of a lifetime. I should not discriminate between the "amateur" and the "professional". Or rather I should discriminate quite often in favour of the amateur, but I should discriminate between the amateur and the expert. It is certain that the present chaos will endure until the Art of poetry has been preached down the amateur gullet, until there is such a general understanding of the fact that poetry is an art and not a pastime; such a knowledge of technique; of technique of surface and technique of content, that the amateurs will cease to try to drown out the masters.

If a certain thing was said once for all in Atlantis or Arcadia, in 450 Before Christ or in 1290 after, it is not for us moderns to go saying it over, or to go obscuring the memory of the dead by saying the same thing with less skill and less conviction.

My pawing over the ancients and semi-ancients has been one struggle to find out what has been done, once for all, better than it can ever be done again, and to find out what remains for us to do, and plenty does remain, for if we still feel the same emotions as those which launched the thousand ships, it is quite certain that we come on these feelings differently, through different nuances, by different intellectual gradations. Each age has its own abounding gifts yet only some ages transmute them into matter of duration. No good poetry is ever written in a manner 20 years old, for to write in such a manner shows conclusively that the writer thinks from books, convention and *cliché*, and not from life, yet a man feeling the divorce of life and his art may naturally try to resurrect a forgotten mode if he finds in that mode some leaven, or if he think he sees in it some element lacking in contemporary art which might unite that art again to its sustenance, life.

In the art of Daniel and Cavalcanti, I have seen that precision which I miss in the Victorians, that explicit rendering, be it of external nature, or of emotion. Their testimony is of the eyewitness, their symptoms are first hand.

As for the 19th century, with all respect to its achievements, I think we shall look back upon it as a rather blurry, messy sort of a period, a rather sentimentalistic, mannerish sort of a period. I say this without any self-righteousness, with no self-satisfaction.

As for there being a "movement" or my being of it, the conception of poetry as a "pure art" in the sense in which I use the term, revived with Swinburne. From the puritanical revolt to Swinburne, poetry had been merely the vehicle – yes, definitely, Arthur Symon's scruples and feelings about the word not withholding – the ox-cart and post-chaise for transmitting thoughts poetic or otherwise. And perhaps the "great Victorians", though it is doubtful, and assuredly the "nineties" continued the development of the art, confining their improvements, however, chiefly to sound and to refinements of manner.

Mr Yeats has once and for all stripped English poetry of its perdamnable rhetoric. He has boiled away all that is not poetic – and a good deal that is. He has become a classic in his own lifetime and *nel mezzo del cammin*. He has made our poetic idiom a thing pliable, a speech without inversions.

Robert Bridges, Maurice Hewlett and Frederic Manning are[5] in their different ways seriously concerned with overhauling the metric, in testing the language and its adaptability to certain modes. Ford Hueffer is making some sort of experiments in modernity. The Provost of Oriel continues his translation of the *Divina Commedia*.

As to 20th century poetry, and the poetry which I expect to see written during the next decade or so, it will, I think, move against poppycock, it will be harder and saner, it will be what Mr Hewlett calls 'nearer the bone'. It will be as much like granite as it can be, its force will lie in its truth, its interpretative power (of course, poetic force does always rest there); I mean it will not try to seem forcible by rhetorical din, and luxurious riot. We will have fewer painted adjectives impeding the shock and stroke of it. At least for myself, I want it so, austere, direct, free from emotional slither.

What is there now, in 1917, to be added? [...]

## ONLY EMOTION ENDURES

'Only emotion endures.' Surely it is better for me to name over
the few beautiful poems that still ring in my head than for me to
search my flat for back numbers of periodicals and rearrange all
that I have said about friendly and hostile writers.

The first 12 lines of Padraic Colum's 'Drover'; his 'O Woman
shapely as a swan, on your account I shall not die'; Joyce's 'I hear
an army'; the lines of Yeats that ring in my head and in the heads
of all young men of my time who care for poetry: Braseal and the
Fisherman, 'The fire that stirs about her when she stirs'; the later
lines of 'The Scholars', the faces of the Magi; William Carlos
Williams's 'Postlude', Aldington's version of 'Atthis', and 'H.D.'s'
waves like pine tops, and her verse in 'Des Imagistes', the first anth-
ology; Hueffer's 'How red your lips are' in his translation from
Von der Vogelweide, his 'Three Ten', the general effect of his 'On
Heaven'; his sense of the prose values or prose qualities in poetry;
his ability to write poems that half-chant and are spoiled by a
musician's additions; beyond these a poem by Alice Corbin, 'One
City Only', and another ending 'But sliding water over a stone'.
These things have worn smooth in my head and I am not through
with them, nor with Aldington's 'In Via Sestina' nor his other
poems in 'Des Imagistes', though people have told me their flaws.
It may be that their content is too much embedded in me for me
to look back at the words.

I am almost a different person when I come to take up the argu-
ment for Eliot's poems.

### NOTES

1. A group of early essays and notes which appeared under this title in
*Pavannes and Divisions* (1918). 'A Few Dont's' was first printed in *Poetry*, I,
6 (March, 1913).

2. This is for rhythm, his vocabulary must of course be found in his native
tongue.

3. Vide infra.

4. Dante, *De Vulgari Eloquentia*.

5. Dec. 1911.

**Editorial note:** On page 23, 'Immortal Aphrodite, on your patterned throne'
is Josephine Balmer's translation of a famous line by Sappho quoted only in
Greek by Pound in his original text.

# W.B. YEATS

William Butler Yeats (1865-1939) was born in Dublin but spent his early life in London, holidaying in Co. Sligo. He was the son of the painter John Butler Yeats. After moving back to Dublin, his earliest writings were much influenced by and influential within the Irish Revival of the 1880s onward. Irish myth and his own mythologised love for Maud Gonne dominate his work up to *The Green Helmet* (1910). The lush symbolism gave way to a starker politicised voice in volumes from *Responsibilities* (1914) onward, partly influenced by events, partly by Ezra Pound, and partly by his ambitious drive to be Ireland's national poet. His activities, both in the Senate of the new state, and in the Abbey Theatre, helped give his poetry a considerable public resonance. The late volumes, *The Tower* (1928) and *The Winding Stair* (1933), achieve a magisterial combination of symbolic resonance and lyric directness which has proved enormously influential in both Irish and British poetry. The *Last Poems* (1939), if anything, heighten and seal his reputation as one of the last century's foremost poets.

His critical writings and essays are illuminating more in respect of his own processes than of those of his contemporaries. Nonetheless many of his insights have become axiomatic, particularly the idea that the poet projects aspects of his concerns through adopting 'masks', and his adaptation of Romantic integrity: poetry arises from an argument with the self, suggesting public engagement of any kind cannot be willed. 'A General Introduction for my Work' was written in 1937.

# *from* A General Introduction for my Work
## (1937/1961)

### I. THE FIRST PRINCIPLE

A poet writes always of his personal life, in his finest work out of its tragedy, whatever it be, remorse, lost love, or mere loneliness; he never speaks directly as to someone at the breakfast table, there is always a phantasmagoria. Dante and Milton had mythologies, Shakespeare the characters of English history or of traditional romance; even when the poet seems most himself, when he is Raleigh and gives potentates the lie, or Shelley 'a nerve o'er which do creep the else unfelt oppressions of this earth', or Byron when 'the soul wears out the breast' as 'the sword outwears its sheath', he is never the bundle of accident and incoherence that sits down to breakfast; he has been reborn as an idea, something intended, complete. A novelist might describe his accidence, his incoherence, he must not; he is more type than man, more passion than type.

He is Lear, Romeo, Oedipus, Tiresias; he has stepped out of a
play, and even the woman he loves is Rosalind, Cleopatra, never
The Dark Lady. He is part of his own phantasmagoria and we
adore him because nature has grown intelligible, and by so doing
a part of our creative power. 'When mind is lost in the light of
the Self,' says the Prashna Upanishad, 'it dreams no more; still in
the body it is lost in happiness.' 'A wise man seek in Self,' says
the Chandogya Upanishad, 'those that are alive and those that are
dead and gets what the world cannot give.' The world knows
nothing because it has made nothing, we know everything because
we have made everything.

## II. SUBJECT MATTER

It was through the old Fenian leader John O'Leary I found my theme.
His long imprisonment, his longer banishment, his magnificent
head, his scholarship, his pride, his integrity, all that aristocratic
dream nourished amid little shops and little farms, had drawn around
him a group of young men; I was but 18 or 19 and had already,
under the influence of *The Faerie Queene* and *The Sad Shepherd*,
written a pastoral play, and under that of Shelley's *Prometheus
Unbound* two plays, one staged somewhere in the Caucasus, the
other in a crater of the moon; and I knew myself to be vague and
incoherent. He gave me the poems of Thomas Davis, said they were
not good poetry but had changed his life when a young man, spoke
of other poets associated with Davis and *The Nation* newspaper,
probably lent me their books. I saw even more clearly than O'Leary
that they were not good poetry. I read nothing but romantic litera-
ture; hated that dry 18th century rhetoric; but they had one quality
I admired and admire: they were not separated individual men;
they spoke or tried to speak out of a people to a people; behind
them stretched the generations. I knew, though but now and then
as young men know things, that I must turn from that modern
literature Jonathan Swift compared to the web a spider draws out
of its bowels; I hated and still hate with an ever growing hatred the
literature of the point of view. I wanted, if my ignorance permitted,
to get back to Homer, to those that fed at his table. I wanted to
cry as all men cried, to laugh as all men laughed, and the Young
Ireland poets when not writing mere politics had the same want,
but they did not know that the common and its befitting language
is the research of a lifetime and when found may lack popular
recognition. [...]

### III. STYLE AND ATTITUDE

Style is almost unconscious. I know what I have tried to do, little what I have done. Contemporary lyric poems, even those that moved me – *The Stream's Secret, Dolores* – seemed too long, but an Irish preference for a swift current might be mere indolence, yet Burns may have felt the same when he read Thomson and Cowper. The English mind is meditative, rich, deliberate; it may remember the Thames valley. I planned to write short lyrics or poetic drama where every speech would be short and concentrated, knit by dramatic tension, and I did so with more confidence because young English poets were at that time writing out of emotion at the moment of crisis, though their old slow-moving meditation returned almost at once. Then, and in this English poetry has followed my lead, I tried to make the language of poetry coincide with that of passionate, normal speech. I wanted to write in whatever language comes most naturally when we soliloquise, as I do all day long, upon the events of our own lives or of any life where we can see ourselves for the moment. I sometimes compare myself with the mad old slum women I hear denouncing and remembering; 'How dare you,' I heard one say of some imaginary suitor, 'and you without health or a home!' If I spoke my thoughts aloud they might be as angry and as wild. It was a long time before I had made a language to my liking; I began to make it when I discovered some 20 years ago that I must seek, not as Wordsworth thought, words in common use, but a powerful and passionate syntax, and a complete coincidence between period and stanza. Because I need a passionate syntax for passionate subject-matter I compel myself to accept those passionate metres that have developed with the language. Ezra Pound, Turner, Lawrence wrote admirable free verse, I could not. I would lose myself, become joyless like those mad old women. The translators of the Bible, Sir Thomas Browne, certain translators from the Greek when translators still bothered about rhythm, created a form midway between prose and verse that seems natural to impersonal meditation; but all that is personal soon rots; it must be packed in ice or salt. Once when I was in delirium from pneumonia I dictated a letter to George Moore telling him to eat salt because it was a symbol of eternity; the delirium passed, I had no memory of that letter, but I must have meant what I now mean. If I wrote of personal love or sorrow in free verse, or in any rhythm that left it unchanged, amid all its accidence, I would be full of self-contempt because of my egotism and indiscretion, and foresee the boredom of my reader. I must choose a traditional stanza, even what I alter

must seem traditional. I commit my emotion to shepherds, herds-
men, camel-drivers, learned men, Milton's or Shelley's Platonist,
that tower Palmer drew. Talk to me of originality and I will turn
on you with rage. I am a crowd, I am a lonely man, I am nothing.
Ancient salt is best packing. The heroes of Shakespeare convey to
us through their looks, or through the metaphorical patterns of
their speech, the sudden enlargement of their vision, their ecstasy
at the approach of death: 'She should have died hereafter,' 'Of
many thousand kisses, the poor last,' 'Absent thee from felicity
awhile.' They have become God or Mother Goddess, the pelican,
'My baby at my breast,' but all must be cold; no actress has ever
sobbed when she played Cleopatra, even the shallow brain of a
producer has never thought of such a thing. The supernatural is
present, cold winds blow across our hands, upon our faces, the
thermometer falls, and because of that cold we are hated by jour-
nalists and groundlings. There may be in this or that detail painful
tragedy, but in the whole work none. I have heard Lady Gregory
say, rejecting some play in the modern manner sent to the Abbey
Theatre, 'Tragedy must be a joy to the man who dies.' Nor is it any
different with lyrics, songs, narrative poems; neither scholars nor
the populace have sung or read anything generation after gener-
ation because of its pain. The maid of honour whose tragedy they
sing must be lifted out of history with timeless pattern, she is one
of the four Maries, the rhythm is old and familiar, imagination
must dance, must be carried beyond feeling into the aboriginal
ice. Is ice the correct word? I once boasted, copying the phrase
from a letter of my father's, that I would write a poem 'cold and
passionate as the dawn.'

When I wrote in blank verse I was dissatisfied; my vaguely medi-
eval *Countess Cathleen* fitted the measure, but our Heroic Age went
better, or so I fancied, in the ballad metre of *The Green Helmet*.
There was something in what I felt about Deirdre, about Cuchulain,
that rejected that Renaissance and its characteristic metres, and
this was a principal reason why I created in dance plays the form
that varies blank verse with lyric metres. When I speak blank verse
and analyse my feelings, I stand at a moment of history when
instinct, its traditional songs and dances, its general agreement, is
of the past. I have been cast up out of the whale's belly though I
still remember the sound and sway that came from beyond its
ribs, and, like the Queen in Paul Fort's ballad, I smell of the fish
of the sea. The contrapuntal structure of the verse, to employ a
term adopted by Robert Bridges, combines the past and present.
If I repeat the first lines of *Paradise Lost* so as to emphasise its

five feet I am among the folk singers – 'Of mán's first dísobédience
ánd the frúit,' but speak it as I should I cross it with another
emphasis, that of passionate prose – 'Of mán's first disobédience
and the frúit,' or 'Of mán's first dísobedience and the frúit'; the
folk song is still there, but a ghastly voice, an unvariable possibility,
an unconscious norm. What moves me and my hearer is a vivid
speech that has no laws except that it must not exorcise the ghostly
voice. I am awake and asleep, at my moment of revelation, self-
possessed in self-surrender; there is no rhyme, no echo of the beaten
drum, the dancing foot, that would overset my balance. When I
was a boy I wrote a poem upon dancing that had one good line:
'They snatch with their hands at the sleep of the skies.' If I sat
down and thought for a year I would discover that but for certain
syllabic limitations, a rejection or acceptance of certain elisions, I
must wake or sleep.

The Countess Cathleen could speak a blank verse which I had
loosened, almost put out of joint, for her need, because I thought
of her as medieval and thereby connected her with the general
European movement. For Deirdre and Cuchulain and all the other
figures of Irish legend are still in the whale's belly. [...]

# T.S. ELIOT

Thomas Stearns Eliot, born in St Louis in 1888, became part of Pound's Modernist shock troops on moving to London in 1914. Championed by his fellow expat, he published a series of increasingly dislocating poems based on his fastidious dissection of Browning and Laforgue ('Prufrock', 1917) and the disturbed nature of his private life, culminating in *The Waste Land* (1922), written after his wife was placed in an asylum and he had suffered a breakdown. A collision of high culture tags and fragments with frenetic jazz rhythms and Eliot's arid preacherly tones, cut and mixed by Pound to flirt with incoherence, *The Waste Land* became the seminal Modernist text. Eliot promptly began backing away from it into the hoped-for certainties of Anglicism, Royalism, and the editorship of Faber and *The Criterion*. *Four Quartets* (1943) marks his final resting place as a poet: austere, abstracted, yet still animated by a neurotic, controlling edge that marks him as the defining voice of the first part of the 20th century.

A massively influential essayist, Eliot's critical writings are infused with the themes of dissociation from contemporary life and anxious engagement with past literature that animate his poetry. Crucial ideas such as the 'objective correlative' and the 'dissociation of sensibility', like many Modernist precepts, are vital aesthetic concepts rather than workable critical models.

# Tradition and the Individual Talent
## (1919)

### I

In English writing we seldom speak of tradition, though we occasionally apply its name in deploring its absence. We cannot refer to 'the tradition' or to 'a tradition'; at most, we employ the adjective in saying that the poetry of So-and-so is 'traditional' or even 'too traditional'. Seldom, perhaps, does the word appear except in a phrase of censure. If otherwise, it is vaguely approbative, with the implication, as to the work approved, of some pleasing archaeological reconstruction. You can hardly make the word agreeable to English ears without this comfortable reference to the reassuring science of archaeology.

Certainly the word is not likely to appear in our appreciations of living or dead writers. Every nation, every race, has not only its own creative, but its own critical turn of mind; and is even more oblivious of the shortcomings and limitations of its critical habits than of those of its creative genius. We know, or think we know,

from the enormous mass of critical writing that has appeared in the
French language the critical method or habit of the French; we
only conclude (we are such unconscious people) that the French
are "more critical" than we, and sometimes even plume ourselves
a little with the fact, as if the French were the less spontaneous.
Perhaps they are; but we might remind ourselves that criticism is
as inevitable as breathing, and that we should be none the worse
for articulating what passes in our minds when we read a book and
feel an emotion about it, for criticising our own minds in their work
of criticism. One of the facts that might come to light in this pro-
cess is our tendency to insist, when we praise a poet, upon those
aspects of his work in which he least resembles anyone else. In these
aspects or parts of his work we pretend to find what is individual,
what is the peculiar essence of the man. We dwell with satisfaction
upon the poet's difference from his predecessors, especially his
immediate predecessors; we endeavour to find something that can
be isolated in order to be enjoyed. Whereas if we approach a poet
without this prejudice we shall often find that not only the best, but
the most individual parts of his work may be those in which the
dead poets, his ancestors, assert their immortality most vigorously.
And I do not mean the impressionable period of adolescence, but
the period of full maturity.

Yet if the only form of tradition, of handing down, consisted in
following the ways of the immediate generation before us in a blind
or timid adherence to its successes, 'tradition' should positively be
discouraged. We have seen many such simple currents soon lost in
the sand; and novelty is better than repetition. Tradition is a matter
of much wider significance. It cannot be inherited, and if you want
it you must obtain it by great labour. It involves, in the first place,
the historical sense, which we may call nearly indispensable to any-
one who would continue to be a poet beyond his 25th year; and the
historical sense involves a perception, not only of the pastness of the
past, but of its presence; the historical sense compels a man to write
not merely with his own generation in his bones, but with a feeling
that the whole of the literature of Europe from Homer and within it
the whole of the literature of his own country has a simultaneous
existence and composes a simultaneous order. This historical sense,
which is a sense of the timeless as well as of the temporal and of
the timeless and of the temporal together, is what makes a writer
traditional. And it is at the same time what makes a writer most
acutely conscious of his place in time, of his own contemporaneity.

No poet, no artist of any art, has his complete meaning alone.
His significance, his appreciation is the appreciation of his relation

to the dead poets and artists. You cannot value him alone; you must set him, for contrast and comparison, among the dead. I mean this as a principle of aesthetic, not merely historical, criticism. The necessity that he shall conform, that he shall cohere, is not one-sided; what happens when a new work of art is created is something that happens simultaneously to all the works of art which preceded it. The existing monuments form an ideal order among themselves, which is modified by the introduction of the new (the really new) work of art among them. The existing order is complete before the new work arrives; for order to persist after the super-vention of novelty, the *whole* existing order must be, if ever so slightly, altered; and so the relations, proportions, values of each work of art toward the whole are readjusted; and this is conformity between the old and the new. Whoever has approved this idea of order, of the form of European, of English literature will not find it preposterous that the past should be altered by the present as much as the present is directed by the past. And the poet who is aware of this will be aware of great difficulties and responsibilities.

In a peculiar sense he will be aware also that he must inevitably be judged by the standards of the past. I say judged, not amputated, by them; not judged to be as good as, or worse or better than, the dead; and certainly not judged by the canons of dead critics. It is a judgment, a comparison, in which two things are measured by each other. To conform merely would be for the new work not really to conform at all; it would not be new, and would therefore not be a work of art. And we do not quite say that the new is more valuable because it fits in; but its fitting in is a test of its value – a test, it is true, which can only be slowly and cautiously applied, for we are none of us infallible judges of conformity. We say: it appears to conform, and is perhaps individual, or it appears individual, and may conform; but we are hardly likely to find that it is one and not the other.

To proceed to a more intelligible exposition of the relation of the poet to the past: he can neither take the past as a lump, an indiscriminate bolus, nor can he form himself wholly on one or two private admirations, nor can he form himself wholly upon one preferred period. The first course is inadmissible, the second is an important experience of youth, and the third is a pleasant and highly desirable supplement. The poet must be very conscious of the main current, which does not at all flow invariably through the most distinguished reputations. He must be quite aware of the obvious fact that art never improves, but that the material of art is never quite the same. He must be aware that the mind of Europe

– the mind of his own country – a mind which he learns in time to
be much more important than his own private mind – is a mind
which changes, and that this change is a development which abandons
nothing *en route*, which does not superannuate either Shakespeare,
or Homer, or the rock drawing of the Magdalenian draughtsmen.
That this development, refinement perhaps, complication certainly,
is not, from the point of view of the artist, any improvement.
Perhaps not even an improvement from the point of view of the
psychologist or not to the extent which we imagine; perhaps only in
the end based upon a complication in economics and machinery.
But the difference between the present and the past is that the
conscious present is an awareness of the past in a way and to an
extent which the past's awareness of itself cannot show.

Someone said: 'The dead writers are remote from us because we
*know* so much more than they did.' Precisely, and they are that
which we know.

I am alive to a usual objection to what is clearly part of my
programme for the *métier* of poetry. The objection is that the doc-
trine requires a ridiculous amount of erudition (pedantry), a claim
which can be rejected by appeal to the lives of poets in any pantheon.
It will even be affirmed that much learning deadens or perverts
poetic sensibility. While, however, we persist in believing that a poet
ought to know as much as will not encroach upon his necessary
receptivity and necessary laziness, it is not desirable to confine
knowledge to whatever can be put into a useful shape for examin-
ations, drawing-rooms, or the still more pretentious modes of
publicity. Some can absorb knowledge, the more tardy must sweat
for it. Shakespeare acquired more essential history from Plutarch
than most men could from the whole British Museum. What is to
be insisted upon is that the poet must develop or procure the con-
sciousness of the past and that he should continue to develop this
consciousness throughout his career.

What happens is a continual surrender of himself as he is at the
moment to something which is more valuable. The progress of an
artist is a continual self-sacrifice, a continual extinction of personality.

There remains to define this process of depersonalisation and its
relation to the sense of tradition. It is in this depersonalisation that
art may be said to approach the condition of science. I therefore
invite you to consider, as a suggestive analogy, the action which
takes place when a bit of finely filiated platinum is introduced into
a chamber containing oxygen and sulphur dioxide.

## II

Honest criticism and sensitive appreciation is directed not upon the poet but upon the poetry. If we attend to the confused cries of the newspaper critics and the susurrus of popular repetition that follows, we shall hear the names of poets in great numbers; if we seek not Blue-book knowledge but the enjoyment of poetry, and ask for a poem, we shall seldom find it. I have tried to point out the importance of the relation of the poem to other poems by other authors, and suggested the conception of poetry as a living whole of all the poetry that has ever been written. The other aspect of this Impersonal theory of poetry is the relation of the poem to its author. And I hinted, by an analogy, that the mind of the mature poet differs from that of the immature one not precisely in any valuation of "personality", not being necessarily more interesting, or having "more to say", but rather by being a more finely perfected medium in which special, or very varied, feelings are at liberty to enter into new combinations.

The analogy was that of the catalyst. When the two gases previously mentioned are mixed in the presence of a filament of platinum, they form sulphurous acid. This combination takes place only if the platinum is present; nevertheless the newly formed acid contains no trace of platinum, and the platinum itself is apparently unaffected: has remained inert, neutral, and unchanged. The mind of the poet is the shred of platinum. It may partly or exclusively operate upon the experience of the man himself; but, the more perfect the artist, the more completely separate in him will be the man who suffers and the mind which creates; the more perfectly will the mind digest and transmute the passions which are its material.

The experience, you will notice, the elements which enter the presence of the transforming catalyst, are of two kinds: emotions and feelings. The effect of a work of art upon the person who enjoys it is an experience different in kind from any experience not of art. It may be formed out of one emotion, or may be a combination of several; and various feelings, inhering for the writer in particular words or phrases or images, may be added to compose the final result. Or great poetry may be made without the direct use of any emotion whatever: composed out of feelings solely. Canto XV of the *Inferno* (Brunetto Latini) is a working up of the emotion evident in the situation; but the effect, though single as that of any work of art, is obtained by considerable complexity of detail. The last quatrain gives an image, a feeling attaching to an image, which "came", which did not develop simply out of what precedes, but which was probably in suspension in the poet's mind until the proper combination arrived for it to add itself to. The poet's mind is in fact a receptacle for seizing and storing up numberless feelings, phrases, images, which remain there until all the particles which can unite to form a new compound are present together.

If you compare several representative passages of the greatest poetry you see how great is the variety of types of combination, and also how completely any semi-ethical criterion of "sublimity" misses the mark. For it is not the "greatness", the intensity, of the emotions, the components, but the intensity of the artistic process, the pressure, so to speak, under which the fusion takes place, that counts. The episode of Paolo and Francesca employs a definite emotion, but the intensity of the poetry is something quite different from whatever intensity in the supposed experience it may give the impression of. It is no more intense, furthermore, than Canto XXVI, the voyage of Ulysses, which has not the direct dependence upon an emotion. Great variety is possible in the process of transmutation of emotion: the murder of Agamemnon, or the agony of Othello, gives an artistic effect apparently closer to a possible original than the scenes from Dante. In the *Agamemnon*, the artistic emotion approximates to the emotion of an actual spectator; in *Othello* to the emotion of the protagonist himself. But the difference between art and the event is always absolute; the combination which is the murder of Agamemnon is probably as complex as that which is the voyage of Ulysses. In either case there has been a fusion of elements. The ode of Keats contains a number of feelings which have nothing particular to do with the nightingale, but which the nightingale, partly perhaps because of its attractive name, and partly because of its reputation, served to bring together.

The point of view which I am struggling to attack is perhaps related to the metaphysical theory of the substantial unity of the soul: for my meaning is, that the poet has, not a "personality" to express, but a particular medium, which is only a medium and not a personality, in which impressions and experiences combine in peculiar and unexpected ways. Impressions and experiences which are important for the man may take no place in the poetry, and those which become important in the poetry may play quite a negligible part in the man, the personality.

I will quote a passage which is unfamiliar enough to be regarded with fresh attention in the light – or darkness – of these observations:

And now methinks I could e'en chide myself
For doating on her beauty, though her death
Shall be revenged after no common action.
Does the silkworm expend her yellow labours
For thee? For thee does she undo herself?
Are lordships sold to maintain ladyships
For the poor benefit of a bewildering minute?
Why does yon fellow falsify highways,
And put his life between the judge's lips,
To refine such a thing – keeps horse and men
To beat their valours for her?...

In this passage (as is evident if it is taken in its context) there is a combination of positive and negative emotions: an intensely strong attraction toward beauty and an equally intense fascination by the ugliness which is contrasted with it and which destroys it. This balance of contrasted emotion is in the dramatic situation to which the speech is pertinent, but that situation alone is inadequate to it. This is, so to speak, the structural emotion, provided by the drama. But the whole effect, the dominant tone, is due to the fact that a number of floating feelings, having an affinity to this emotion by no means superficially evident, have combined with it to give us a new art emotion.

It is not in his personal emotions, the emotions provoked by particular events in his life, that the poet is in any way remarkable or interesting. His particular emotions may be simple, or crude, or flat. The emotion in his poetry will be a very complex thing, but not with the complexity of the emotions of people who have very complex or unusual emotions in life. One error, in fact, of eccentricity in poetry is to seek for new human emotions to express; and in this search for novelty in the wrong place it discovers the perverse. The business of the poet is not to find new emotions, but to use the ordinary ones and, in working them up into poetry, to express feelings which are not in actual emotions at all. And emotions which he has never experienced will serve his turn as well as those familiar to him. Consequently, we must believe that 'emotion recollected in tranquillity' is an inexact formula. For it is neither emotion, nor recollection, nor, without distortion of meaning, tranquillity. It is a concentration, and a new thing resulting from the concentration, of a very great number of experiences which to the practical and active person would not seem to be experiences at all; it is a concentration which does not happen consciously or of deliberation. These experiences are not 'recollected', and they finally unite in an atmosphere which is 'tranquil' only in that it is a passive attending upon the event. Of course this is not quite the whole story. There is a great deal, in the writing of poetry, which must be conscious and deliberate. In fact, the bad poet is usually unconscious where he ought to be conscious, and conscious where he ought to be unconscious. Both errors tend to make him 'personal'. Poetry is not a turning loose of emotion, but an escape from emotion; it is not the expression of personality, but an escape from personality. But, of course, only those who have personality and emotions know what it means to want to escape from these things.

### III

ὁ δὲ νοῦς ἴσως θειότερόν τι καὶ ἀπαθές ἐστιν.

This essay proposes to halt at the frontier of metaphysics or mysticism, and confine itself to such practical conclusions as can be applied by the responsible person interested in poetry. To divert interest from the poet to the poetry is a laudable aim: for it would conduce to a juster estimation of actual poetry, good and bad. There are many people who appreciate the expression of sincere emotion in verse, and there is a smaller number of people who can appreciate technical excellence. But very few know when there is an expression of significant emotion, emotion which has its life in the poem and not in the history of the poet. The emotion of art is impersonal. And the poet cannot reach this impersonality without surrendering himself wholly to the work to be done. And he is not likely to know what is to be done unless he lives in what is not merely the present, but the present moment of the past, unless he is conscious, not of what is dead, but of what is already living.

# ROBERT GRAVES

Robert Graves (1895-1985) was born in Wimbledon and educated at Charterhouse and Oxford. His first poems were published while he was serving alongside Siegfried Sassoon in the First World War, and his prolific output included essays, biographies, fiction and children's books, as well as works on Greek and Hebrew mythology. But he saw himself primarily as a poet; and if his early work was associated with the 'Georgians', his friendship with the American poet Laura Riding encouraged different directions in his work, and inspired his attempt to reconnect poet and Muse in *The White Goddess* (1948). At its best, Graves's poetry combines lyricism with an unusual, self-reflexive insight into the poet's own processes. A series of *Collected Poems* appeared from 1938 onwards.

In 1949, Graves condensed his critical writings from the early 20s into a series of 'Observations', reprinted here. Besides his idea of the 'poetic trance', Graves's distinction between the outward and the inward ear remains an important one.

## *from* Observations on Poetry 1922–1925
### (1953)

### THE POETIC TRANCE

The nucleus of every poem worthy of the name is rhythmically formed in the poet's mind, during a trance-like suspension of his normal habits of thought, by the supra-logical reconciliation of conflicting emotional ideas. The poet learns to induce the trance in self-protection whenever he feels unable to resolve an emotional conflict by simple logic. If interrupted during this preliminary process of composition he will experience the disagreeable sensations of a sleep-walker disturbed; and if able to continue until the draft is completed will presently come to himself and wonder: was the writer really he?

As soon as he has thus dissociated himself from the poem, the secondary phase of composition begins: that of testing and correcting on commonsense principles, so as to satisfy public scrutiny, what began as a private message to himself from himself – yet taking care that nothing of poetic value is lost or impaired. For the reader of the poem must fall into a complementary trance if he is to appreciate its full meaning. The amount of revision needed depends largely on the strength and scope of the emotional disturbance and the degree of trance. In a light trance, the critical sense is not completely suspended; but there is a trance that comes so close to sleep that what is written in it can hardly be distinguished from ordinary dream-poetry: the rhymes are inaccurate, the phrasing eccentric, the texture clumsy, the syntax rudimentary, the thought-connections ruled by free-association, the atmosphere charged with unexplained emotion.

The classical instance of a poem composed in deep trance is Cole-ridge's *Kubla Khan*. Though the thought-connections in the pub-lished version remain characteristically obscure, it is clear that Coleridge revised the first draft considerably after his unfortunate interruption by the 'gentleman from Porlock'. I believe that if it could be recovered we should find, for instance, that *Abora* rhymed with *dulcimer*:

> I saw an Abyssinian maid
> And on a dulcimer she played –
> A damsel with a dulcimer,
> Singing of Mount Abora.

The published version runs:

> A damsel with a dulcimer
> In a vision once I saw:
> It was an Abyssinian maid,
> And on her dulcimer she played,
> Singing of Mount Abora.

Here *saw* is too self-conscious an assonance, and too far distant from *Abora*, to have been part of the original laudanum-dream.

Poetry as the reconciliation of conflicting emotional ideas may be illustrated by crucial lines from Elizabethan and Jacobean drama. When Lady Macbeth complains: 'All the perfumes of Arabia will not sweeten this little hand' the conflict is between her ambition to command the luxuries of queenship and her fear of divine retribution as a murderess: between 'All the perfumes of Arabia will sweeten my little hands' and 'Nothing will ever cleanse this hand of blood.'

When Ferdinand views the dead body of the Duchess of Malfi, in Webster's play, and says: 'Cover her face: mine eyes dazzle: she died young', the word 'dazzle' conveys two simultaneous emotions: sun-dazzled awe at loveliness, tear-dazzled grief for early death.

When Marlowe's Doctor Faustus is waiting for the clock to strike and the Devil to exact his debt, he cries: 'That Time may cease and midnight never come! / *O lente, lente currite noctis equi.*' Prosaic commentators have remarked on the inappropriate over-sweetness of the quotation, 'Go slowly, slowly, coursers of the night,' originally spoken by an Ovidian lover with his arms around the mistress from whom he must part at dawn. But Marlowe has chosen it both to mark the distance which the scholar Faustus has travelled since his first dry Latin quotation: *'Bene disserere est finis logices'* ('Is to dispute well, Logick's chiefest end') and to combine in a single expression mawkish sensuality with agonised fear of the eternal bonfire.

Such poetry has a therapeutic effect on the minds of readers similarly disturbed by conflicting emotions. The Greeks presented this notion mythically in the fable of Perseus, the hero who rode Pegasus. The polished shield given him by the Goddess Athene mirrored the Gorgon with no hurtful effect and enabled him to behead her at his ease. Poetic drama to the Greeks was thus a rite of spiritual cleansing. [...]


RHYME

Rhymes properly used are the good servants whose presence at the dinner-table gives the guests a sense of opulent security; never awkward or over-clever, they hand the dishes silently and professionally. You can trust them not to interrupt the conversation or allow their personal disagreements to come to the notice of the guests; but some of them are getting very old for their work.

Milton, Spenser and Campion all used rhyme though agreeing to condemn it as a barbarism, there being no rhymes in the Greek and Latin classics which were regarded as the foundation of civilised literature. Now that English poetry is accepted as an independent tradition, rhyme is generally approved even by Classicists, but with the proviso that it must on no account appear to guide the sense: it must come unexpectedly and yet inevitably, like presents at Christmas, and convey the comforting sense of free will within predestination. The chimes must answer one another harmoniously and clearly, whatever the poetic context; and though there are licensed exceptions to this rule, known as near-rhymes and sight-rhymes – e.g. *have* and *grave*; *earth* and *hearth*; *love* and *remove* – where the pronunciation of one or other of the words has changed in the course of the last four centuries, the Classicist professes to be outraged by such 'Cockney' rhymes as *dawn* and *morn*, *thought* and *sort*. He far prefers 'French rhymes', i.e. *groan* and *grown*, *poor* and *pour*, which at least have the authority of Chaucer.

Modern anti-Classicists either reject rhyme as an impediment to free poetic expression – a 'silly ornament' Mr Flint has lately called it – or modify the harmony of its chimes to suit the context. It has been found, for example, that to rhyme a stressed syllable with an unstressed, e.g. *spent* with *moment*, *dish* with *famish*, or one unstressed syllable with another, e.g. *melon* with *Mammon* and *Babylon*, gives the effect of uncertainty, incompleteness, suspense. Wilfred Owen's use of assonantal French rhymes in 'Strange Meeting': *escaped*, *scooped*; *groined*, *groaned*; *bestirred*, *stared* – to convey the heavy, fateful, nightmarish atmosphere of the Hindenburg Tunnel in which the meeting took place – has been much admired and imitated. Miss Edith Sitwell and others use rhyme as a means of arraigning the ethical and philosophical structure on which Classicism rests: not only using half-rhymes, French rhymes, assonances, Cockney rhymes, e.g. *board* and *fraud*, and false rhymes, e.g. *bath* and *laugh*, but letting the rhymes seem to guide the sense:

> The wind's bastinado
> Whipt on the calico
> Skin of the Macaroon
> And the black Picaroon
> Beneath the galloon
> Of the midnight sky...

– thus advancing a view of life as founded in error, boredom and ugliness and ruled by caprice. Granted, Miss Sitwell does not regard herself as a revolutionary and will even on occasion proclaim herself a traditionalist; but that is no more than bearing lightly home the handle of the family pitcher which has gone to the well once too often. [...]

## THE OUTWARD AND INWARD EARS

Though the poet ought to write as if his work were intended to be read aloud, in practice the reading aloud of a poem distracts attention from its subtler properties by emphasising the more obvious ones. The outward ear is easily deceived. A beautiful voice can make magic even with bad or fraudulent poetry which the eye, as the most sophisticated organ of sense, would reject at once; for the eye is in close communication with the undeceivable inward ear. [...]

## TEXTURE

Classicists pay great attention to the texture of poetry; their aim is euphony and, within the strict metrical patterns approved by tradition, variety. "Texture" covers the interrelations of all vowels and consonants in a poem considered as mere sound. The skilled craftsman varies the vowel sounds as if they were musical notes so as to give an effect of melodic richness; uses liquid consonants, labials and open vowels for smoothness; aspirates and dentals for force; gutturals for strength; sibilants for flavour, as a cook uses salt. His alliteration is not barbarously insistent, as in Anglo-Saxon poems or *Piers Plowman*, but concealed by the gradual interlacement of two or three alliterative sequences. He gauges the memory-length of the reader's inward ear and plants the second word of an alliterative pair at a point where the memory of the first has begun to blur but has not yet faded. He varies his word-endings, keeping a careful eye on *-ing* and *-y*, and takes care not to interrupt the smooth flow of the line, if this can possibly be avoided, by close correspondence between terminal consonants and the initial consonants that follow them – e.g. *break ground, maid's sorrow, great toe*. Non-Classicists either disregard texture as another of the heavy chains clamped on the naked limbs of poetry, or use their understanding of it for deliberate exercises in cacophony or dislocation: by judicious manipulation of vowels and consonants a line can be made to limp, crawl, scream, bellow and make other ugly or sickening noises. In a passage from *The Waste Land* Mr T.S. Eliot, though a master craftsman of musical verse, amuses himself by letting a line snuffle and clear its throat realistically:

> Madame Sosostris, famous clairvoyante,
> *Had a bad cold, nevertheless*
> Is known to be the wisest woman in Europe.

# ROBERT FROST

Robert Frost (1874-1963) was born in San Francisco, and moved to New England at the age of 11. He studied, sporadically, at Dartmouth and Harvard, interspersed with work as a shoe-maker, newspaperman and farmer. He relocated to England in 1912, where he befriended Ezra Pound and Edward Thomas, and where he published his first two collections, *A Boy's Will* (1913) and the best-selling *North of Boston* (1914). In 1915 he returned to the US, settling on a small New Hampshire farm where he cultivated chickens and a public image for himself as something of a sage. *Mountain Interval* (1916) brought national fame for such poems as 'The Road Not Taken' and 'Out, Out –', and his following book, *New Hampshire* (1923), won him the first of four Pulitzer Prizes. Through the 30s, however, Frost was beset by family tragedy, reflected in what was perhaps his last key work, *The Witness Tree* (1942).

Frost's idiom is colloquial and formal (he compared the writing of free verse to the playing of tennis with the net down). It is also profoundly lyrical, and his pursuit of the 'sound of sense' runs directly counter to Modernist ideas about movement, image, and economy of phrase. And yet it is Frost's influence upon contemporary British and Irish poetry has been so far-reaching; an influence that (along with Auden and Yeats) has possibly outweighed the impression of Modernism.

# The Figure a Poem Makes
### (1939)

Abstraction is an old story with the philosophers, but it has been like a new toy in the hands of the artists of our day. Why can't we have any one quality of poetry we choose by itself? We can have in thought. Then it will go hard if we can't in practice. Our lives for it.

Granted no one but a humanist much cares how sound a poem is if it is only *a* sound. The sound is the gold in the ore. Then we will have the sound out alone and dispense with the inessential. We do till we make the discovery that the object in writing poetry is to make all poems sound as different as possible from each other, and the resources for that of vowels, consonants, punctuation, syntax, words, sentences, metre are not enough. We need the help of context – meaning – subject matter. That is the greatest help towards variety. All that can be done with words is soon told. So also with metres – particularly in our language where there are virtually but two, strict iambic and loose iambic. The ancients with many were still poor if they depended on metres for all tune. It is painful to watch our sprung-rhythmists straining at the point of omitting one short from a foot for relief from monotony. The possibilities for tune from the dramatic tones of meaning struck across the rigidity of a limited metre are endless. And we are back in poetry as merely one more art of having something to say, sound or unsound. Probably better if sound, because deeper and from wider experience.

Then there is this wildness whereof it is spoken. Granted again that it has an equal claim with sound to being a poem's better half. If it is a wild tune, it is a poem. Our problem then is, as modern abstractionists, to have the wildness pure; to be wild with nothing to be wild about. We bring up as aberrationists, giving way to undirected associations and kicking ourselves from one chance suggestion to another in all directions as of a hot afternoon in the life of a grasshopper. Theme alone can steady us down. Just as the first mystery was how a poem could have a tune in such a straightness as metre, so the second mystery is how a poem can have wildness and at the same time a subject that shall be fulfilled.

It should be of the pleasure of a poem itself to tell how it can. The figure a poem makes. It begins in delight and ends in wisdom. The figure is the same as for love. No one can really hold that the ecstasy should be static and stand still in one place. It begins in delight, it inclines to the impulse, it assumes direction with the first line laid down, it runs a course of lucky events, and ends in a clarification of life – not necessarily a great clarification, such as sects and cults are founded on, but in a momentary stay against confusion. It has denouement. It has an outcome that though unforeseen was predestined from the first image of the original mood – and indeed from the very mood. It is but a trick poem and no poem at all if the best of it was thought of first and saved for the last. It finds its own name as it goes and discovers the best waiting for it in some final phrase at once wise and sad – the happy-sad blend of the drinking song.

No tears in the writer, no tears in the reader. No surprise for the writer, no surprise for the reader. For me the initial delight is in the surprise of remembering something I didn't know I knew. I am in a place, in a situation, as if I had materialised from cloud or risen out of the ground. There is a glad recognition of the long lost and the rest follows. Step by step the wonder of unexpected supply keeps growing. The impressions most useful to my purpose seem always those I was unaware of and so made no note of at the time when taken, and the conclusion is come to that like giants we are always hurling experience ahead of us to pave the future with against the day when we may want to strike a line of purpose across it for somewhere. The line will have the more charm for not being mechanically straight. We enjoy the straight crookedness of a good walking stick. Modern instruments of precision are being used to make things crooked as if by eye and hand in the old days.

I tell how there may be a better wildness of logic than of inconsequence. But the logic is backward, in retrospect, after the act. It must be more felt than seen ahead like prophecy. It must be a revelation, or a series of revelations, as much for the poet as for the reader. For it to be that there must have been the greatest freedom of the material to move about in it and to establish relations in it regardless of time and space, previous relation, and everything but affinity. We prate of freedom. We call our schools free because we are not free to stay away from them till we are 16 years of age. I have given up my democratic prejudices and now willingly set the lower classes free to be completely taken care of by the upper classes. Political freedom is nothing to me. I bestow it right and left. All I would keep for myself is the freedom of my material – the condition of body and mind now and then to summons aptly from the vast chaos of all I have lived through.

Scholars and artists thrown together are often annoyed at the puzzle of where they differ. Both work from knowledge; but I suspect they differ most importantly in the way their knowledge is come by. Scholars get theirs with conscientious thoroughness along projected lines of logic; poets theirs cavalierly and as it happens in and out of books. They stick to nothing deliberately, but let what will stick to them like burrs where they walk in the fields. No acquirement is on assignment, or even self-assignment. Knowledge of the second kind is much more available in the wild free ways of wit and art. A schoolboy may be defined as one who can tell you what he knows in the order in which he learned it. The artist must value himself as he snatches a thing from some previous order in time and space into a new order with not so much as a ligature clinging to it of the old place where it was organic.

More than once I should have lost my soul to radicalism if it had been the originality it was mistaken for by its young converts. Originality and initiative are what I ask for my country. For myself the originality need be no more than the freshness of a poem run in the way I have described: from delight to wisdom. The figure is the same as for love. Like a piece of ice on a hot stove the poem must ride on its own melting. A poem may be worked over once it is in being, but may not be worried into being. Its most precious quality will remain its having run itself and carried away the poet with it. Read it a hundred times: it will for ever keep its freshness as a metal keeps its fragrance. It can never lose its sense of a meaning that once unfolded by surprise as it went.

# HART CRANE

Hart Crane was born in Ohio in 1899, the son of a confectionery manufacturer, and had a turbulent upbringing in which he saw his parents separate at an early age. He gave up college to work as a labourer in a Cleveland shipyard and, later, in his father's factory, until relations between the two men soured and were finally broken off altogether. In the 1920s he moved to Brooklyn where he later wrote his landmark poem *The Bridge* (1930) – a visionary celebration of the New World and its possibilities. Crane saw himself as the direct inheritor of Walt Whitman, similarly 'concerned with the future of America' and its promise of a new moral consciousness. Yet Crane himself saw little of that promise. Tormented by poverty, alcohol, broken relationships, and a sense of his own critical failings, he wavered on the brink of serious depression. On 27 April 1932, returning from Havana to New York, Crane walked to the stern of the boat and leapt to his death.

Poetry, Crane outlines here, bridges the gap between the imagination and the 'seething, confused cosmos' of lived experience. But so unstable has this cosmos become that a poet can no longer rely on the great themes of human speculation ('love, beauty, death, renascence') to convey the same universality that once they might. Instead, poetry must re-energise language to discover 'a new hierarchy of faith': spiritual, moral, a new word to put forth into the world. And the key to this, for Crane, is a 'logic of metaphor' that allows us to connect the imaginative and the real. This piece was written in 1925.

# General Aims and Theories
## (1925/1937)

When I started writing 'Faustus & Helen' it was my intention to embody in modern terms (words, symbols, metaphors) a contemporary approximation to an ancient human culture or mythology that seems to have been obscured rather than illumined with the frequency of poetic allusions made to it during the last century. The name of Helen, for instance, has become an all-too-easily employed crutch for evocation whenever a poet felt a stitch in his side. The real evocation of this (to me) very real and absolute conception of beauty seemed to consist in a reconstruction in these modern terms of the basic emotional attitude toward beauty that the Greeks had. And in so doing I found that I was really building a bridge between so-called classic experience and many divergent realities of our seething, confused cosmos of today, which has no formulated mythology yet for classic poetic reference or for religious exploitation.

So I found 'Helen' sitting in a street car; the Dionysian revels of her court and her seduction were transferred to a Metropolitan roof garden with a jazz orchestra; and the *katharsis* of the fall of Troy I saw approximated in the recent World War. The importance of this scaffolding may easily be exaggerated, but it gave me a series of correspondences between two widely separated worlds on which to sound some major themes of human speculation – love, beauty, death, renascence. It was a kind of grafting process that I shall doubtless not be interested in repeating, but which is consistent with subsequent theories of mine on the relation of tradition to the contemporary creating imagination.

It is a terrific problem that faces the poet today – a world that is so in transition from a decayed culture toward a reorganisation of human evaluations that there are few common terms, general denominators of speech that are solid enough or that ring with any vibration or spiritual conviction. The great mythologies of the past (including the Church) are deprived of enough façade to even launch good raillery against. Yet much of their traditions are operative still – in millions of chance combinations of related and unrelated detail, psychological reference, figures of speech, precepts, etc. These are all a part of our common experience and the terms, at least partially, of that very experience when it defines or extends itself.

The deliberate program, then, of a "break" with the past or tradition seems to me to be a sentimental fallacy...The poet has a right to draw on whatever practical resources he finds in books or otherwise about him. He must tax his sensibility and his touch-stone of experience for the proper selections of these themes and details, however – and that is where he either stands, or falls into useless archaeology.

I put no particular value on the simple objective of "modernity". The element of the temporal location of an artist's creation is of very secondary importance; it can be left to the impressionist or historian just as well. It seems to me that a poet will accidentally define his time well enough simply by reacting honestly and to the full extent of his sensibilities to the states of passion, experience and rumination that fate forces on him, first hand. He must, of course, have a sufficiently universal basis of experience to make his imagination selective and valuable. His picture of the "period", then, will simply be a by-product of his curiosity and the relation of his experience to a postulated "eternity".

I am concerned with the future of America, but not because I think that America has any so-called par value as a state or as a group of people... It is only because I feel persuaded that here are destined to be discovered certain as yet undefined spiritual quantities, perhaps a new hierarchy of faith not to be developed so completely elsewhere. And in this process I like to feel myself as a potential factor; certainly I must speak in its terms and what discoveries I may make are situated in its experience.

But to fool one's self that definitions are being reached by merely referring frequently to skyscrapers, radio antennae, steam whistles, or other surface phenomena of our time is merely to paint a photograph. I think that what is interesting and significant will emerge only under the conditions of our submission to, and examination and assimilation of the organic effects on us of these and other fundamental factors of our experience. It can certainly not be an organic expression otherwise. And the expression of such values may often be as well accomplished with the vocabulary and blank verse of the Elizabethans as with the calligraphic tricks and slang used so brilliantly at times by an impressionist like Cummings.

It may not be possible to say that there is, strictly speaking, any "absolute" experience. But it seems evident that certain aesthetic experience (and this may for a time engross the total faculties of the spectator) can be called absolute, inasmuch as it approximates a formally convincing statement of a conception or apprehension of life that gains our unquestioning assent, and under the conditions of which our imagination is unable to suggest a further detail consistent with the design of the aesthetic whole.

I have been called an 'absolutist' in poetry, and if I am to welcome such a label it should be under the terms of the above definition. It is really only a *modus operandi* however, and as such has been used organically before by at least a dozen poets such as Donne, Blake, Baudelaire, Rimbaud, etc. I may succeed in defining it better by contrasting it with the impressionistic method. The impressionist is interesting as far as he goes – but his goal has been reached when he has succeeded in projecting certain selected factual details into his reader's consciousness. He is really not interested in the *causes* (metaphysical) of his materials, their emotional derivations or their utmost spiritual consequences. A kind of retinal registration is enough, along with a certain psychological stimulation. And this is also true of your realist (of the Zola type), and to a certain extent of the classicist, like Horace, Ovid, Pope, etc.

Blake meant these differences when he wrote:

We are led to believe in a lie
When we see *with* not *through* the eye.

The impressionist creates only with the eye and for the readiest surface of the consciousness, at least relatively so. If the effect has been harmonious or even stimulating, he can stop there, relinquishing entirely to his audience the problematic synthesis of the details into terms of their own personal consciousness.

It is my hope to go *through* the combined materials of the poem, using our "real" world somewhat as a spring-board, and to give the poem *as a whole* an orbit or predetermined direction of its own. I would like to establish it as free from my own personality as from any chance evaluation on the reader's part. (This is, of course, an impossibility, but it is a characteristic worth mentioning.) Such a poem is at least a stab at a truth, and to such an extent may be differentiated from other kinds of poetry and called "absolute". Its evocation will not be toward decoration or amusement, but rather toward a state of consciousness, an 'innocence' (Blake) or absolute beauty. In this condition there may be discoverable under new forms certain spiritual illuminations, shining with a morality essentialised from experience directly, and not from previous precepts or preconceptions. It is as though a poem gave the reader as he left it a single, new *word*, never before spoken and impossible to actually enunciate, but self-evident as an active principle in the reader's consciousness henceforward.

As to technical considerations: the motivation of the poem must be derived from the implicit emotional dynamics of the materials used, and the terms of expression employed are often selected less for their logical (literal) significance than for their associational meanings. Via this and their metaphorical inter-relationships, the entire construction of the poem is raised on the organic principle of a "logic of metaphor", which antedates our so-called pure logic, and which is the genetic basis of all speech, hence consciousness and thought-extension.

These dynamics often result, I'm told, in certain initial difficulties in understanding my poems. But on the other hand I find them at times the only means possible for expressing certain concepts in any forceful or direct way whatever. To cite two examples:– when, in 'Voyages' (II), I speak of 'adagios of islands', the reference is to the motion of a boat through islands clustered thickly, the rhythm of the motion, etc. And it seems a much more direct and creative statement than any more logical employment of words such as 'coasting slowly through the islands,' besides ushering in a whole world of music. Similarly in 'Faustus and Helen' (III) the speed and tense altitude of an aeroplane are much better suggested by the idea of 'nimble blue plateaus' – *implying* the aeroplane and its speed against a contrast of stationary elevated earth. Although the statement is pseudo in relation to formal logic – it *is* completely logical in relation to the truth of the imagination, and there is expressed a concept of speed and space that could not be handled so well in other terms.

In manipulating the more imponderable phenomena of psychic motives, pure emotional crystallisations, etc., I have had to rely even more on these dynamics of inferential mention, and I am doubtless still very unconscious of having committed myself to what seems nothing but obscurities to some minds. A poem like 'Possessions' really cannot be technically explained. It must rely (even to a large extent with myself) on its organic impact on the imagination to successfully imply its meaning. This seems to me to present an exceptionally difficult problem, however, considering the real clarity and consistent logic of many of the other poems.

I know that I run the risk of much criticism by defending such theories as I have, but as it is part of a poet's business to risk not only criticism – but folly – in the conquest of consciousness I can only say that I attach no intrinsic value to what means I use beyond their practical service in giving form to the living stuff of the imagination.

New conditions of life germinate new forms of spiritual articulation. And while I feel that my work includes a more consistent extension of traditional literary elements than many contemporary poets are capable of appraising, I realise that I am utilising the gifts of the past as instruments principally; and that the voice of the present, if it is to be known, must be caught at the risk of speaking in idioms and circumlocutions sometimes shocking to the scholar and historians of logic. Language has built towers and bridges, but itself is inevitably as fluid as always.

# E.E. CUMMINGS

E(dward) E(stlin) Cummings (1894-1962) began experimenting with Modernist forms of writing while a student at Harvard. Born in Cambridge, Massachusetts, he studied art in Paris, returning to New York in 1924 where his first collection of poems, *Tulips and Chimneys*, had just been published to some acclaim. Influenced by Gertrude Stein and the Imagists, Cummings nevertheless developed a distinctive, chaotic lyricism that was both sensuous and individualistic in its commitment to 'feeling' and to being 'nobody-but-yourself'. Modernist in technique and romantic in declaration, it is his technique that rescues his poems from sentimentality, and that same sentiment that rescues his technique from sheer trickery. His love lyrics can be erotic and affecting, his satire scabrous and shocking. To the delight of his followers, but the despair of his critics, he maintained the style for which he was so recognised throughout his career.

An obsession with 'The Verb', Cummings writes in his forward to *is 5* (and in his work verbs often take the place of nouns), is the poet's leap of faith, the act that changes the place of things. But rife though his syntactic play is, play alone is not enough – 'since feeling is first', he warns in the same collection, anyone 'who pays any attention / to the syntax of things / will never wholly kiss you'.

# Foreword to *is 5*
## (1926)

On the assumption that my technique is either complicated or original or both,the publishers have politely requested me to write an introduction to this book.

At least my theory of technique,if I have one,is very far from original;nor is it complicated. I can express it in fifteen words,by quoting The Eternal Question And Immortal Answer of burlesk,viz. 'Would you hit a woman with a child? – No, I'd hit her with a brick.' Like the burlesk comedian, I am abnormally fond of that precision which creates movement.

If a poet is anybody,he is somebody to whom things made matter very little – somebody who is obsessed by Making. Like all obsessions,the Making obsession has disadvantages;for instance, my only interest in making money would be to make it. Fortunately,however,I should prefer to make almost anything else,including locomotives and roses. It is with roses and locomotives(not to mention acrobats Spring electricity Coney Island the 4th of July the eyes of mice and Niagara Falls)that my "poems" are competing.

They are also competing with each other,with elephants,and with El Greco.

Ineluctable preoccupation with The Verb gives a poet one priceless advantage:whereas nonmakers must content themselves with the merely undeniable fact that two times two is four,he rejoices in a purely irresistible truth(to be found,in abbreviated costume,upon the title page of the present volume).

# GERTRUDE STEIN

Gertrude Stein (1874-1946) was the principal female figure in that remarkable generation of Americans who settled in Europe at the turn of the last century. She arrived in Paris in 1902 and established herself as an associate of Picasso and the French avant-garde. Her poetry, though seen as secondary to her large outpouring of prose works, nonetheless marks perhaps the most thoroughgoing effort to match the radical change wrought on Western art by Cubism. Where Cubism reconfigured perspective, Stein reconstructed syntax and played with the referential nature of language in *Tender Buttons* (1914), *Stanzas in Meditation* (1956), and an extraordinary exploration, almost a deconstruction, of sensuality, 'Lifting Belly'. Her work, often criticised for its lack of referentiality and prolixity, can achieve an exalted, unpompous tone and is frequently both hilarious and entertaining. Her influence on subsequent generations of American poets, particularly Robert Duncan and Frank O'Hara, has been marked.

Her essay 'Poetry and Grammar' (collected in *Look at Me Now and Here I Am*, 1967) projects the grammatical units of a sentence and even its punctuation as the main antagonists of any piece of writing, and posits that in poetry the main character is the noun. Poems are affairs of vocabulary, of engaging with the act of naming.

# Explaining 'a rose is a rose is a rose'
## (1934/1947)

Now listen. Can't you see that when language was new – as it was with Chaucer and Homer – the poet could use the name of a thing and the thing was really there. He could say 'O moon', 'O sea', 'O love', and the moon and the sea and love were really there. And can't you see that after hundreds of years had gone by and thousands of poems had been written, he could call on those words and find that they were just worn out literary words. The excitingness of pure being had withdrawn from them; they were just rather stale literary words. Now the poet has to work in the excitingness of pure being; he has to get back that intensity into the language. We all know that it's hard to write poetry in a late age; and we know that you have to put some strangeness, as something unexpected, into the structure of the sentence in order to bring back vitality into the noun. Now it's not enough to be bizarre; the strangeness in a sentence structure has to come from the poetic gift, too. That's why it's doubly hard to be a poet in a late age. Now you all have seen hundreds of poems about roses and you know in your bones

that the rose is not there. All those songs that sopranos sing as
encores about 'I have a garden! oh, what a garden!'... Now listen!
I'm no fool. I know that in daily life we don't go around saying
'... is a ... is a ... is a ...' Yes, I'm no fool; but I think that in that
line the rose is red for the first time in English poetry for a hun-
dred years.

# WALLACE STEVENS

Wallace Stevens (1879-1955) exploited a dichotomy between his exterior life (comfortably middle-class American) and the interior world of the poet (richly symbolic and metaphysical) to produce a body of work that is almost a sub-version of his environment. His daily routines as vice-president of an insurance company in Connecticut appeared to involve a self-abnegation to bourgeois values. But in the astonishing baroque vocabulary of *Harmonium* (1923) and the more symbolically-charged work of his middle period, *The Man with the Blue Guitar* (1937), and above all in the late poems of *Transport to Summer* (1947), in particular, 'Notes Toward a Supreme Fiction', he reveals himself as a self-appointed priest of his own cult of the imagination. Capable of an extraordinarily sensual response to his transcendental subject-matter, his mastery of tone has proven significant to another conflater of the mundane with the transformative powers of language, John Ashbery.

*The Necessary Angel* (1951), his collection of essays, is in many ways as striking as his poetry. Stevens aligns himself with a Shelleyan vision of the poet as the creator of the imaginative models by which we, knowingly or not, live our lives. In a sense, he posits poetry as the supreme ideology.

## *from* Adagia
### (1934-40/1957)

To give a sense of the freshness or vividness of life is a valid purpose for poetry. A didactic purpose justifies itself in the mind of the teacher; a philosophical purpose justifies itself in the mind of the philosopher. It is not that one purpose is as justifiable as another but that some purposes are pure others impure. Seek those purposes that are purely the purposes of the pure poet.

The poet makes silk dresses out of worms.

The public of the poet. The public of the organist is the church in which he improvises.

Merit in poets is as boring as merit in people.

Authors are actors, books are theatres.

An attractive view: The aspects of earth of interest to a poet are the casual ones, as light or color, images.

Definitions are relative. The notion of absolutes is relative.

Life is an affair of people not of places. But for me life is an affair of places and that is the trouble. [...]

Literature is the better part of life. To this it seems inevitably necessary to add provided life is the better part of literature.

Thought is an infection. In the case of certain thoughts it becomes an epidemic.

It is life that we are trying to get at in poetry.

After one has abandoned a belief in god, poetry is that essence which takes its place as life's redemption.

Art, broadly, is the form of life or the sound or color of life. Considered as form (in the abstract) it is often indistinguishable from life itself.

The poet seems to confer his identity on the reader. It is easiest to recognise this when listening to music – I mean this sort of thing: the transference.

Accuracy of observation is the equivalent of accuracy of thinking.

A poem is a meteor.

An evening's thought is like a day of clear weather.

The loss of a language creates confusion or dumbness.

The collecting of poetry from one's experience as one goes along is not the same thing as merely writing poetry. [...]

A grandiose subject is not an assurance of a grandiose effect but, most likely, of the opposite.

Art involves vastly more than the sense of beauty.

Life is the reflection of literature.

As life grows more terrible, its literature grows more terrible.

Poetry and materia poetica are interchangeable terms.

Usage is everything. (Les idées sont destinées à être déformées à l'usage. Reconnaître ce fait est une preuve de désintéressement. Georges Braque, *Verve* No. 2).

The imagination wishes to be indulged.

A new meaning is the equivalent of a new word.

Poetry is not personal. [...]

Poetry is a means of redemption. [...]

The poem reveals itself only to the ignorant man.

The relation between the poetry of experience and the poetry of rhetoric is not the same thing as the relation between the poetry of reality and that of the imagination. Experience, at least in the case of a poet of any scope, is much broader than reality.

To a large extent, the problems of poets are the problems of painters and poets must often turn to the literature of painting for a discussion of their own problems.

Weather is a sense of nature. Poetry is a sense.

Abstraction is a part of idealism. It is in that sense that it is ugly.

There are two opposites: the poetry of rhetoric and the poetry of experience.

In poetry at least the imagination must not detach itself from reality.

Not all objects are equal. The vice of imagism was that it did not recognise this.

The poet must put the same degree of intentness into his poetry as, for example, the traveller into his adventure, the painter into his painting.

All poetry is experimental poetry.

The bare image and the image as a symbol are the contrast: the image without meaning and the image as meaning. When the image is used to suggest something else, it is secondary. Poetry, as an imaginative thing, consists of more than lies on the surface. [...]

In poetry, you must love the words, the ideas and images and rhythms with all your capacity to love anything at all. [...]

What we see in the mind is as real to us as what we see by the eye.

Poetry must be irrational.

The purpose of poetry is to make life complete in itself.

Poetry increases the feeling for reality.

The mind is the most powerful thing in the world. [...]

Consider

I
That the whole world is material for poetry.

II
That there is not a specifically poetic material.

One reads poetry with one's nerves.

The poet is the intermediary between people and the world in which they live and, also, between people as between themselves; but not between people and some other world. [...]

Poetry is not the same thing as the imagination taken alone. Nothing is itself taken alone. Things are because of interrelations or interactions.

The final belief is to believe in a fiction, which you know to be a fiction, there being nothing else. The exquisite truth is to know that it is a fiction and that you believe in it willingly.

I
All of our ideas come from the natural world: Trees = umbrellas.

II
There is nothing so offensive to a man of intellectual principle as unprincipled thinking.

Wine and music are not good until afternoon. But poetry is like prayer in that it is most effective in solitude and in the times of solitude as, for example, in the earliest morning. [...]

The great objective is the truth not only of the poem but of poetry.

Poetry is a poetic conception, however expressed. A poem is poetry expressed in words. But in a poem there is a poetry of words. Obviously, a poem may consist of several poetries. [...]

As the reason destroys, the poet must create.

The exquisite environment of fact. The final poem will be the poem of fact in the language of fact. But it will be the poem of fact not realised before. [...]

To live in the world but outside of existing conceptions of it.

It is the explanations of things that we make to ourselves that disclose our character:
    The subjects of one's poems are the symbols of one's self or of one of one's selves.

Poetry has to be something more than a conception of the mind. It has to be a revelation of nature. Conceptions are artificial. Perceptions are essential.

A poem should be part of one's sense of life.

To read a poem should be an experience, like experiencing an act. [...]

Money is a kind of poetry.

Poetry is an effort of a dissatisfied man to find satisfaction through words, occasionally of the dissatisfied thinker to find satisfaction through his emotions.

It is not every day that the world arranges itself in a poem. [...]

In the presence of extraordinary actuality, consciousness takes the place of imagination.

Everything tends to become real; or everything moves in the direction of reality.

There is an intensely pejorative aspect of the idea of the real. The opposite should be the case. Its own poetry is actual.

One does not write for any reader except one.

Every man dies his own death.

The writer who is content to destroy is on a plane with the writer who is content to translate. Both are parasites.

The thing said must be the poem not the language used in saying it. At its best the poem consists of both elements.

A poet looks at the world somewhat as a man looks at a woman.

To have nothing to say and to say it in a tragic manner is not the same thing as to have something to say.

The poem is a nature created by the poet.

The aesthetic order includes all other orders but is not limited to them. [...]

Perhaps there is a degree of perception at which what is real and what is imagined are one: a state of clairvoyant observation, accessible or possibly accessible to the poet or, say, the acutest poet. [...]

Realism is a corruption of reality. [...]

I don't think we should insist that the poet is normal or, for that matter, that anybody is. [...]

Poetry is a purging of the world's poverty and change and evil and death. It is a present perfecting, a satisfaction in the irremediable poverty of life. [...]

The thing seen becomes the thing unseen. The opposite is, or seems to be, impossible.

To study and to understand the fictive world is the function of the poet.

When one is young everything is physical; when one is old everything is psychic. [...]

Which is correct: whether, if I respect my ancestors I am bound
to respect myself or if I respect myself I am bound to respect my
ancestors? [...]

I believe in the image.

The tongue is an eye. [...]

The time will come when poems like Paradise will seem like very
triste contraptions.

The poet is a stronger life.

The great conquest is the conquest of reality. It is not to present
life, for a moment, as it might have been.

A poem is a pheasant.

How has the human spirit ever survived the terrific literature with
which it has had to contend? [...]

Poetry is metaphor.

The word must be the thing it represents otherwise it is a symbol.
It is a question of identity.

When the mind is like a hall in which thought is like a voice speak-
ing, the voice is always that of someone else.

In dramatic poetry the imagination attaches itself to a heightened
reality. Degrees or planes of reality.

It is necessary to propose an enigma to the mind. The mind always
proposes a solution.

There must be something of the peasant in every poet. [...]

The body is the great poem. [...]

The poet is the priest of the invisible.

Society is a sea.

Metaphor creates a new reality from which the original appears to be unreal.

The transition from make believe for one's self to make believe for others is the beginning, or the end, of poetry in the individual.

The acquisitions of poetry are fortuitous: trouvailles. (Hence, its disorder.)

Exhibitionism attaches and is not inherent. [...]

The eye sees less than the tongue says. The tongue says less than the mind thinks.

Reality is the motif.

We have to step boldly into man's interior world or not at all. [...]

It is manner that becomes stale.

Description is an element, like air or water.

The reading of a poem should be an experience. Its writing must be all the more so.

A poem is a café. (Restoration.)

Poets acquire humanity.

Thought tends to collect in pools.

The reason is a part of nature and is controlled by it. [...]

The poet comes to words as nature comes to dry sticks.

Words are the only melodeon. [...]

*Esthétique* is the measure of a civilisation: not the sole measure, but a measure.

Poetry must resist the intelligence almost successfully.

The romantic exists in precision as well as in imprecision.

Literature is based not on life but on propositions about life, of which this is one.

Life is a composite of the propositions about it.

A change of style is a change of subject. [...]

The feeling or the insight is that which quickens the words, not the other way round. [...]

Everything accomplishes itself: fulfills itself. [...]

The full flower of the actual, not the California fruit of the ideal. [...]

Poetry is not limited to a single effect, as, for example, overt reality.

Poetry is a search for the inexplicable.

Poems are new subjects.

Ignorance is one of the sources of poetry.

Poetry is a pheasant disappearing in the brush.

We never arrive intellectually. But emotionally we arrive constantly (as in poetry, happiness, high mountains, vistas).

The imagination consumes & exhausts some element of reality.

The poet is a god or The young poet is a god. The old poet is a tramp.

If the mind is the most terrible force in the world, it is, also, the only force that defends us against terror. (or)

The mind is the most terrible force in the world principally in this that it is the only force that can defend us against itself. The modern world is based on this pensée.

The poet represents the mind in the act of defending us against itself. [...]

Every poem is a poem within a poem: the poem of the idea within the poem of the words.

The poetic view of life is larger than any of its poems (a larger thing than any poem); and to recognise this is the beginning of the recognition of the poetic spirit.

On the death of some men the world reverts to ignorance.

Poetry is the gaiety (joy) of language.

Words are everything else in the world. [...]

If the answer is frivolous, the question was frivolous. [...]

Eventually an imaginary world is entirely without interest.

To be at the end of fact is not to be at the beginning of the imagination but it is to be at the end of both. [...]

What is meant by interest? Is it a form of liking?

One cannot spend one's time in being modern when there are so many more important things to be.

The man who asks questions seeks only to reach a point where it will no longer be necessary for him to ask questions.

I have no life except in poetry. No doubt that would be true if my whole life was free for poetry.

The more intensely one feels something that one likes the more one is willing for it to be what it is.

The mind is not equal to the demands of oratory, poetry etc.

There is a nature that absorbs the mixedness of metaphors. [...]

Imagination applied to the whole world is vapid in comparison to imagination applied to a detail.

It is easier to copy than to think, hence fashion. Besides a community of originals is not a community.

There must be some wing on which to fly.

Poetry is a cure of the mind.

Most modern reproducers of life, even including the camera, really repudiate it. We gulp down evil, choke at good. [...]

Nothing could be more inappropriate to American literature than its English source since the Americans are not British in sensibility.

Poetry is a response to the daily necessity of getting the world right. [...]

Reality is the spirit's true centre.

A poem need not have a meaning and like most things in nature often does not have.

Newness (not novelty) may be the highest individual value in poetry. Even in the meretricious sense of newness a new poetry has value. [...]

To 'subtilise experience' = to apprehend the complexity of the world, to perceive the intricacy of appearance.

Poetry is often a revelation of the elements of appearance.

Literature is the abnormal creating an illusion of the normal. [...]

The theory of poetry is the life of poetry. Christianity is an exhausted culture. [...]

Reality is the object seen in its greatest common sense.

Poetry constantly requires a new relation.

Reality is not what it is. It consists of the many realities which it can be made into. [...]

Poetry is, (and should be,) for the poet, a source of pleasure and satisfaction, not a source of honors.

# W.H. AUDEN

Wystan Hugh Auden was born in York in 1907, and grew up near Birmingham before attending Christ Church, Oxford. He became obsessed in childhood with the lead-mining landscape of the Pennines, and this became a powerful symbol in his work. While at Oxford he met Christopher Isherwood and Stephen Spender, the latter publishing his first collection, *Poems*, in 1928. Early Auden is utterly distinctive: hard-toned and hard to follow, stripped-down and Anglo-Saxon. The success of 30s volumes like *Look, Stranger* (1936), led to him being seen as the voice of a generation. Radically political, culturally sweeping poems like 'Spain' and the Chinese sonnet sequence 'In Time of War' seemed to fulfil this viewpoint. In 1939, however, he decided to settle in America, becoming more meditative, more Christian, and still more stylistically-rounded. A series of long poems appeared, including *The Age of Anxiety* (1947), but the significant work of this second period was in the trio of books, *Nones*, *The Shield of Achilles* and *Homage to Clio* (1951, 1955, 1960). The perspective encompasses great lengths of history, the intimacy of tone is assured, and the technical grasp is faultless. Late Auden is quieter still, and sometimes wiser still. He died in Vienna in 1973.

Auden's essays, mostly written late in his career, have his characteristic blend of mandarin eccentricity and piercing observation. The poet, once seen as the psychological healer of his culture, becomes the creator of useful analogies for the perfections only God can achieve.


## *from* The Virgin and the Dynamo
### (1962)

The subject-matter of the scientist is a crowd of natural events at all times; he presupposes that this crowd is not real but apparent, and seeks to discover the true place of events in the system of nature. The subject-matter of the poet is a crowd of historical occasions of feeling recollected from the past; he presupposes that this crowd is real but should not be, and seeks to transform it into a community. Both science and art are primarily spiritual activities, whatever practical applications may be derived from their results. Disorder, lack of meaning, are spiritual not physical discomforts, order and sense spiritual not physical satisfactions.

It is impossible, I believe, for any poet, while he is writing a poem, to observe with complete accuracy what is going on, to define with any certainty how much of the final result is due to subconscious activity over which he has no control, and how much is due to conscious artifice. All one can say with certainty is negative. A poem does not compose itself in the poet's mind as a child grows in its mother's womb; *some* degree of conscious participation by the poet is necessary, *some* element of craft is always present. On the other hand, the writing of poetry is not, like carpentry, simply a craft; a carpenter can decide to build a table according to certain specifications and know before he begins that the result will be exactly what he intended, but no poet can know what his poem is going to be like until he has written it. The element of craftsmanship in poetry is obscured by the fact that all men are taught to speak and most to read and write, while very few men are taught to draw or paint or write music. Every poet, however, in addition to the everyday linguistic training he receives, requires a training in the poetic use of language. Even those poets who are most vehemently insistent upon the importance of the Muse and the vanity of conscious calculation must admit that, if they had never read any poetry in their lives, it is unlikely that they would have written any themselves. If, in what follows, I refer to the poet, I include under that both his Muse and his mind, his subconscious and conscious activity.

The subject-matter of a poem is comprised of a crowd of recollected occasions of feeling, among which the most important are recollections of encounters with sacred beings or events. This crowd the poet attempts to transform into a community by embodying it in a verbal society. Such a society, like any society in nature, has its own laws; its laws of prosody and syntax are analogous to the laws of physics and chemistry. Every poem must presuppose – sometimes mistakenly – that the history of the language is at an end.

One should say, rather, that a poem is a natural organism, not an inorganic thing. For example, it is rhythmical. The temporal recurrences of rhythm are never identical, as the metrical notation would seem to suggest. Rhythm is to time what symmetry is to space. Seen from a certain distance, the features of a human face seem symmetrically arranged, so that a face with a nose a foot long or a left eye situated two inches away from the nose would appear monstrous. Close up, however, the exact symmetry disappears; the size and position of the features vary slightly from face to face and, indeed, if a face could exist in which the symmetry were mathematically perfect, it would look, not like a face, but like a lifeless mask. So with rhythm. A poem may be described as being written in iambic pentameters, but if every foot in every line were identical, the poem would sound intolerable to the ear. I am sometimes inclined to think that the aversion of many modern poets and their readers to formal verse may be due to their association of regular repetition and formal restrictions with all that is most boring and lifeless in modern life, road drills, time-clock punching, bureaucratic regulations.

It has been said that a poem should not mean but be. This is not quite accurate. In a poem, as distinct from many other kinds of verbal societies, meaning and being are identical. A poem might be called a pseudo-person. Like a person, it is unique and addresses the reader personally. On the other hand, like a natural being and unlike a historical person, it cannot lie. We may be and frequently are mistaken as to the meaning or the value of a poem, but the cause of our mistake lies in our own ignorance or self-deception, not in the poem itself.

The nature of the final poetic order is the outcome of a dialectical struggle between the recollected occasions of feeling and the verbal system. As a society the verbal system is actively coercive upon the occasions it is attempting to embody; what it cannot embody truthfully it excludes. As a potential community the occasions are passively resistant to all claims of the system to embody them which they do not recognise as just; they decline all unjust persuasions. As members of crowds, every occasion competes with every other, demanding inclusion and a dominant position to which they are not necessarily entitled, and every word demands that the system shall modify itself in its case, that a special exception shall be made for it and it only.

In a successful poem, society and community are one order and the system may love itself because the feelings which it embodies are all members of the same community, loving each other and it. A poem may fail in two ways; it may exclude too much (banality), or attempt to embody more than one community at once (disorder).

In writing a poem, the poet can work in two ways. Starting from an intuitive idea of the kind of community he desires to call into being, he may work backwards in search of the system which will most justly incarnate that idea, or, starting with a certain system, he may work forward in search of the community which it is capable of incarnating most truthfully. In practice he nearly always works simultaneously in both directions, modifying his conception of the ultimate nature of the community at the immediate suggestions of the system, and modifying the system in response to his growing intuition of the future needs of the community.

A system cannot be selected completely arbitrarily nor can one say that any given system is absolutely necessary. The poet searches for one which imposes just obligations on the feelings. "Ought" always implies "can" so that a system whose claims cannot be met must be scrapped. But the poet has to beware of accusing the system of injustice when what is at fault is the laxness and self-love of the feelings upon which it is making its demands.

Every poet, consciously or unconsciously, holds the following absolute presuppositions, as the dogmas of his art:

1. A historical world exists, a world of unique events and unique persons, related by analogy, not identity. The number of events and analogical relations is potentially infinite. The existence of such a world is a good, and every addition to the number of events, persons and relations is an additional good.

2. The historical world is a fallen world, i.e., though it is good that it exists, the way in which it exists is evil, being full of unfreedom and disorder.

3. The historical world is a redeemable world. The unfreedom and disorder of the past can be reconciled in the future.

It follows from the first presupposition that the poet's activity in creating a poem is analogous to God's activity in creating man after his own image. It is not an imitation, for were it so, the poet would be able to create like God *ex nihilo*; instead, he requires pre-existing occasions of feeling and a pre-existing language out of which to create. It is analogous in that the poet creates not necessarily according to a law of nature but voluntarily according to provocation.

It is untrue, strictly speaking, to say that a poet should not write poems unless he must; strictly speaking it can only be said that he should not write them unless he can. The phrase is sound in practice, because only in those who can and when they can is the motive genuinely compulsive.

In those who profess a desire to write poetry, yet exhibit an incapacity to do so, it is often the case that their desire is not for creation but for self-perpetuation, that they refuse to accept their own mortality, just as there are parents who desire children, not as new persons analogous to themselves, but to prolong their own existence in time. The sterility of this substitution of identity for analogy is expressed in the myth of Narcissus. When the poet speaks, as he sometimes does, of achieving immortality through his poem, he does not mean that he hopes, like Faust, to live for ever, but that he hopes to rise from the dead. In poetry as in other matters the law holds good that he who would save his life must lose it; unless the poet sacrifices his feelings completely to the poem so that they are no longer his but the poem's, he fails.

It follows from the second presupposition, that a poem is a witness to man's knowledge of evil as well as good. It is not the duty of a witness to pass moral judgment on the evidence he has to give, but to give it clearly and accurately; the only crime of which a witness can be guilty is perjury. When we say that poetry is beyond good and evil, we simply mean that a poet can no more change the facts of what he has felt than, in the natural order, parents can change the inherited physical characteristics which they pass on to their children. The judgement good-or-evil applies only to the intentional movements of the will. Of our feelings in a given situation which are the joint product of our intention and the response to the external factors in that situation it can only be said that, given an intention and the response, they are appropriate or inappropriate. Of a recollected feeling it cannot be said that it is appropriate or inappropriate because the historical situation in which it arose no longer exists.

Every poem, therefore, is an attempt to present an analogy to that paradisal state in which Freedom and Law, System and Order are united in harmony. Every good poem is very nearly a Utopia. Again, an analogy, not an imitation; the harmony is possible and verbal only.

It follows from the third presupposition that a poem is beautiful or ugly to the degree that it succeeds or fails in reconciling contradictory feelings in an order of mutual propriety. Every beautiful poem presents an analogy to the forgiveness of sins; an analogy, not an imitation, because it is not evil intentions which are repented of and pardoned but contradictory feelings which the poet surrenders to the poem in which they are reconciled.

The effect of beauty, therefore, is good to the degree that, through its analogies, the goodness of created existence, the historical fall into unfreedom and disorder, and the possibility of regaining paradise through repentance and forgiveness are recognised. Its effect is evil to the degree that beauty is taken, not as analogous to, but identical with goodness, so that the artist regards himself or is regarded by others as God, the pleasure of beauty taken for the joy of Paradise, and the conclusion drawn that, since all is well in the work of art, all is well in history. But all is not well there.

# LOUIS MacNEICE

Louis MacNeice worked as a writer and producer for BBC Radio. He was born in Belfast in 1907 and educated at Oxford, where his poetry began to attract attention in the early 1930s, publishing alongside his contemporaries Spender, Auden and Day Lewis ('Macspaunday', as they were known). MacNeice's long association with these poets, and his own bitter ambivalence to the politics of Ireland, saw the question of his own "Irishness" underrepresented in his own lifetime; although he has been substantially "reclaimed" by subsequent generations of Irish poets. *Poems* (1935) and *Letters from Iceland* (with Auden, 1937) are among his key works, but it was the extended *Autumn Journal* (1939), written at the height of the Munich crisis, that won MacNeice his greatest acclaim as a poet of great personal and public balance. He died from pneumonia in 1963, caught making radio productions in a damp cave, and his *Collected Poems* appeared three years later.

The poet is 'the still, small voice' of society, MacNeice writes – its conscience, its morality, but never its dogmatist: propaganda is someone else's responsibility. The poet is committed to honesty, to writing what 'comes out of life': after all there can be no duty to write, but there can be no poetry without commitment.

# A Statement

### (1938)

I have been asked to commit myself about poetry. I have committed myself already so much *in* poetry that this seems almost superfluous. I think that the poet is only an extension – or, if you prefer it, a concentration – of the ordinary man. The content of poetry comes out of life. Half the battle is the selection of material. The poet is both critic and entertainer. He should select subjects therefore which (a) he is in a position to criticise, and (b) other people are likely to find interesting. The poet at the moment will tend to be moralist rather than æsthete. But his morality must be honest; he must not merely retail other people's dogma. The world no doubt needs propaganda, but propaganda (unless you use the term, as many do, very loosely indeed) is not the poet's job. He is not the loudspeaker of society, but something much more like its still, small voice. At his highest he can be its conscience, its critical faculty, its grievous instinct. He will not serve his world by wearing blinkers. The world today consists of specialists and intransigents. The poet, by contrast, should be synoptic and elastic in his sympathies. It is quite possible therefore that at some period his duty as a poet may conflict with his duty as a man. In that case he can stop writing, but he must not degrade his poetry even in the service of a good cause; for bad poetry won't serve it much anyway. It is still, however, possible to write honestly without feeling that the time for honesty is past.

# HUGH MacDIARMID

Hugh MacDiarmid, or more properly, Christopher Murray Grieve, was born in 1892 in the Scottish borders. He served as a medical orderly during the First World War, returning with a store of frustrated energy, which for 20 years, from 1920 on, he expended in shaking up Scottish literature. He was a reiver of vocabularies, raiding Jamieson's Scots Dictionary to produce an intellectualised poetry in Scots, rejuvenated by unfamiliar words. In *Sangschaw* (1925) and *Penny Wheep* (1926), the Scots word is treated almost as Pound treated the image: as a source of energy. His long masterpiece, 'A Drunk Man Looks at the Thistle' (1926), combined his garrulity and striking vocabulary with tightly interlocking symbols, portraying the Scot as the archetypal Modernist. Subsequent attempts to repeat the feat are either disconnected (*To Circumjack Cencrastus*, 1930) or incomplete (*Clann Albann*). In 1933, after divorce and remarriage, MacDiarmid settled in the Shetlands and in conditions of some poverty produced his most balanced book, *Stony Limits* (1934), in which he tried his acquisitive skills on the vocabulary of science. Breakdown and a radical reformation of his poetics produced a prosaic late poetry in English, often employing collage. His supposedly crowning work, *Mature Art*, remains unassembled.

MacDiarmid made his living as a journalist, and his massive prose output is uneven. In this editorial for *The Scottish Chapbook*, he is typically asserting his own practice is in line with whatever sounds most radical in European thought, but his underlying faith in the power of language, particularly Scots, is what comes through.

# *from* A Theory of Scots Letters
(1923)

## I

[...] I venture to day that whoever has understood the meaning of "disinterestedness" is not far-off understanding the goal of human culture.

A.R. ORAGE, The Criteria of Culture

Nationalism in literature is the reaction of a distinctive essential of the spirit to the various time-influences to which it is subjected. And that which gives a recognisable if hardly definable unity to the work of all true Scottish writers, whether in English or the Vernacular, is a quality of 'disinterestedness' in the sense in which Orage uses it...Consider in this connection what Professor Gregory Smith says in this passage from his most searching and stimulating book, *Scottish Literature*:

There is more in the Scottish antithesis of the real and fantastic than is to be explained by the familiar rules of rhetoric...The one invades the other without warning. They are the 'polar twins' of the Scottish Muse...The douce travesty which stands for the Scot with the general (the methodical, level-headed, self-conscious creature of popular tradition) never says as much as he thinks; he is as calm as a country Sabbath morn on the cantrips of his mind. But he is not the Scot who steps forth self-expressed in the Makars old and new despite the accidents or thwarts of history which stayed or appeared to stay the freer play of his fancy...This mingling, even of the most eccentric kind, is an indication to us that the Scot, in that fashion which takes all things as granted, is at his ease in both rooms of life, and turns to fun and even profanity with no misgivings. We owe part of our strength to this freedom in passing from one mood to another. It takes some people more time than they can spare to see the absolute propriety of a gargoyle's grinning at the elbow of a kneeling saint!

Is not that precisely why the most advanced literature today is unintelligible to many highly educated people even? Professor Gregory Smith has in these words described the great vital characteristic of Scottish literature – a distinguishing faculty, which it can only shape forth poorly in English, but which is potentially expressible in the Vernacular to which it belongs. It is the predominant feature of Scots Literature old and new, and yet, do not the same phrases ('taking all things as granted', 'freedom in passing from one mood to another') sum up the essential tendencies of the most advanced schools of thought in every country in Europe today? We base our belief in the possibility of a great Scottish Literary Renaissance, deriving its strength from the resources that lie latent and almost unsuspected in the Vernacular, upon the fact that the genius of our Vernacular enables us to secure with comparative ease the very effects and swift transitions which other literatures are for the most part unsuccessfully endeavouring to cultivate in languages that have a very different and inferior bias. Whatever the potentialities of the Doric may be, however, there cannot be a revival in the real sense of the word – a revival of the spirit as distinct from a mere renewed vogue of the letter – unless these potentialities are in accord with the newest and truest tendencies of human thought. We confess to having been discouraged when thinking of the Vernacular Movement by the fact that the seal of its approval is so largely set upon the traditional and the conventional. The real enemy is he who cries: 'Hands off our fine old Scottish tongue.' If all that the Movement is to achieve is to preserve specimens of Braid Scots, archaic, imitative, belonging to a type of life that has passed and cannot return, in a sort of museum department of our consciousness – set apart from our vital preoccupations – it is a movement which not only cannot claim our support but compels our opposition. The rooms of thought are choc-a-bloc with far too much dingy old rubbish as it is. There are too many vital problems clamouring for attention.

It is a different matter, however, if an effort is to be made to really revive the Vernacular – to encourage the experimental exploitation of the unexplored possibilities of Vernacular expression. 'The letter killeth but the spirit giveth life.' Only in so far as the Vernacular has unused resources corresponding better than English does to the progressive expression of the distinctive characteristics of Scottish life – however much these may have been submerged, subverted, or camouflaged, by present conditions (we shall deal later with the question of the relationship between literature and politics) – has it possibilities of literary value. If the cultural level of work in the Doric is not capable of being raised to equal that in any other living language – if the Doric has not certain qualities which no other language possesses and qualities at that of consequence to modern consciousness as a whole – then all that can be hoped for is a multiplication of equivalents in the Vernacular to work that has already been better achieved in other languages without any special contribution at all from Scotland to the expressive resource of modern life. The Doric unquestionably has a past and, to a very much more limited extent, a present. The question is whether it has a future which will enable it successfully to compete, at any rate along specialised lines, with other languages. Our interest, therefore, should centre not so much in what has been done in the Doric as in what has not but may be done in it. No literature can rest on its laurels. [...]

For our part we frankly confess that a living dog is worth any number of dead lions, and we unreservedly accept Thomas Hardy's definition 'that literature is the written expression of revolt against accepted things'.

We have been enormously struck by the resemblance – the moral resemblance – between Jamieson's *Etymological Dictionary of the Scottish Language* and James Joyce's *Ulysses*. A *vis comica* that has not yet been liberated lies bound by desuetude and misappreciation in the recesses of the Doric: and its potential uprising would be no less prodigious, uncontrollable, and utterly at variance with conventional morality than was Joyce's tremendous outpouring. The Scottish instinct is irrevocably, continuously, opposed to all who 'are at ease in Zion'. [...]

And one of the most distinctive characteristics of the Vernacular, part of its very essence, is its insistent recognition of the body, the

senses. [...] In other words, in Meredith's phrase, the Vernacular
can never consent to 'forfeit the beast wherewith we are crost'.
This explains the unique blend of the lyrical and the ludicrous in
primitive Scots sentiment. It enables us to realise very clearly just
what Matthew Arnold meant when he called Burns 'a beast with
splendid gleams' – and the essence of the genius of our race, is, in
our opinion, the reconciliation it effects between the base and the
beautiful, recognising that they are complementary and indispens-
able to each other.

## II

The Scottish Vernacular is the only language in Western Europe
instinct with those uncanny spiritual and pathological perceptions
alike which constitute the uniqueness of Dostoevesky's work, and
word after word of Doric establishes a blood-bond in a fashion at
once infinitely more thrilling and vital and less explicable than those
deliberately sought after by writers such as D.H. Lawrence in the
medium of English which is inferior for such purposes because it
has [an] entirely different natural bias which has been so confirmed
down the centuries as to be insusceptible of correction. The Scots
Vernacular is a vast storehouse of just the very peculiar and subtle
effects which modern European literature in general is assiduously
seeking and, if the next century is to see an advance in mental science
equal to that which last century has marked in material science,
then the resumption of the Scots Vernacular into the mainstream
of European letters, in a fashion which the most enthusiastic Ver-
nacularist may well hesitate to hope for, is inevitable. The Vernacular
is a vast unutilised mass of lapsed observation made by minds whose
attitudes to experience and whose speculative and imaginative ten-
dencies were quite different from any possible to Englishmen and
Anglicised Scots today. It is an inchoate Marcel Proust – a Dosto-
eveskian debris of ideas – an inexhaustible quarry of subtle and
significant sound.

As a recent writer on the revival of Irish Gaelic (in which novels
as well as poems and plays are now being written) remarks,

> the best work done in Gaelic reveals a part of Irish life that has been
> long silent, with a freshness due to sources that have remained com-
> paratively uninfluenced by alien imagination... Most of the writers of
> the so-called Irish Literary Revival of a decade or so back were ignorant
> of Gaelic. Even Synge had probably only a patois knowledge... A school
> is now arising among young men having the advantage of an educated
> knowledge of the tongue, and even the distinctiveness of their work in
> English is more marked. The new generation will doubtless be increas-
> ingly bilingual and in possession of the literary traditions of Gaelic life.

The revival of Scots Vernacular is being retarded simply because of the fact that the majority of writers in the Vernacular have only a patois knowledge of it – not an educated knowledge – and are not to any useful extent in possession of its literary traditions apart from Burns: while they confine their efforts to a little range of conventional forms.

A writer in the *Glasgow Herald* recently pointed out that reflexly the distinctive humour of our Vernacular fulfilled at least three invaluable functions.

> It stimulates the wits and the descriptive and reflective powers. It keeps alive a spirit of brave and virile gaiety. By pricking the bladders of pride and pretension, and nourishing the independence and self-respect of the stepchildren of Fortune, it brings all sorts and conditions of men to a greatest common measure of sheer humanity, and is thus a powerful preservative of the true spirit of democracy...The democratic spirit of the Scottish Vernacular speech and literature is strongly allied with an ethical bent which is all the stronger for its fearless realism and its freedom from didacticism or sentiment, and also with an element of pathos that has suffered somewhat from its dilution and exploitation by certain writers of the Kailyard School.

The writer goes on to say 'jalouse, dwam, dowie, gurlie, mavis, carline, crouse, gawkie, blate, gaucie, and thrawn are chance selections from a long list of fine old words that usefully express shades of meaning which English either ignores or renders very imperfectly'. To that may be added the fact that the Vernacular abounds in terms which short-circuit conceptions that take sentences to express in English. Take only one – *Guyfaul*. It takes nine English words to convey its meaning. It means 'Hungry for his meat but not very hungry for his work'.

Just as physiologically we have lost certain powers possessed by our forefathers – the art of wiggling our ears, for example, or of moving our scalps this way and that – so we have lost (but may perhaps re-acquire) wordforming faculties peculiar to the Doric for the purposes of both psychological and nature description. There are words and phrases in the Vernacular which thrill me with a sense of having been produced as a result of mental processes entirely different from my own and much more powerful. They embody observations of a kind which the modern mind makes with increasing difficulty and weakened effect. Take the word *birth*, for instance, meaning a current in the sea caused by a furious tide but taking a different course from it – a contrary motion. It exemplifies a fascinating, exceedingly adroit and purely Scottish application of metaphor. Then there are natural occurrences and phenomena of all kinds which have apparently never been noted by the English mind. No words exist for them in English. For instance – *water-gaw* – for an indistinct rainbow; *yow-trummle* – meaning the cold weather in July after the sheepshearing; *cavaburd* – meaning a thick fall of snow; and *blue bore* – meaning a patch of blue in a cloudy sky. Another feature of the Doric which I will not illustrate here is the fashion in which diverse attitudes of mind or shades of temper are telescoped into single words or phrases, investing the whole speech with subtle flavours of irony, commiseration, realism and humour which cannot be reproduced in English. In onomatopoetic effect, too, the Doric has a wider range and infinitely richer resources than English while the diversity of inherent bias is revealed in un-mistakable fashion.

Whatever the potentialities of the Doric may be, however, there cannot be a revival in the real sense of the word – a revival of the spirit as distinct from a mere renewed vogue of the letter – unless these potentialities are in accord with the newest tendencies of human thought.

# BASIL BUNTING

Basil Bunting was born in Northumberland in 1900, and returned there in the latter part of his life. The intervening period was filled with travel to exotic locations, and Ezra Pound. In 1933, Pound published a considerable selection of Bunting's work in the *Active Anthology*, alongside Zukofsky, among others. Bunting appeared to remain in Pound's shadow for many years. His experiences in Persia (now Iran) furnished him with the subject-matter of *The Spoils* (1951) as well as several of his odes, and these poems combine an exquisite musicality with trenchant insights into British imperialism. His return to the North-East was followed by the emergence in Newcastle of poets interested in Modernism and American poetry, and his career achieved a second flowering of productivity and acknowledgement with readings at the Morden Tower and the publication of *Briggflatts* (1966), which applies his technical insights to his native ground and language. Structurally it has an integrity, based on a reading of sonata form, that surpasses his old master's capacity to organise *The Cantos*, while thematically it recalls Wordsworth's *Prelude*.

Bunting's critical writings can overplay the analogy with musical form, but at their best display the rigour of ear and attention that marks him as a Northern master of Modernism, comparable to Hugh MacDiarmid for scope and achievement.

# The Poet's Point of View
### (1966)

Poetry, like music, is to be heard. It deals in sound – long sounds and short sounds, heavy beats and light beats, the tone relations of vowels, the relations of consonants to one another which are like instrumental colour in music. Poetry lies dead on the page, until some voice brings it to life, just as music, on the stave, is no more than instructions to the player. A skilled musician can imagine the sound, more or less, and a skilled reader can try to hear, mentally, what his eyes see in print: but nothing will satisfy either of them till his ears hear it as real sound in the air. Poetry must be read aloud.

Reading in silence is the source of half the misconceptions that have caused the public to distrust poetry. Without the sound, the reader looks at the lines as he looks at prose, seeking a meaning. Prose exists to convey meaning, and no meaning such as prose conveys can be expressed as well in poetry. That is not poetry's business.

Poetry is seeking to make not meaning, but beauty; or if you insist on misusing words, its "meaning" is of another kind, and lies in the relation to one another of lines and patterns of sound, perhaps harmonious, perhaps contrasting and clashing, which the hearer feels rather than understands, lines of sound drawn in the air which stir deep emotions which have not even a name in prose. This needs no explaining to an audience which gets its poetry by ear. It has neither time nor inclination to seek a prose meaning in poetry.

Very few artists have clear, analytical minds. They do what they do because they must. Some think about it afterwards in a muddled way and try unskilfully to reason about their art. Thus theories are produced which mislead critics and tyros, and sometimes disfigure the work of artists who try to carry out their own theories.

There is no need of any theory for what gives pleasure through the ear, music or poetry. The theoreticians will follow the artist and fail to explain him. The sound, whether it be in words or notes, is all that matters. It is perfectly possible to delight an audience by reading poetry of sufficient quality in a language it does not know. I have seen some of Goethe, some of Hafez, produce nearly the same effect they would have produced on an audience familiar with German or Persian.

Composers are not always the best players of their own compositions, nor poets the best readers of their own verses, though the composer and the poet can always bring out something that might otherwise be lost. Some lack a voice, or have not learned to control it. Some are so immersed in the mechanics of their craft that they, for instance, make an exaggerated pause at the line's end and lose the swing of the metre. Some have mannerisms, such as the constant repetition of a particular cadence, producing an effect rather like the detestable noise parsons make in church. Such defects no doubt sicken some people of poetry readings.

Actors, on the other hand, have the defects of their profession. They cannot bear to leave their beautiful voices in the dark, they must use the whole range on poems that need only a short scale. They are trained for the stage, to make the most of every contrast, and are apt to make poetry sound theatrical. Nevertheless, actors and poets alike, if they but speak the lines, will give you more of a poem than you can get by reading it in silence.

Do not let the people who set examinations kid you that you are any nearer understanding a poem when you have parsed and analysed every sentence, scanned every line, looked up the words in the Oxford Dictionary and the allusions in a library of reference

books. That sort of knowledge will make it harder for you to under-
stand the poem because, when you listen to it, you will be distracted
by a multitude of irrelevant scraps of knowledge. You will not hear
the meaning, which is in the sound.

All the arts are plagued by charlatans seeking money, or fame,
or just an excuse to idle. The less the public understands the art,
the easier it is for charlatans to flourish. Since poetry reading
became popular, they have found a new field, and it is not easy
for the outsider to distinguish the fraud from the poet. But it is a
little less difficult when poetry is read aloud. Claptrap soon bores.
Threadbare work soon sounds thin and broken backed.

There were mountebanks at the famous Albert Hall meeting, as
well as a poet or two, but the worst, most insidious charlatans fill
chairs and fellowships at universities, write for the weeklies or work
for the BBC or the British Council or some other asylum for
obsequious idlers. In the 18th century it was the Church. If these
men had to read aloud in public, their empty lines, without reson-
ance, would soon give them away.

# WILLIAM CARLOS WILLIAMS

William Carlos Williams (1883-1963) first met Ezra Pound and H.D. at Pennsylvania University. Unlike them he remained in the States, working as a doctor in Rutherford, New Jersey. Like them he wrote a poetry which dispensed with 19th century tradition. His language was marked by a focus on the energies of American English, and his poetry, which appeared in numerous collections such as *Spring and All* (1923), *An Early Martyr* (1935) and *Journey to Love* (1955), is marked by the distinctive dynamic of his free verse line. More than his contemporaries, he was open to urban diversity and the diversity of means at his disposal to depict it. Instrumental in the creation of Objectivism, involved in the early career of Allen Ginsberg, influencing writers as far afield as Tom Leonard and Miroslav Holub, Williams helped to change poetry's modes of perception. His major work, the long poem *Paterson* (1946-1958), is an examination of the interrelation of individual and city, deploying historical documents and contemporary linguistic artefacts like letters, shopping lists, adverts. It is held together by his triumphant and transformative sureness of ear.

His prose reflects with slightly less focus the concerns of his poetry, particularly the necessity to renew poetic language (*In the American Grain*, 1925), and the workings of the poetic eye ('No ideas but in things'). His meditations on a possible unit within the free verse line, the variable foot, remain as fascinating as they are convoluted.

# On Measure – Statement for Cid Corman
## (1954)

Verse – we'd better not speak of poetry lest we become confused – verse has always been associated in men's minds with "measure", i.e., with mathematics. In scanning any piece of verse, you "count" the syllables. Let's not speak either of rhythm, an aimless sort of thing without precise meaning of any sort. But measure implies something that can be measured. Today verse has lost all measure.

Our lives also have lost all that in the past we had to measure them by, except outmoded standards that are meaningless to us. In the same way our verses, of which our poems are made, are left without any metrical construction of which you can speak, any recognisable, any new measure by which they can be pulled together. We get sonnets, etc, but no one alive today, or half alive, seems to see anything incongruous in that. They cannot see that poems cannot any longer be made following a Euclidian measure, "beautiful" as this may make them. The very grounds for our

beliefs have altered. We do not live that way any more; nothing in
our lives, at bottom, is ordered according to that measure; our
social concepts, our schools, our very religious ideas, certainly our
understanding of mathematics are greatly altered. Were we called
upon to go back to what we believed in the past we should be lost.
Only the construction of our poems – and at best the construction
of a poem must engage the tips of our intellectual awareness – is
left shamefully to the past.

A relative order is operative elsewhere in our lives. Even the
divorce laws recognise that. Are we so stupid that we can't see the
same things apply to the construction of modern verse, to an art
which hopes to engage the attention of a modern world? If men
do not find in the verse they are called on to read a construction
that interests them or that they believe in, they will not read your
verses and I, for one, do not blame them. What will they find out
there that is worth bothering about? So, I understand, the young
men of my generation are going back to Pope. Let them. They
want to be read at least with some understanding of what they are
saying and Pope is at least understandable; a good master. They
have been besides scared by all the wild experimentation that pre-
ceded them so that now they want to play it safe and to conform.

They have valid reasons for what they are doing – of course
not all of them are doing it, but the English, with a man such as
Christopher Fry prominent among them, lead the pack. Dylan
Thomas is thrashing around somewhere in the wings but he is
Welsh and acknowledges no rule – he cannot be of much help to
us. Return as they may to the classics for their models it will not
solve anything for them. They will still, later, have to tackle the
fundamental problems which concern verse of a new construction to
conform with our age. Their brothers in the chemical laboratory,
from among whom their most acute readers will come if they know
what is good for them, must be met on a footing that will not be
retrograde but equal to their own. Though they may recognise
this theoretically there is no one who dares overstep the conven-
tional mark.

It's not only a question of daring, no one has instructed them
differently. Most poems I see today are concerned with what they
are *saying*, how profound they have been given to be. So true is
this that those who write them have forgotten to make poems at
all of them. Thank God we're not musicians, with our lack of
structural invention we'd be ashamed to look ourselves in the face
otherwise. There is nothing interesting in the construction of our
poems, nothing that can jog the ear out of its boredom. I for one

can't read them. There is nothing in their metrical construction to attract me, so I fall back on e. e. cummings and the disguised conventions that he presents which are at least amusing – as amusing as 'Doctor Foster went to Gloucester, in a shower of rain.' Ogden Nash is also amusing, but not amusing enough.

The thing is that "free verse" since Whitman's time has led us astray. He was taken up, as were the leaders of the French Revolution before him with the abstract idea of freedom. It slopped over into all their thinking. But it was an idea lethal to all order, particularly to that order which has to do with the poem. Whitman was right in breaking our bounds but, having no valid restraints to hold him, went wild. He didn't know any better. At the last he resorted to a loose sort of language with no discipline about it of any sort and we have copied its worst feature, just that.

The corrective to that is forgetting Whitman, for instinctively he was on the right track, to find a new discipline. Invention is the mother of art. We must invent new modes to take the place of those which are worn out. For want of this we have gone back to worn-out modes with our tongues hanging out and our mouths drooling after "beauty" which is not even in the same category under which we are seeking it. Whitman, great as he was in his instinctive drive, was also the cause of our going astray. I among the rest have much to answer for. No verse can be free, it must be governed by some measure, but not by the old measure. There Whitman was right but there, at the same time, his leadership failed him. The time was not ready for it. We have to return to some measure but a measure consonant with our time and not a mode so rotten that it stinks.

We have no measure by which to guide ourselves except a purely intuitive one which we feel but do not name. I am not speaking of verse which has long since been frozen into a rigid mould signifying its death, but of verse which shows that it has been touched with some dissatisfaction with its present state. It is all over the page at the mere whim of the man who composed it. This will not do. Certainly an art which implies a discipline as the poem does, a rule, a measure, will not tolerate it. There is no measure to guide us, no recognisable measure.

Relativity gives us the cue. So, again, mathematics comes to the rescue of the arts. Measure, an ancient word in poetry, something we have forgotten in its literal significance as something measured, becomes related again with the poetic. We have today to do with the poetic, as always, but a *relatively* stable foot, not a rigid one. That is all the difference. It is that which must become the object

of our search. Only by coming to that realisation shall we escape
the power of these magnificent verses of the past which we have
always marveled over and still be able to enjoy them. We live in a
new world, pregnant with tremendous possibility for enlightenment
but sometimes, being old, I despair of it. For the poem which has
always led the way to the other arts as to life, being explicit, the
only art which is explicit, has lately been left to fall into decay.

Without measure we are lost. But we have lost even the ability
to count. Actually we are not as bad as that. Instinctively we have
continued to count as always but it has become not a conscious
process and being unconscious has descended to a low level of the
invention. There are a few exceptions but there is no one among us
who is consciously aware of what he is doing. I have accordingly
made a few experiments which will appear in a new book shortly.
What I want to emphasise is that I do not consider anything I have
put down there as final. There will be other experiments but all
will be directed toward the discovery of a new measure, I repeat,
a new measure by which may be ordered our poems as well as our
lives.

# LOUIS ZUKOFSKY

Born in 1904 in New York City of Yiddish-speaking parents, and educated at Columbia, Louis Zukofsky lived and worked most of his life in New York. With William Carlos Williams he became the central figure in the Objectivist school of poetry; and in 1931, Pound secured him the task of editing the now famously influential 'Objectivist' issue of *Poetry* magazine. A descendant of Imagism and its techniques, Objectivism gave similar attention to the precision and cadence of writing, but placed an increasingly formal emphasis upon the poem and the poet as artefacts in the world. Zukofsky collected his shorter volumes in *All* (1966), but it was his long, ambitious 24-part poem '*A*' for which his writing will be remembered, published over a 38-year period and collected upon his death in 1978. A rich and idiosyncratic melee of history, poetics and autobiography, Zukofsky's work is characterised by an attention to the sonic and the intellectual properties of language. And yet, perhaps more important than the work itself, has been his influence on a younger generation of poets, notably Creeley, Duncan and the Black Mountain college.

A prime expression of Objectivist thought, 'A Statement for Poetry' shows how – through sound, image, and the interplay of concepts – a poem becomes 'another created thing in the world, to affect and be judged by it'.

# A Statement for Poetry
## (1950/1967)

Any definition of poetry is difficult because the implications of poetry are complex – and that despite the natural, physical simplicity of its best examples. Thus poetry may be defined as an order of words that as movement and tone (rhythm and pitch) approaches in varying degrees the wordless art of music as a kind of mathematical limit. Poetry is derived obviously from everyday existence (real or ideal).

Whoever makes it may very well consider a poem as a design or construction. A contemporary American poet says: 'A poem is a small (or large) machine made of words.' The British mathematician George Hardy has envied poetry its fineness of immediate logic. A scientist may envy its bottomless perception of relations which, for all its intricacies, keeps a world of things tangible and whole. Perhaps poetry is what Hideki Yukawa is looking for when, with reference to his latest theory of particles that possess not only charge and mass but also dimensions in space, he says: 'This problem of infinity is a disease that must be cured. I am very eager to be healthy.'

'Poetry is something more philosophic and of graver import than history.' (Aristole, *Poetics* 9.) True or not this statement recalls that poetry has contributed intense records to history. The rhythmic or intoned utterance that punctuates the movement of a body in a dance or ritual, aware of dead things as alive, as it fights animals and earth; Homer's heavenly singer who gave pleasure at a feast in a society accomplished in husbandry and craft, whose group beliefs *saw* the Muses presiding over the harmony that moved the words; the dry passages of Lucretius forced by his measures to sing despite their regard for abstract patterns of thought, beginnings of atomic speculation: the stages of culture are concretely delineated in these three examples.

Poetry has always been considered more literary than music, though so-called pure music may be literary in a communicative sense. The parts of a fugue, Bach said, should behave like reasonable men in an orderly discussion. But music does not depend mainly on the human voice, as poetry does, for rendition. And it is possible in imagination to divorce speech of all graphic elements, to let it become a movement of sounds. It is this musical horizon of poetry (which incidentally poems perhaps never reach) that permits anybody who does not know Greek to listen and get something out of the poetry of Homer: to "tune in" to the human tradition, to its voice which has developed among the sounds of natural things, and thus escape the confines of a time and place, as one hardly ever escapes them in studying Homer's grammar. In this sense poetry is international.

The foregoing definition of poetry has been, for the most part, cultural in its bearings. But what specifically is good poetry? It is precise information on existence out of which it grows, and information of its own existence, that is, the movement (and tone) of words. Rhythm, pulse, keeping time with existence, is the distinction of its technique. This integrates any human emotion, any discourse, into an order of words that exists as another created thing in the world, to affect it and be judged by it. Condensed speech is most of the method of poetry (as distinguished from the essentially discursive art of prose). The rest is ease, pause, grace. If read properly, good poetry does not argue its attitudes or beliefs; it exists independently of the reader's preferences for one kind of "subject" or another. Its conviction is in its mastery or technique. The length of a poem has nothing to do with its merits as composition in which each sound of a word is weighed, though obviously it is possible to have more of a good thing – a wider range of things felt, known, and conveyed.

The oldest recorded poems go back to the Egyptian *Chapters of Coming Forth by Day*, some of whose hieroglyphs were old by 3000 BC. The human tradition that survives the esoteric significance of these poems remains, as in these lines praising the sun:

> Millions of years have passed, we cannot count their number,
> Millions of years shall come. You are above the years.

It is quite safe to say that the *means* and *objects* of poetry (cf. Aristotle's *Poetics*) have been constant, that is, recognisably human, since *c*. 3000 BC.

I. The Means of Poetry: *Words* – consisting of *syllables*, in turn made up of *phones* that are denoted by *letters* that were once graphic symbols or pictures. Words grow out of effects of

A. Sight, touch, taste, smell
B. Hearing
C. Thought with respect to other words, the interplay of concepts.

II. The Objects of Poetry: *Poems* – rhythmic compositions of words whose components are

A. Image
B. Sound
C. Interplay of Concepts (judgments of other words either abstract or sensible, or both at once).

Some poems make use of – i.e. resolve – all three components. Most poems use only A and B. Poems that use B and C are less frequent, though C is a poetic device (invention) at least as old as Homer's puns on the name of Odysseus: 'the man of all odds', 'how odd I see you Od-ysseus.' (cf. also the earlier, homophonic devices of syllabaries.)

A. *Image.* Composed groups of words used as symbols for things and states of sight, touch, taste and smell present an image. For example: Homer's 'a dark purple wave made an arch over them like a mountain cave'; the image of Hades evoked by the 11th book of *The Odyssey*; or the landscape and journey which is all of *The Odyssey* – the homecoming of Odysseus.

> cf. Weight, grandeur, and energy in writing are very largely produced, dear pupil, by the use of "images". (That at least is what some people call the actual mental pictures.) For the term Imagination is applied in general to an idea which enters the mind from any source and engenders speech, but the word has now come to be used of passages where, inspired by strong emotion, you seem to see what you describe and bring it vividly before the eyes of your audience. That imagination

means one thing in oratory and another in poetry you will yourself
detect, and also that the object of poetry is to enthral, of prose writing
to present ideas clearly, though both indeed aim at this latter and at
excited feeling.

[LONGINUS (213-73), *On the Sublime*, XV, 2]

**B.** *Sound.* Besides the imitation in words of natural sound (the
sound of the sea in Homer, the sound of birds in 'Bare ruined
choirs where late the sweet birds sang'), the component of sound
in poetry, as conveyed by rendition, comprises sound that is

1. Spoken (e.g. 'and we'll talk with them too, / Who loses and
   who wins, who's in, / who's out,' – *King Lear*)
2. Declaimed (e.g., Milton's *Paradise Lost*)
3. Intoned or Chanted (e.g. words used in a liturgical monotone)
4. Sung (to a melody, i.e. a musical phrase or idea. Some of the
   best examples in English are Campion's poems, Shakespeare's
   songs – which have been set to music by Purcell, Johnson,
   Arne – and Burns' songs written to folk tunes.)

**C.** *Interplay of Concepts.* This component affects compositions in
which words involve other words in common or contrasting logical
implications, and to this end it employs sound, and sometimes
image, as an accessory. The elements of grammar and rhetorical
balance (v.s., Shakespeare's 'who's *in*, who's *out*') contribute to
this type of poetry. (Examples: most of Donne's poems, Andrew
Marvell's 'The Definition of Love', George Herbert's 'Heaven',
Lord Rochester's 'Ode to Nothing', Fitzgerald's translation of
*Rubaiyat*, Eliot's 'The Hollow Men'.)

From the preceding analysis of the components of poems it is clear
that their forms are achieved as a dynamics of speech and sound,
that is, as a resolution of their interacting rhythms – with no loss
of value to any word at the expense of the movement. In actual
practice, this dynamics works out standards of measure – or metres.
The good poems of the past have developed the "science" of prosody
in the same way that the effective use of words has developed the
logic of grammar. But poetry, though it has its constants, is made
in every age.

Prosody analyses poems according to line lengths and groups of
lines or verses as vehicles of rhythm, varieties of poetic feet or units
of rhythm (analogous to a measure in music) *and* their variants
(e.g., unexpected inversions of accent, unexpected "extra" syllables),
rhymes *and* their variants (e.g. consonance, assonance, perfect rhyme
– i.e. the same sound rhymes with itself, etc), rhyming patterns,

stanzas or strophes, fixed forms and free verse. No verse is "free", however, if its rhythms inevitably carry the words in contexts that do not falsify the function of words as speech probing the possibilities and attractions of existence. This being the practice of poetry, prosody as such is of secondary interest to the poet. He looks, so to speak, into his ear as he does at the same time into his heart and intellect. His ear is sincere, if his words convey his awareness of the range of differences and subtleties of duration. He does not measure with handbook, and is not a pendulum. He may find it right to count syllables, or their relative lengths and stresses, or to be sensitive to all these metrical factors. As a matter of fact, the good poets do all these things. But they do not impose their count on what is said or made – as may be judged from the impact of their poems.

Symmetry occurs in all the arts as they develop. It is usually present in some form in most good poetry. The stanza was perhaps invented in an attempt to fit a tune to more words than it had notes: the words were grouped into stanzas permitting the tune to be repeated. But existence does not foster this technique in all times indiscriminately. The least unit of a poem must support the stanza; it should never be inflicted on the least unit. As Sidney wrote in his *Apology* (1595): 'One may be a poet without versing, and a versifier without poetry.'

The best way to find out about poetry is to read the poems. That way the reader becomes something of a poet himself: not because he "contributes" to the poetry, but because he finds himself subject of its energy.

# CHARLES OLSON

Charles Olson (1910-70) was born in Worcester, Massachusetts, and educated at Harvard, Yale and Wesleyan. In 1948 he took a teaching position at Black Mountain College in North Carolina, where he was to be joined by Creeley, Duncan, Dorn and company for the most radical collective experiment with form that American poetry has known. These poets, together with Levertov, Paul Blackburn and others, began publishing their work in *Origin* and *Black Mountain Review* through the 1950s, ever guided by Olson's principles of 'projective' verse. Perversely, perhaps, these principles have come to overshadow Olson's actual work, with his poetry frequently relegated to an expression of his poetics (notably, his long poem 'The Kingfisher' from *In Cold Hell, in Thicket* (1953), and his life work *The Maximus Poems*, collected in 1983).

'Projective Verse' is one of the defining poetics of the 20th century. Not only a manifesto for the Black Mountain school, it crystallises the logical developments of American Modernism after Pound and Williams. Projective writing is 'open' and organic: famously, 'FORM IS NEVER MORE THAN AN EXTENSION OF CONTENT' (Olson capitalised to stress importance). While this idea carries across much from Imagism and Objectivism, the distinction is one of movement. Olson believes that a poem is propelled by *kinetics* – that is, by the energy of the poet's own breath transformed into language, and recorded typographically on the page. The layout of the poem, then – its line-breaks and its pause for 'breath' – is crucial to the conveyance of sense.

## *from* Projective Verse
### (1950)

PROJECTIVE                                                                         VERSE

    (projectile            (percussive         (prospective
                             *vs.*

The NON-Projective

*(or what a French critic calls 'closed' verse, that verse which print bred and which is pretty much what we have had, in English & American, and have still got, despite the work of Pound & Williams:*

*it led Keats, already a hundred years ago, to see it (Wordsworth's, Milton's) in the light of 'the Egotistical Sublime'; and it persists, at this latter day, as what you might call the private-soul-at-any-public-wall)*

Verse now, 1950, if it is to go ahead, if it is to be of *essential* use, must, I take it, catch up and put into itself certain laws and possibilities of the breath, of the breathing of the man who writes as well as of his listenings. (The revolution of the ear, 1910, the trochee's heave, asks it of the younger poets.) [...]

First, some simplicities that a man learns, if he works in OPEN, or what can also be called COMPOSITION BY FIELD, as opposed to inherited line, stanza, over-all form, what is the "old" base of the non-projective.

(1) the *kinetics* of the thing. A poem is energy transferred from where the poet got it (he will have some several causations), by way of the poem itself to, all the way over to, the reader. Okay. Then the poem itself must, at all points, be a high energy-construct and, at all points, an energy-discharge. So: how is the poet to accomplish same energy, how is he, what is the process by which a poet gets in, at all points, energy at least the equivalent of the energy which propelled him in the first place, yet an energy which is peculiar to verse alone and which will be, obviously, also different from the energy which the reader, because he is a third term, will take away?

This is the problem which any poet who departs from closed form is specially confronted by. And it involves a whole series of new recognitions. From the moment he ventures into FIELD COMPOS-ITION – puts himself in the open – he can go by no track other than the one the poem under hand declares for itself. Thus he has to behave, and be, instant by instant, aware of some several forces just now beginning to be examined. (It is much more, for example, this push, than simply such a one as Pound put, so wisely, to get us started: 'the musical phrase', go by it, boys, rather than by, the metronome.)

(2) is the *principle*, the law which presides conspicuously over such composition, and, when obeyed, is the reason why a project-ive poem can come into being. It is this: FORM IS NEVER MORE THAN AN EXTENSION OF CONTENT. (Or so it got phrased by one, R. Creeley, and it makes absolute sense to me, with this pos-sible corollary, that right form, in any given poem, is the only and exclusively possible extension of content under hand.) There it is, brothers, sitting there, for USE.

Now (3) the *process* of the thing, how the principle can be made so to shape the energies that the form is accomplished. And I think it can be boiled down to one statement (first pounded into my head by Edward Dahlberg): ONE PERCEPTION MUST IMMEDIATELY AND DIRECTLY LEAD TO A FURTHER PERCEPTION. It means exactly what it says, is a matter of, at *all* points (even, I should say, of our management of daily reality as of the daily work) get on with it, keep moving, keep in, speed, the nerves, their speed, the perceptions, theirs, the acts, the split second acts, the whole business, keep it moving as fast as you can, citizen. And if you also set up as a poet, USE USE USE the process at all points, in any given poem always, always one perception must must must MOVE, INSTANTER, ON ANOTHER!

So there we are, fast, there's the dogma. And its excuse, its usableness, in practice. Which gets us, it ought to get us, inside the machinery, now, 1950, of how projective verse is made.

If I hammer, if I recall in, and keep calling in, the breath, the breathing as distinguished from the hearing, it is for cause, it is to insist upon a part that breath plays in verse which has not (due, I think, to the smothering of the power of the line by too set a concept of foot) has not been sufficiently observed or practised, but which has to be if verse is to advance to its proper force and place in the day, now, and ahead. I take it that PROJECTIVE VERSE teaches, is, this lesson, that that verse will only do in which a poet manages to register both the acquisitions of his ear *and* the pressures of his breath.

Let's start from the smallest particle of all, the syllable. It is the king and pin of versification, what rules and holds together the lines, the larger forms, of a poem. I would suggest that verse here and in England dropped this secret from the late Elizabethans to Ezra Pound, lost it, in the sweetness of meter and rime, in a honey-head. (The syllable is one way to distinguish the original success of blank verse, and its falling off, with Milton.)

It is by their syllables that words juxtapose in beauty, by these particles of sound as clearly as by the sense of the words which they compose. In any given instance, because there is a choice of words, the choice, if a man is in there, will be, spontaneously, the obedience of his ear to the syllables. The fineness, and the practice, lie here, at the minimum and source of speech.

> O western wynd, when wilt thou blow
> And the small rain down shall rain
> O Christ that my love were in my arms
> And I in my bed again

It would do no harm, as an act of correction to both prose and verse as now written, if both rime and meter, and, in the quantity words, both sense and sound, were less in the forefront of the mind than the syllable, if the syllable, that fine creature, were more allowed to lead the harmony on. With this warning, to those who would try: to step back here to this place of the elements and minims of language, is to engage speech where it is least careless – and least logical. Listening for the syllables must be so constant and so scrupulous, the exaction must be so complete, that the assurance of the ear is purchased at the highest – 40 hours a day – price. For from the root out, from all over the place, the syllable comes, the figures of, the dance:

'Is' comes from the Aryan root, *as*, to breathe. The English 'not' equals the Sanskrit *na*, which may come from the root *na*, to be lost, to perish. 'Be' is from *bhu*, to grow.

I say the syllable, king, and that it is spontaneous, this way: the ear, the ear which has collected, which has listened, the ear, which is so close to the mind that it is the mind's, that it has the mind's speed...

it is close, another way: the mind is brother to this sister and is, because it is so close, is the drying force, the incest, the sharpener...

it is from the union of the mind and the ear that the syllable is born.

But the syllable is only the first child of the incest of verse (always, that Egyptian thing, it produces twins!). The other child is the LINE. And together, these two, the syllable *and* the line, they make a poem, they make that thing, the – what shall we call it, the Boss of all, the "Single Intelligence". And the line comes (I swear it) from the breath, from the breathing of the man who writes, at the moment that he writes, and thus is, it is here that, the daily work, the WORK, gets in, for only he, the man who writes, can declare, at every moment, the line its metric and its ending – where its breathing, shall come to, termination.

The trouble with most work, to my talking, since the breaking away from traditional lines and stanzas, and from such wholes as, say, Chaucer's *Troilus* or S's *Lear*, is: contemporary workers go lazy RIGHT HERE WHERE THE LINE IS BORN.

Let me put it baldly. The two halves are:
>        the HEAD, by way of the EAR, to the SYLLABLE
>        the HEART, by way of the BREATH, to the LINE

And the joker? that it is in the 1st half of the proposition that, in composing, one lets-it-rip; and that it is in the 2nd half, surprise, it is the LINE that's the baby that gets, as the poem is getting made, the attention, the control, that it is right here, in the line, that the shaping takes place, each moment of the going.

I am dogmatic, that the head shows in the syllable. The dance of the intellect is there, among them, prose or verse. Consider the best minds you know in this here business: where does the head show, is it not, precise, here, in the swift currents of the syllable?

can't you tell a brain when you see what it does, just there? It is true, what the master says he picked up from Confusion: all the thots men are capable of can be entered on the back of a postage stamp. So, is it not the PLAY of a mind we are after, is not that that shows whether a mind is there at all?

And the threshing floor for the dance? Is it anything but the LINE? And when the line has, is, a deadness, is it not a heart which has gone lazy, is it not, suddenly, slow things, similes, say, adjectives, or such, that we are bored by?

For there is a whole flock of rhetorical devices which have now to be brought under a new bead, now that we sight with the line. Simile is only one bird who comes down, too easily. The descriptive functions generally have to be watched, every second, in projective verse, because of their easiness, and thus their drain on the energy which composition by field allows into a poem. *Any* slackness takes off attention, that crucial thing, from the job in hand, from the *push* of the line under the hand at the moment, under the reader's eye, in his moment. Observation of any kind is, like argument in prose, properly previous to the act of the poem, and, if allowed in, must be so juxtaposed, apposed, set in, that it does not, for an instant, sap the going energy of the content towards its form.

It comes to this, this whole aspect of the newer problems. (We now enter, actually, the large area of the whole poem, into the FIELD, if you like, where all the syllables and all the lines must be managed in their relations to each other.) It is a matter, finally, of OBJECTS, what they are, what they are inside a poem, how they got there, and, once there, how they are to be used. This is something I want to get to in another way, but for the moment, let me indicate this, that every element in a open poem (the syllable, the line, as well as the image, the sound, the sense) must be taken up as participants in the kinetic of the poem just as solidly as we are accustomed to take what we call the objects of reality; and that these elements are to be seen as creating the tensions of a poem just as totally as do those other objects create what we know as the world.

The objects which occur at every given moment of composition (of recognition, we can call it) are, can be, must be treated exactly as they do occur therein and not by any ideas or preconceptions from outside the poem, must be handled as a series of objects in field in such a way that a series of tensions (which they also are) are made to *hold*, and to hold exactly inside the content and the context of the poem which has forced itself, through the poet and them, into being.

Because breath allows *all* the speech-force of language back in (speech is the "solid" of verse, is the secret of a poem's energy), because, now, a poem has, by speech, solidity, everything in it can now be treated as solids, objects, things; and, though insisting upon the absolute difference of the reality of the verse from that other dispersed and distributed thing, yet each of these elements of a poem can be allowed to have the play of their separate energies and can be allowed, once the poem is well composed, to keep, as those other objects do, their proper confusions.

Which brings us up, immediately, bang, against tenses, in fact against syntax, in fact against grammar generally, that is, as we have inherited it. Do not tenses, must they not also be kicked around anew, in order that time, that other governing absolute, may be kept, as must the space-tensions of a poem, immediate, contemporary to the acting-on-you of the poem? I would argue that here, too, the LAW OF THE LINE, which projective verse creates, must be hewn to, obeyed, and that the conventions which logic has forced on syntax must be broken open as quietly as must the too set feet of the old line. But an analysis of how far a new poet can stretch the very conventions on which communication by language rests, is too big for these notes, which are meant, I hope it is obvious, merely to get things started.

Let me just throw in this. It is my impression that *all* parts of speech suddenly, in composition by field, are fresh for both sound and percussive use, spring up like unknown, unnamed vegetables in the patch, when you work it, come spring. Now take Hart Crane. What strikes me in him is the singleness of the push to the nominative, his push along that one arc of freshness, the attempt to get back to word as handle. (If logos is word as thought, what is word as noun, as, pass me that, as Newman Shea used to ask, at the galley table, put a jib on the blood, will ya.) But there is a loss in Crane of what Fenollosa is so right about, in syntax, the sentence as first act of nature, as lightning, as passage of force from subject to object, quick in this case, from Hart to me, in every case, from me to you, the VERB, between two nouns. Does not Hart miss the advantages, by such an isolated push, miss the point of the whole front of syllable, line, field, and what happened to all language, and to the poem, as a result?

I return you now to London, to beginnings, to the syllable, for the pleasures of it, to intermit:

If music be the food of love, play on,
give me excess of it, that, surfeiting,
the appetite may sicken, and so die.
That strain again. It had a dying fall,
o, it came over my ear like the sweet sound
that breathes upon a bank of violets,
stealing and giving odour.

What we have suffered from, is manuscript, press, the removal of verse from its producer and its reproducer, the voice, a removal by one, by two removes from its place of origin and its destination. For the breath has a double meaning which Latin had not yet lost.

The irony is, from the machine has come one gain not yet sufficiently observed or used, but which leads directly on toward projective verse and its consequences. It is the advantage of the typewriter that, due to its rigidity and its space precisions, it can, for a poet, indicate exactly the breath, the pauses, the suspensions even of syllables, the juxtapositions even of parts of phrases, which he intends. For the first time the poet has the stave and the bar a musician has had. For the first time he can, without the convention of rime and meter, record the listening he has done to his own speech and by that one act indicate how he would want any reader, silently or otherwise, to voice his work.

It is time we picked the fruits of the experiments of Cummings, Pound, Williams, each of whom has, after his way, already used the machine as a scoring to his composing, as a script to its vocalisation. It is now only a matter of the recognition of the conventions of composition by field for us to bring into being an open verse as formal as the closed, with all its traditional advantages.

If a contemporary poet leaves a space as long as the phrase before it, he means that space to be held, by the breath, an equal length of time. If he suspends a word or syllable at the end of a line (this was most Cummings' addition) he means that time to pass that it takes the eye – that hair of time suspended – to pick up the next line. If he wishes a pause so light it hardly separates the words, yet does not want a comma – which is an interruption of the meaning rather than the sounding of the line – follow him when he uses a symbol the typewriter has ready to hand:

> 'What does not change / is the will to change'

Observe him, when he takes advantage of the machine's multiple margins, to juxtapose:

> 'Sd he:
>     to dream takes no effort
>         to think is easy
>             to act is more difficult
>             but for a man to act after he has taken thought, this!
>     is the most difficult thing of all'

Each of these lines is a progressing of both the meaning and the breathing forward, and then a backing up, without a progress or any kind of movement outside the unit of time local to the idea.

There is more to be said in order that this convention be recognised, especially in order that the revolution out of which it came may be so forwarded that work will get published to offset the reaction now afoot to return verse to inherited forms of cadence and rime. But what I want to emphasise here, by this emphasis on the typewriter as the personal and instantaneous recorder of the poet's work, is the already projective nature of verse as the sons of Pound and Williams are practising it. Already they are composing as though verse was to have the reading its writing involved, as though not the eye but the ear was to be its measurer, as though the intervals of its composition could be so carefully put down as to be precisely the intervals of its registration. For the ear, which once had the burden of memory to quicken it (rime & regular cadence were its aids and have merely lived on in print after the oral necessities were ended) can now again, that the poet has his means, be the threshold of projective verse. [...]

# ROBERT CREELEY

Robert Creeley, born in 1926 in Arlington, Massachusetts, remains strongly associated with the Black Mountain College where he taught in the 50s, alongside John Cage, Merce Cunningham, and the great influence on his work, Charles Olson. He is the finest exponent of the American tradition of the non-tradition, insisting like Williams Carlos Williams and Olson on the need of the contemporary US poet to 'realise the world anew', instead of looking to Europe. This he does in a series of works from the early 50s on, including *For Love: Poems 1950-1960*, *Pieces* (1969) and *A Day Book* (1972). His early focus on one type of intimacy, the interiority of the lover, was succeeded in the 70s by as intimate a focus on the nature of perception. The effect is a significant variation on his literary New England antecedents: angst-ridden, pained "confessions" in which identification with the first-person "I" is continually disturbed. Instead of a Creeley poem arising from the circumstances of life, it turns our attention back to those circumstances with quiet and sometimes unnerving effect.

Following Olson's depiction of the poem as operating within an open field of free verse possibilities, Creeley's credo is very much that the poem functions as a discharger of energy.

# To Define

## (1953)

The process of definition is the intent of the poem, or is to that sense – 'Peace comes of communication.' Poetry stands in no need of any sympathy, or even goodwill. One acts from bottom, the root is the purpose quite beyond any kindness.

A poetry can act on this: 'A poem is energy transferred from where the poet got it (he will have some several causations), by way of the poem itself to, all the way over to, the reader.' One breaks the line of aesthetics, or that outcrop of a general division of knowledge. A sense of the KINETIC impels recognition of force. Force is, and therefore stays.

The means of a poetry are, perhaps, related to Pound's sense of the *increment of association*; usage coheres value. Tradition is an aspect of what anyone is now thinking – not what someone once thought. We make with what we have, and in this way anything is worth looking at. A tradition becomes inept when it blocks the necessary conclusion; it says we have felt nothing, it implies others have felt more.

A poetry denies its end in any *descriptive* act, I mean any act which leaves the attention outside the poem. Our anger cannot exist usefully without its objects, but a description of them is also a perpetuation. There is that confusion – one wants the thing to act on, and yet hates it. *Description* does nothing, it includes the object – it neither hates nor loves.

If one can junk these things, of the content which relates only to denial, the negative, the impact of dissolution – act otherwise, on other things. There is no country. Speech is an assertion of one man, by one man. 'Therefore each speech having its own character the poetry it engenders will be peculiar to that speech also in its own intrinsic form.'

# DENISE LEVERTOV

Denise Levertov (1923-97) was born in England but emigrated to America in 1948, where she became involved with the Objectivist and Black Mountain schools, effectively becoming the strongest woman poet of a group including Roberts Creeley and Duncan. Her work owes much structurally to William Carlos Williams in its tight, energetic free verse, but she has a visionary approach to the natural world and to the dynamics of being human which is her most distinctive quality. Volumes like *O Taste and See* (1964), *Freeing the Dust* (1975) and *A Door in the Hive* (1989), show her remarkable consistency of voice and clarity of eye. Throughout her career she pursued a radical political agenda, which lent authority to her intense observations of nature and society.

Her prose evades the sometimes stentorian emphasis on the theoretical freedoms of free verse found in Olson and Creeley, but enunciates the same principles with a convincing directness.

# 'I believe poets are instruments'
## (1960)

I believe poets are instruments on which the power of poetry plays.

But they are also *makers*, craftsmen: It is given to the seer to see, but it is then his responsibility to communicate what he sees, that they who cannot see may see, since we are 'members one of another.'

I believe every space and comma is a living part of the poem and has its function, just as every muscle and pore of the body has its function. And the way the lines are broken is a functioning part essential to the poem's life.

I believe content determines form, and yet that content is discovered only *in* form. Like everything living, it is a mystery. The revelation of form itself can be a deep joy; yet I think form *as means* should never obtrude, whether from intention or carelessness, between the reader and the essential force of the poem, it must be so fused with that force.

I do not believe that a violent imitation of the horrors of our times is the concern of poetry. Horrors are taken for granted. Disorder is ordinary. People in general take more and more "in their stride" – hides grow thicker. I long for poems of an inner harmony in utter contrast to the chaos in which they exist. Insofar as poetry has a social function it is to awaken sleepers by other means than shock.

I think of Robert Duncan and Robert Creeley as the chief poets among my contemporaries.

# MARIANNE MOORE

Marianne Moore (1887-1972) belongs to the first generation of American Modernism, and is perhaps one of its most individual practitioners. She knew H.D. at Bryn Mawr and gained Pound's praise as early as 1915. Her verse is immediately recognisable with its complex syllabics and its apparently limited subject-matter which, as she put it, displays 'an inordinate interest in animals and athletes'. Beneath the seeming naivety and certain eccentricity, however, is a vigorous moral integrity and delicious wit. Her books include *Observations* (1924) and *Like a Bulwark* (1956). Her *Collected Poems* appeared in 1968.

As with many of her poems, her comments on form have a distinctly acerbic bearing on the grandiosities of others.

## 'I tend to write in a patterned arrangement'
### (1938)

I tend to write in a patterned arrangement, with rhymes; stanza as it follows stanza being identical in number of syllables and rhyme-plan, with the first stanza. (Regarding the stanza as a unit, rather than the line, I sometimes divide a word at the end of a line, relying on a general straightforwardness of treatment to counteract the mannered effect.) I have a liking for the long syllable followed by three (or more) short syllables, – 'ly*ing on the* air *there is a* bird,' and for the inconspicuous or light rhyme, – 'let' in flageolet, for instance, being rhymed with 'set' in the lines,

Its leaps should be set
to the flageolet.

I try to secure an effect of flowing continuity and am more and more impressed by the many correspondences between verse and instrumental music. I am against the stock phrase and an easier use of words in verse than would be tolerated in prose. I feel that form is the outward equivalent of a determining inner conviction, and that the rhythm is the person.

# ELIZABETH BISHOP

Elizabeth Bishop (1911-1979) was born in Worcester, Massachusetts; her father died before her first birthday, and from the age of five she never saw her mother. She met Marianne Moore in 1934, and Robert Lowell in 1947, forming long and well-documented friendships with both poets. Bishop travelled widely, settling in Brazil in 1951 with her lover Lota Soares, where they lived until Lota's death in 1967. She divided her remaining years between travelling, teaching at Harvard, and life in Brazil. Her literary output was patient and meticulous (it took her 16 years to draft her poem 'The Moose'); she published only four volumes of poems in her lifetime, each of them much celebrated: *North and South* (1946), *Poems* (1955), *Questions of Travel* (1965) and *Geography III* (1976). A *Complete Poems* was published in 1969, and again in 1983; her *Collected Prose* appeared in 1984, a *Selected Letters* in 1994.

Bishop rarely professed a "poetics", but here she reveals her belief in exhaustive reading, of learning through imitation and submergence in another's work, and the separation of writing and criticism. Even then, the act of writing remains 'a mystery & a surprise, and after that a great deal of hard work.'

# Letter to Miss Pierson
## (1975/1994)

May 28th, 1975

I am answering you because (1) You enclosed a stamped, self-addressed envelope. (This happens very rarely.) (2) You think that poetry discussion groups are 'a bloody bore' – and, although there are exceptions, in general I agree with you completely.

I think you have set up difficulties for yourself that perhaps don't really exist at all. I don't know what 'poetic tools & structures' are, unless you mean traditional forms. Which one can use or not, as one sees fit. If you feel you are 'moralising' too much – just cut the morals off – or out. (Quite often young poets tend to try to tie everything up neatly in 2 or 3 beautiful last lines, and it is quite surprising how the poems are improved if the poet can bear to sacrifice those last, pat, beautiful lines.) Your third problem – why shouldn't the poet appear in the poem? There are several tricks – 'I' or 'we' or 'he' or 'she' or even 'one' – or somebody's name. Someone *is* talking, after all – but of course the idea is to prevent that particular tone of voice from growing monotonous.

From what you say, I think perhaps you are actually trying too hard – or reading too much *about* poetry and not enough poetry.

Prosody – metrics – etc are fascinating – but they all came *afterwards*, obviously. And I always ask my writing classes NOT to read criticism.

Read a lot of poetry – all the time – and *not* 20th-century poetry. Read Campion, Herbert, Pope, Tennyson, Coleridge – anything at all almost that's any good, from the past – until you find out what you really like, by yourself. Even if you try to imitate it exactly – it will come out quite different. Then the great poets of our own century – Marianne Moore, Auden, Wallace Stevens – and not just 2 or 3 poems each, in anthologies – read ALL of somebody. Then read his or her life, and letters, and so on. (And by all means read Keats's Letters.) Then see what happens.

That's really all I can say. It can't be done, apparently, by will-power and study alone – or by being "with it" – but I really don't know *how* poetry gets to be written. There is a mystery & a surprise, and after that a great deal of hard work.

P.S. If you don't have a poetry library at hand – I recommend the five small volumes edited by Auden and Pearson, with very good introductions, *Poets of the English Language*. They come in paperback now. [*Handwritten*:] This is a borrowed machine; please forgive the untidiness.

[*In margin*:] But perhaps by (3) you meant the "family" poem – about one's grandfather or how one broke away from Mother, etc? I am a bit tired of those.

# ROBERT LOWELL

Robert Lowell was born in 1911, in Boston, Massachusetts, into the same New England family as the poet Amy Lowell. He studied at Harvard, completing at Kenyon College, Ohio, where he formed a life-long friendship with Randall Jarrell. Throughout his life, Lowell was afflicted by torturing bouts of manic depression – what he called his 'jaundice of the spirit' – and when in 1977 he died from a heart attack in the back of a New York taxi, his third wife described his passing as 'a suicide of wish'. *Lord Weary's Castle* appeared in 1946, but it was *Life Studies* (1959) that really marked Lowell as a major poet. Arguably one of the defining collections of the 20th century, *Life Studies* established the ground for the so-called 'confessional' school of poetry, and concluded with the poem 'Skunk Hour' that Lowell writes about here. *For the Union Dead* (1964) and *Near the Ocean* (1967) would establish Lowell as America's unofficial laureate; and his controversial *Imitations* (1961) have been influential in the art of "translation".

The poet must know their intention, Lowell writes, but not know it too well. And certainly their task is not one of explanation – a poem (and a poet) must retain their 'private secrets'. Poetry – 'real poetry', he calls it – comes not from the confession but the imagination.

# On 'Skunk Hour'
## (1962)

### I. THE MEANING

The author of a poem is not necessarily the ideal person to explain its meaning. He is as liable as anyone else to muddle, dishonesty, and reticence. Nor is it his purpose to provide a peg for a prose essay. Meaning varies in importance from poem to poem, and from style to style, but always it is only a strand and an element in the brute flow of composition. Other elements are pictures that please or thrill for themselves, phrases that ring for their music or carry some buried suggestion. For all this the author is an opportunist, throwing whatever comes to hand into his feeling for start, continuity, contrast, climax, and completion. It is imbecile for him not to know his intentions, and unsophisticated for him to know too explicitly and fully.

Three papers by three poets [John Berryman, John Frederick Nims, Richard Wilbur] on another's poem! Perhaps they should be considered as short stories and variants on my original. I shall comment on them later; here, I only want to say that I learned much from them. Very little of what I had in mind is untouched on; much that never occurred to me has been granted me. What I didn't intend often seems now at least as valid as what I did. My complaint is not that I am misunderstood but that I am overunderstood. I am seen through.

I am not sure whether I can distinguish between intention and interpretation. I think this is what I more or less intended. The first four stanzas are meant to give a dawdling more or less amiable picture of a declining Maine sea town. I move from the ocean inland. Sterility howls through the scenery, but I try to give a tone of tolerance, humor, and randomness to the sad prospect. The composition drifts, its direction sinks out of sight into the casual, chancy arrangements of nature and decay. Then all comes alive in stanzas V and VI. This is the dark night. I hoped my readers would remember John of the Cross's poem. My night is not gracious, but secular, puritan, and agnostic. An existentialist night. Somewhere in my mind was a passage from Sartre or Camus about reaching some point of final darkness where the one free act is suicide. Out of this comes the march and affirmation, an ambiguous one, of my skunks in the last two stanzas. The skunks are both quixotic and barbarously absurd, hence the tone of amusement and defiance. 'Skunk Hour' is not entirely independent, but the anchor poem in its sequence.

## II. HOW THE POEM WAS WRITTEN

What I can describe and what no one else can describe are the circumstances of my poem's composition. I shan't reveal private secrets. John Berryman's pathological chart comes frighteningly close to the actual event. When I first read his paper, I kept saying to myself, 'Why, he is naming the very things I wanted to keep out of my poem.' In the end, I had to admit that Berryman had hit a bull's-eye, and often illuminated matters more searchingly and boldly than I could have wished. Is his account true? I cannot decide, the truth here depends on what psychologists and philosophers one accepts. Berryman comes too close for comfort.

'Skunk Hour' was begun in mid-August 1957 and finished about a month later. In March of the same year, I had been giving readings on the West Coast often reading six days a week and sometimes twice on a single day. I was in San Francisco, the era and setting of Allen Ginsberg and all about, very modest poets were waking up prophets. I became sorely aware of how few poems I had written, and that these few had been finished at the latest three or four

years earlier. Their style seemed distant, symbol-ridden, and wil-
fully difficult. I began to paraphrase my Latin quotations, and to
add extra syllables to a line to make it clearer and more colloquial.
I felt my old poems hid what they were really about, and many
times offered a stiff, humorless, and even impenetrable surface. I
am no convert to the 'beats'. I know well, too, that the best poems
are not necessarily poems that read aloud. Many of the greatest
poems can only be read to one's self, for inspiration is no substitute
for humor, shock, narrative, and a hypnotic voice, the four musts
for oral performance. Still, my own poems seemed like prehistoric
monsters dragged down into the bog and death by their ponderous
armor. I was reciting what I no longer felt. What influenced me
more than San Francisco and reading aloud was that for some
time I had been writing prose. I felt that the best style for poetry
was none of the many poetic styles in English, but something like
the prose of Chekhov or Flaubert.

When I returned to my home, I began writing lines in a new
style. No poem, however, got finished and soon I left off and tried
to forget the whole headache. Suddenly, in August, I was struck
by the sadness of writing nothing and having nothing to write, of
having, at least, no language. When I began writing 'Skunk Hour',
I felt that most of what I knew about writing was a hindrance.

The dedication is to Elizabeth Bishop, because rereading her
suggested a way of breaking through the shell of my old manner.
Her rhythms, idiom, images, and stanza structure seemed to belong
to a later century. 'Skunk Hour' is modeled on Miss Bishop's 'The
Armadillo', a much better poem and one I had heard her read and
had later carried around with me. Both 'Skunk Hour' and 'The
Armadillo' use short line stanzas, start with drifting description,
and end with a single animal.

This was the main source. My others were Hölderlin's 'Brod
und Wein', particularly the moon lines:

Sich! und das Schattenbild unserer Erde, der Mond,
kommet geheim nun auch; die Schwärmerische, die Nacht kommt
'vohl' mit Sternen und 'wohl' wenig bekummert um uns,

and so forth. I put this in long straggling lines and then added
touches of Maine scenery till I saw I was getting nowhere. Another
source, probably undetectable now, was Annette von Droste-Hül-
shoff's 'Amletzten Tage des Jahres'. She, too, uses a six-line stanza
with short lines. Her second stanza is as follows:

's ist tiefe Nacht!
Ob wohl ein Auge offen noch?
In diesen Mauern ruttelt dein

Verrinnen, Zeit! Mir schaudert; doch
Es will die letzte Stunde sein
Einsam durchwacht.

Geschehen all…

Here and elsewhere, my poem and the German poem have the same
shudders and situation.

'Skunk Hour' was written backward, first the last two stanzas, I
think, and then the next-to-last two. Anyway, there was a time when
I had the last four stanzas much as they now are and nothing
before them. I found the bleak personal violence repellent. All was
too close, though watching the lovers was not mine, but from an
anecdote about Walt Whitman in his old age. I began to feel that
real poetry came, not from fierce confessions, but from something
almost meaningless but imagined. I was haunted by an image of a
blue china doorknob. I never used the doorknob, or knew what it
meant, yet somehow it started the current of images in my open-
ing stanzas. They were written in reverse order, and at last gave
my poem an earth to stand on, and space to breathe.

## III. THE CRITICS

I don't think I intended either the Spartan boy holding the fox or
Satan's feeling of sexual deprivation while he watched Adam and
Eve in the Garden. I may have, but I don't remember. The red
fox stain was merely meant to describe the rust reddish color of
autumn on Blue Hill, a Maine mountain near where we were living.
I had seen foxes playing on the road one night, and I think the words
have sinister and askew suggestions.

I can't imagine anything more thorough than Nims's stanza-by-
stanza exposition. Almost all of it is to the point. I get a feeling of
going on a familiar journey, but with another author and another
sensibility. This feeling is still stronger when I read Wilbur's essay.
Sometimes he and I are named as belonging to the same school,
what *Time* magazine calls 'the couth poets'. Sometimes we are set in
battle against one another. I have no idea which, if either, is true.
Certainly, we both in different ways owe much to the teaching and
practice of John Crowe Ransom. Certainly, his essay embodies and
enhances my poem. With Berryman, too, I go on a strange journey!
Thank God, we both come out clinging to spars, enough floating
matter to save us, though faithless.

# RANDALL JARRELL

Randall Jarrell (1914-65) was born in Nashville, Tennessee, and studied at Vanderbilt University under John Crowe Ransom's so-called 'fugitive' poetics (a forerunner, in fact, to the New Criticism), although Jarrell's own work displays little of its influence. Around the time of his first collection (*Blood for a Stranger*, 1942), he began to establish a reputation for sharp and often witty criticism, and by the publication of his essays *Poetry and the Age* (1953) his standing as a critic far outstripped his profile as a poet. Jarrell's poetry is fused with dream, myth and fairy-tale, and at times moves arrestingly between the real and surreal in his war poems *Little Friend, Little Friend* (1945) and *Losses* (1948). Shortly after completing his last collection, *The Lost World* (1965), he was struck by manic depression, and attempted suicide; he was killed in a bizarre traffic accident having wandered onto the highway at dusk.

Jarrell loathed being asked for manifestos, believing it was not for the poet to comment on their own work. Nevertheless, in his 'Answers to Questions' he is unusually candid about his art, expressing a belief in a loosely formal lyricism, where rhyme is 'irregular, live, and heard', and where image and symbol are not the foundations upon which to build. Perhaps most striking of all is his connection between meaning and experience.

# Answers to Questions
## (1950)

1. (*oral quality*). All my poems are meant to be said aloud; many of them are dramatic speeches or scenes.

2. (*audience*). I don't know whom they are written for – for the usual audience that reads poetry from age to age, I believe, and not for the more specialised audience that reads modern poetry. It seems to me that the poet's responsibility is to his subject-matter, but that one of the determining conditions of the poem is the hypothetical normal audience for which he writes it. No one would say that a mathematician or scientist is chiefly or directly responsible to his readers; it is a mistake to say that a poet is.

3. (*language*). I try to make the language fit the poem. Since the poem is one of my actions, it will have a family resemblance to other actions and poems of mine, but I do not try to make it have one. As the cartwright in Chuangtse says, 'When I make the spokes too tight, they won't fit the wheel, and when I make them too loose, they will not hold. I have to make them just right. I feel them with my hands and judge them with my heart. There is something about it which I cannot put down in words. I cannot

teach that feeling to my own son, and my own son cannot learn it from me.' And he finishes as anyone would like to finish: 'Therefore, at the age of 70, I am good at making wheels.'

4. (*overtones*). If the poem has a quiet or neutral ground, a delicate or complicated figure can stand out against it; if the ground is exaggerated and violent enough, no figure will.

5. (*levels of meaning*). It is better to have the child in the chimney-corner moved by what happens in the poem, in spite of his ignorance of its real meaning, than to have the poem a puzzle to which that meaning is the only key. Still, complicated subjects make complicated poems, and some of the best poems can move only the best readers; this is one more question of curves of normal distribution. I have tried to make my poems plain, and most of them are plain enough; but I wish that they were more difficult because I had known more.

6. (*subjects*). Half my poems are about the war, half are not. Some of their usual subjects are: airplanes and their crews, animals, ballet, carriers, children, concentration camps, the dead and dying, dreams, forests, graves, hospitals, letters, libraries, love, *Märchen*, moralities, people in extreme situations, prisoners, soldiers, the State, training camps, Western scientific and technical development – in short, *la condition humaine*. Some of these I enjoy writing about, others I could not help writing about. Ordinarily the poems are dramatic or have implied narratives; few are pure lyrics.

7. (*imagery*). Images seem to me means, not ends; I often reread Proust, and almost never reread Virginia Woolf.

8. (*symbols*). In works of art almost anything stands for more than itself; but this *more*, like Lohengrin, vanishes when it names itself.

9. (*rhyme*). Rhyme as an automatic structural device, automatically attended to, is attractive to me, but I like it best irregular, live, and heard.

10. (*line-endings*). I assume that the reader will indicate line-endings when he reads the poem aloud; if he doesn't he is reading it as prose.

11. (*the structure of the total poem; what makes its unity?*) An answer would take too many pages.

12. (*meter*). Most of my poems are written in ordinary iambic verse, regular or irregular according to the poem. Once upon a time I wrote accentual verse; I've used irregular anapaests for special-case poems, syllabic verse for translations of Corbière, and so on.

The questionnaire also says that *Any statement you make about the ethical-philosophical relation of the poet to his writing will be most welcome*. My poems show what this relation actually is for me; what

I say that it should be matters less. I *think* that I am relatively in-
different to the poem-as-performance-of-the-poet, and try to let
the poem have a life of its own; the reader of the poem can know
whether or not this is true.

To write in this way about one's own poetry is extremely unpleas-
ant and unnatural. A successful poem says what a poet wants to
say, and more, with particular finality. The remarks he makes about
his poems are incidental when the poem is good, and embarrassing
or absurd when it is bad – and he is not permitted to say how the
good poem is good, and may never know how the bad poem is
bad. It is better to write about other people's poetry. But to be in
this anthology one had to write about one's own; and to have you
read the poems, I was willing to write this prose.

# KEITH DOUGLAS

Keith Douglas (1920-44) was probably the finest English poet of the Second World War, indeed only the Scots Gaelic poet Sorley MacLean can be said to have produced work of comparable stature. A precocious writer, whose undergraduate work had already absorbed and recast the influence of Auden, Douglas's time in the North African desert, recounted in the disturbingly entertaining prose of *Alamein to Zem Zem*, proved the catalyst into his brief mature period. In poems like 'Vergissmeinnicht' and 'How to Kill' he perfected a tone of dry horrified detachment, both from what he was witnessing and his own necessary actions within the theatre of war. His best poems combine a brittle experimental brilliance with a sensuous understanding of form, a contrast he often extends into subject-matter, juxtaposing the battlefield and the civilisation it is supposed to be defending. He was killed by shrapnel four days after the D-Day landings.

His prose writings sometimes seem less mature than the poetry they comment on, but Douglas is always capable of the sudden, arresting shift in perspective.

## 'Poetry is like a man'
### (1940)

Poetry is like a man, whom thinking you know all his movements and appearance you will presently come upon in such a posture that for a moment you can hardly believe it a position of the limbs you know. So thinking you have set the bounds to the nature of poetry, you shall as soon discover something outside your bounds which they should evidently contain.

The expression "bad poetry" is meaningless: critics still use it, forgetting that bad poetry is not poetry at all.

Nor can prose and poetry be compared any more than pictures and pencils: the one is instrument and the other art. Poetry may be written in prose or verse, or spoken extempore.

For it is anything expressed in words, which appeals to the emotions either in presenting an image or picture to move them; or by the music of words affecting them through the senses; or in stating some truth whose eternal quality exacts the same reverence as eternity itself.

In its nature poetry is sincere and simple.

Writing which is poetry must say what the writer has himself to say, not what he has observed others to say with effect, nor what he thinks will impress his hearers because it impressed him hearing it. Nor must he waste any more words over it than a mathematician: every word must work for its keep, in prose, blank verse, or rhyme.

And poetry is to be judged not by what the poet has tried to say; only by what he has said.

# DYLAN THOMAS

Dylan Thomas was born in Swansea in 1914, and came to prominence in the late 30s. His early work was full of a very Welsh-seeming verbal flourish and modish surrealistic recombinations of his narrow stock of sensuous imagery, and was seen as an antidote to the spare, searching voice of Auden, especially when that poet departed for America in 1939. Thomas became the central figure of the 40s New Romanticism and the booze-sodden Soho it thrived in. His radio work exposed a marvellous reading voice to the public, making him one of the few poets who are still read widely. But the excess both in his writing and his lifestyle told: although later Thomas displays greater discipline and less narcissism, it is also more variable in quality. Nonetheless, Dylan Thomas's contribution to the canon of the last century's poetry includes 12 or 15 poems, utterly distinctive and memorable, including 'Fern Hill', 'Poem in October', 'Do Not Go Gentle into That Good Night' and 'In My Craft or Sullen Art'. He died in New York in 1953, having attempted to apply his beer-drinking techniques to American hard liquor.

Thomas's prose can be as funny and loquacious as his conversation, but his writings on poetry also reveal the intense commitment to shaping that is part of his achievement, the entirely sober emphasis on craft.

## *from* Notes on the Art of Poetry
### (1951/1961)

To your third question – Do I deliberately utilise devices of rhyme, rhythm, and word-formation in my writing – I must, of course, answer with an immediate, Yes. I am a painstaking, conscientious, involved and devious craftsman in words, however unsuccessful the result so often appears, and to whatever wrong uses I may apply my technical paraphernalia, I use everything and anything to make my poems work and move in the directions I want them to: old tricks, new tricks, puns, portmanteau-words, paradox, allusion, paranomasia, paragram, catachresis, slang, assonantal rhymes, vowel rhymes, sprung rhythm. Every device there is in language is there to be used if you will. Poets have got to enjoy themselves sometimes, and the twistings and convolutions of words, the inventions and contrivances, are all part of the joy that is part of the painful, voluntary work. [...]

What is my definition of Poetry?

I, myself, do not read poetry for anything but pleasure. I read only the poems I like. This means, of course, that I have to read a lot of poems I don't like before I find the ones I do, but, when I *do* find the ones I do, then all I can say is, 'Here they are', and read them to myself for pleasure.

Read the poems you like reading. Don't bother whether they're "important", or if they'll live. What does it matter what poetry *is*, after all? If you want a definition of poetry, say: 'Poetry is what makes me laugh or cry or yawn, what makes my toenails twinkle, what makes me want to do this or that or nothing', and let it go at that. All that matters about poetry is the enjoyment of it, however tragic it may be. All that matters is the eternal movement behind it, the vast undercurrent of human grief, folly, pretension, exaltation, or ignorance, however unlofty the intention of the poem.

You can tear a poem apart to see what makes it technically tick, and say to yourself, when the works are laid out before you, the vowels, the consonants, the rhymes or rhythms, 'Yes, this is *it*. This is why the poem moves me so. It is because of the craftsmanship.' But you're back again where you began.

You're back with the mystery of having been moved by words. The best craftsmanship always leaves holes and gaps in the works of the poem so that something that is *not* in the poem can creep, crawl, flash, or thunder in.

The joy and function of poetry is, and was, the celebration of man, which is also the celebration of God.

# W.S. GRAHAM

W.S. Graham was born in Greenock in 1918, but established himself as a poet in London before settling near St Ives in Cornwall in the company of the artists who influenced his later work. The West Coast of Scotland forms a background of loss to his impassioned speculative poetry. His first books were very much under the influence of Dylan Thomas – only the primacy given to the associative powers of language indicates the direction to be taken in *The White Threshold* (1949) and the brilliant long poem *The Nightfishing*, which cast its metaphysical nets in the same year (1955) as the Movement promulgated its very different agenda. As a result Graham vanished for 15 years. His two late books, *Malcolm Mooney's Land* (1970) and *Implements in Their Places* (1977) focussed on abstraction, on the space generated by a poem, between writer and reader, a space occupied by 'The beast that lives on silence'. The austerity of this, much admired by Harold Pinter, is coloured by the Cornish landscape and the directness of the voice: the reader is addressed as friend or lover, existentially remote but nonetheless cherished.

Given the primacy Graham attached to the act of poetry, his prose writings are few, but place their emphasis on the overwhelming affect of language, emotional and intellectual, both on its user and its recipient.

# Notes on a Poetry of Release
## (1946)

### 1

The original diseases and cures of those fictional problems of Morality (involving Politics and our each illusion of a Liberty) live in each of us and express through how we lift a cup, walk, or blow the dandelion seeds into the air to tell the time. Let me be the poet writing in a disguise of the first person about the intricate marriage between those problems and the poem and the searching reader. Though those problems move me as a man to varied action I try to put them out (at least as a conscious direction) when I begin to make my poem. Those problems move me and work to success-fully direct the outside accidents and me through accident. With words my material and immediate environment I am at once half-way the victim and halfway the successful traveller. There is the involuntary war between me and that environment flowing in on me from all sides and there is the poetic outcome. I am not the victim of my environment. History does not repeat itself. I am the bearer of that poetic outcome. History continually arrives as differently as our most recent minute on earth. The labourer going home in the dusk shouts his goodnight across the road and History has a new score on its track. The shape is changed a little. History as a crowd divides and divides into its population where I am a member and at last I am left to say my history has my eyes and mouth and a little likeness of my father. Time and time again I am scored by the others and their words and the diseases and cures war and change in their part of me. First I'll put them aside for my poem is to be a successful construction of words, a construction in which anyhow those cures will act whether the poem is about a pinhead or Lanarkshire.

The most difficult thing for me to remember is that a poem is made of words and not of the expanding heart, the overflowing soul, or the sensitive observer. A poem is made of words. It is words in a certain order, good or bad by the significance of its addition to life and not to be judged by any other value put upon it by imagining how or why or by what kind of man it was made. It is easy to strive to make a poem out of the wrong material like a table out of water. It is easy to mistake a poem for a different thing with a different function and to be sad when it does not put out what it is not. In the end then are those still words on the paper and arranged half-victim to the physical outside, half-victim to my Morality's origins, out of this dying and bearing language. All the poet's knowledge and experience (as far as the people who wait outside his gates are concerned) is contained in the language which is obstacle and vehicle at the same time. The shape of all of us is in this language. Our riches and poverties have affected every word. For the language is a changing creature continually being killed-off, added-to and changed like a river over its changing speakers. The language changes along with all of us and is headline litmus record wreckage pyramid shame and accomplishment of all we do and have done and (through Poetry) might do. Each word is touched by and filled with the activity of every speaker. Each word changes every time it is brought to life. Each single word uttered twice becomes a new word each time. You cannot twice bring the same word into sound.

It is a good direction to believe that this language which is so scored and impressed by the commotion of all of us since its birth can be arranged to in its turn impress significantly for the good of each individual. Let us endure the sudden affection of the language.

## 2

I must begin with first the illusion of an intention. The poem begins to form from the first intention. But the intention is already breaking into another. The first intention begins me but of

course continually shatters itself and is replaced by the child of the
new collision. I try to have the courage to let the last intention be
now a dead step and to allow myself to be taken in hand. Yet I must
not lose my responsibility, being that explorer who shoots the sun,
carries samples of air back to civilisation, and looks his forward.
The poem is more than the poet's intention. The poet does not
write what he knows but what he does not know. A man's imagin-
ing suddenly may inherit the handclapping centuries of his one
minute on earth. He has to explore the imagination by using the
language as his pitch. On it he must construct (intuitively to an
organic as true as a tree) an apparatus which will work and to a
special purpose. It is no help to think of the purpose as being to
'transfuse recollected emotion' or to 'report significantly' or indeed
to think of it as a putting-across of anything. The poem itself is
dumb but has the power of release. Its purpose is that it can be
used by the reader to find out something about himself. Words
are ambiguous. He must face it that words are ambiguous, but
realise that this has to do with the fundamental force of poetry
and is to be used to a positive end. The poem is not a handing
out of the same packet to everyone, as it is not a thrown-down
heap of words for us to choose the bonniest. The poem is the
replying chord to the reader. It is the reader's involuntary reply.

What is to be done? To bisect the angle between God and Man
and find the earliest distance between heart and head. To join Man
and Word and project his consciousness of the prophetic in the
language into the world. To be the labourer carrying the bricks of
his time and on the scaffolding of an unknown construction. To
bring about the reader's Involuntary Belief. To present before him
an addition to the world like this which Blake made where the
reader is left not to agree or disagree as to its rightness but to
answer from a new cave flooded to light,

> For every thing that lives is holy, life delights in life;
> Because the soul of sweet delight can never be defil'd.
> Fires inwrap the earthly globe, yet man is not consum'd;
> Amidst the lustful fires he walks: his feet become like brass,
> His knees and thighs like silver, & his breast and head like gold.

I go my way. Then I find the muse laughing her fill in the Atholl
Arms, fixing her face genteel not to be thought the whore she is.
She's drunk and says, 'give us Kevin Barry', but singing's stopped
this long time, and the bar is thumped like a drum at the least
hint of a note. Glasses go over and we are all at words. Shapes of
language (right out of the gasp and gesture of speech) spill round
our ears and I am at once the man of technique who books the

phrases of drinking and affection so that later I might explore the mechanics of their memorableness and vitality. Down the page I've written, 'fairly his mile', 'anyhow here's Mary will tell you right', 'have you lately heard tell'; and like the unrehearsed possibilities of a dream beginnings, endings, and those swift metaphors of the moment break into sound in the ear. An organic rhetoric is built up which charges and maintains the formal mechanics of poetry. The syntax holds and a poem's infinite number of overtones are magnified to a greater memorableness. A poem is charged to that power of release that even to one man it goes on speaking again and again beyond behind its speaking words, a space of continual messages behind the words like behind Joyce's words like this:

> It's something fails us. First we feel. Then we fall. And let her rain now if she likes. Gently or strongly as she likes. Anyway, let her rain for my time is come. I done me best when I was let. Thinking always if I go all goes. A hundred cares, a tithe of troubles and is there one who understands me? One in a thousand of years of the nights?

I try to remember those adventures along those lines of words. Though do I move along words in a poem when, after all, as I am at the last word and look back I find the first word changed and a new word there, for it is part of the whole poem and its particular life depends on the rest of the poem. The meaning of a word in a poem is never more than its position. The meaning of a poem is itself, not less a comma. But then to each man it comes into new life. It is brought to life by the reader and takes part in the reader's change. Even the poet as a man who searches continually is a new searcher with his direction changing at every step.

> For ever as the seeker turns
> His worshipping eyes on prophetic patterns
> Of shape arising from all men
> He changes through, he shall remain
> Continually stripped and clothed again.

Let the poem be a still thing, a mountain constructed, an addition to the world. It will have its own special function and purpose, to be that certain mountain. And there is the reader going on to it with his never-before exploration after his perfect hunger's daily changing bread. A poem is a mountain made out of the containing, almost physical language, and with the power to release a man into his own completely responsible world larger than that outward solid geography.

> Man setteth an end to darkness,
> And searcheth out to the furthest bound
> The stones of thick darkness and of the shadow of death.

He breaketh open a shaft away from where men sojourn;
They are forgotten of the foot that passeth by;
They hang afar from men, they swing to and fro.

(The Book of Job)

It is a good direction to believe that this language which is so scored and impressed by the commotion of all of us since its birth can be arranged to in its turn impress significantly for the benefit of each individual. Let us endure the sudden affection of the language.

# PATRICK KAVANAGH

Born in 1904 in Iniskeen, Co. Monaghan, the focal point for his early work, Kavanagh was a member of the Irish peasantry Yeats liked to pronounce upon. His early work, *Ploughman and Other Poems* (1936) and the novel *The Green Fool* (1938), was well received, and he moved to Dublin to take up the literary life. What he encountered caused him to reject much of his work as 'stage-Irish', though many early lyrics are admirable for their deft confluence of the immediate and the transcendent. It is his middle period on which his reputation has been founded, *The Great Hunger* (1942) providing the necessary shock of antithesis to Yeatsian idealisations of the peasant's lot, as did the quasi-autobiography *Tarry Flynn* (1948) in prose. His constant quarrelling with the literary establishment in Dublin began to sour his work with cynicism, until he contracted and recovered from lung cancer, whereon his poetry opened out into a graceful final phase, in which his powers of humour and improvisation regain and exceed the lyricism of the early poems.

Since his death in 1967, Kavanagh's reputation for cruel wit and offensiveness has often preceded him. Yet he is now regarded as the most important Irish poet of the generation succeeding Yeats. His championing of the rural and the individual, of things that are of 'no importance to newspapers and politicians', has provided an inspiration to figures as diverse as Heaney and Paul Durcan. If the poet is to ignite the 'dancing flame' of imagination, then they must become impersonal, and, crucially, learn how not to care.


## *from* Self Portrait
### (1967)

I dislike talking about myself in a direct way. The self is only interesting as an illustration. For some reason, whenever we talk about our personal lives they turn out to be both irrelevant and untrue – even when the facts are right, the mood is wrong.

English publishers and newspapers are mad for personal data, especially about people from Ireland. They love Irishmen. America is now even worse. And the unfortunate peoples of my island home lap up all that vulgarity when it is dished out to them.

The quality that most simple people fear – and by simple people I mean terrified, ignorant people – is the comic spirit, for the comic spirit is the ultimate sophistication which they do not understand and therefore fear. [...]

A poet is never one of the people. He is detached, remote, and the life of small-time dances and talk about football would not be for him. He might take part but could not belong.

A poet has to have an audience – half a dozen or so. Landor, who said he esteemed ten a sufficient audience, was very optimistic. I know about half a dozen and these are mainly London-based. It may be possible to live in total isolation but I don't understand how. The audience is as important as the poet. There is no audience in Ireland, though I have managed to build up out of my need a little audience for myself.

The real problem is the scarcity of a right audience which draws out of a poet what is best in him. The Irish audience that I came into contact with tried to draw out of me everything that was loud, journalistic and untrue. Such as:

My soul was an old horse
Offered for sale in twenty fairs.

Anthologists everywhere keep asking for this. Also asked for is another dreadful job about Mother Ireland:

It would never be summer
    always autumn
After a harvest always lost.

Thank God, I control the copyrights in these poems and nobody can use them. What the alleged poetry-lover loved was the Irishness of a thing. Irishness is a form of anti-art. A way of posing as a poet without actually being one. The *New Lines* poets of today have invented a similar system.

They are also sympathetic to the Irish thing.

No young person today would think of coming to live in Dublin as a metropolis. A new awareness is in the air. A couple of years ago I remember a young chap accosting me in a Dublin street. He was from the southern part of Ireland and he was on his way to Rome – to take up the poetry trade. He was right too. At least something might happen to him there, a rich woman might take a fancy to his poetry and keep him in the decency and comfort which are a necessity of the poet.

I pause here to emphasise that I have no belief in the virtue of a place. Many misguided persons imagine that living in France or Italy is the equivalent of a liberal education. French in particular is the language of art. Still, Dublin hasn't the possibilities for getting hitched up to a rich woman, and this is about the only way a true poet can remain true and keep up an adequate supply of good whiskey. [...]

Another great experience I had was my law case, hereinafter to be known as The Trial or Trial and Error, mostly error. Curious thing is that an event so seemingly large at the time disappears in the perspective of a few years. What seems of public importance is never of any importance. Stupid poets and artists think that by taking subjects of public importance it will help their work to survive. There is nothing as dead and damned as an important thing. The things that really matter are casual, insignificant little things, things you would be ashamed to talk of publicly. You are ashamed and then after years someone blabs and you find that you are in the secret majority. Such is fame. [...]

In those days in Dublin the big thing besides being Irish was peasant quality. They were all trying to be peasants. They had been at it for years but I hadn't heard. And I was installed as the authentic peasant, and what an idea that was among rascals pretending to have an interest in poetry. Although the literal idea of the peasant is of a farm labouring person, in fact a peasant is all that mass of mankind which lives below a certain level of consciousness. They live in the dark cave of time unconscious and they scream when they see the light. They take offence easily, their degree of insultability is very great. I have written:

> But I, trained in the slum pubs of Dublin
> Among the most offensive class of all
> The artisans – am equal to the problem;
> I let it ride and there is nothing over.
> I understand through all these years
> That my difference in their company is an intrusion
> That tears at the sentimental clichés.
> They can see my heart squirm when their star rendites
> The topmost twenty in the lowered lights.
> No sir, I did not come unprepared.

Which brings me to something that I might say is the very heart of the matter of human contentment or as near as we can get. This is the secret of learning how not to care. Not caring is really a sense of values and feeling of confidence. A man who cares is not the master. And one can observe this in the matter of simple singing in the rain or in a pub. The fellows who around Christmas sing in pubs are not just chaps enjoying themselves. Enjoying themselves has nothing to do with it. They are *expressing* themselves. This is their art, their reason for existence. And they are usually very humble and ashamed of their own selves, for they always assume the part of some singing star or other. No wonder I squirm. I do not blame them; few people have the courage to be themselves. And when they do appear themselves it is all put on with spade-fulls of bravado. It took me many years to learn or relearn not to care. The heart of a song singing it, or a poem writing it, is not caring. I will sing now and give the poems later:

On Raglan Road on an autumn day
    I met her first and knew
That her dark hair could weave a snare
    that I might one day rue.
I saw the danger yet I walked
    upon the enchanted way
And I said let grief be a fallen leaf
    at the dawning of the day.

In the beginning of my versing career I had hit on the no-caring
jag but there was nobody to tell me that I was on the right track:

My black hills have never seen the sun rising
Eternally they look north to Armagh.

There are two kinds of simplicity, the simplicity of going away
and the simplicity of return. The last is the ultimate in sophistica-
tion. In the final simplicity we don't care whether we appear fool-
ish or not. We talk of things that earlier would embarrass. We are
satisfied with being ourselves, however small. So it was that on
the banks of the Grand Canal between Baggot and Leeson Street
bridges in the warm summer of 1955, I lay and watched the green
waters of the canal. I had just come out of hospital. I wrote:

Leafy-with-love banks and the green waters of the canal
Pouring redemption for me, that I do
The will of God, wallow in the habitual, the banal
Grow with nature again as before I grew.

And so in this moment of great daring I became a poet. Except for
brief moments in my very early years I had not been a poet. The
poems in *A Soul for Sale* are not poetry and neither is *The Great
Hunger*. There are some queer and terrible things in *The Great
Hunger*, but it lacks the nobility and repose of poetry. The trouble
is that there are so few who would know a poem from a hole in
the ground.

It is possible on the other hand to recognise a poet, for the animal
is recognisable. The main feature about a poet, if you ever happen
to meet one – and that's a remote chance, for I can't be everywhere
at the one time – the main feature is his humorosity. Any touch of
boringness and you are in the wrong shop.

Beautiful women, I am glad to say, are capable of recognising
the baste. Recently a man was presented to me as being a great
poet. He wrote in Irish. I expressed me doubts and the introducer
said: 'How can you tell when you don't know the language?' That
was a sore one, but I was able for it. I said, 'I can't bawl like a
cow but I'd know a cow if I saw one.'

That a poet is born, not made, is well known. But this does not mean that he was a poet the day he was physically born. For many a good-looking year I wrought hard at versing but I would say that, as a poet, I was born in or about 1955, the place of my birth being the banks of the Grand Canal.

Thirty years earlier Shancoduff's watery hills could have done the trick, but I was too thick to take the hint. Curious this, how I had started off with the right simplicity, indifferent to crude reason and then ploughed my way through complexities and anger, hatred and ill-will towards the faults of man, and came back to where I started. For one of the very earliest things I wrote, even pre-dating Shancoduff, started this way:

> Child do not go
> Into the dark places of soul
> For there the grey wolves whine,
> The lean grey wolves

In that little thing I had become airborne and more; I had achieved weightlessness. And then I heard about having one's roots in the soil, of being a peasant. And I raged at Monaghan and the clay and all to that. But poetry has to do with the reality of the spirit, of faith and hope and sometimes even charity. It is a point of view. A poet is a theologian.

Arts councils and the like love to believe in the poet as a simple singer piping down the valleys wild. When Shelley said that poets were the real legislators of the world he was right, although he may not have fully understood his rightness. A poet is an original who inspires millions of copies. That's all education consists of – the copying of a good model. [...]

# LANGSTON HUGHES

Langston Hughes was born in 1902 in Joplin, Missouri, and was a central figure in the Harlem Renaissance of the 20s. In 1921, 'The Negro Speaks of Rivers' became his first poem to be published nationwide, and his debut collection, *The Weary Blues* followed in 1926. He was the first African-American to make a living from writing, and his pioneering efforts brought black literature and music to national attention, undoubtedly opening the way for a subsequent generation of black writers. The syncopated rhythms of his 'jazz poetry' were absorbed even further afield: not only by the Beats and the East and West Coast scenes of the 50s, but in Britain, in the work of Christopher Logue, Michael Horovitz, and the 'Underground' poets Trocchi, Mitchell and others. For some, Hughes's writing was not militant enough (he sought 'change through the force of his art'), but his hymns to civil rights remain some of the most moving and memorable ever written, including his Whitmanesque 'I, too, sing America'. He founded black theatre groups in Harlem, Chicago and Los Angeles, and prolifically published poetry, short stories and cultural history, as well as two autobiographies and a *Selected Poems* (1959). He died in 1967.

'How to be a Bad Writer' is not all tongue-in-cheek – it plays seriously with questions of roots and subject-matter. But it also reveals what Hughes believes can and cannot be said by a black writer: that as a gay man in the time of civil rights his racial loyalty is public, while his sexuality must remain secretive.

# How to Be a Bad Writer
## (IN TEN EASY LESSONS)

### (1949/50)

1. Use all the clichés possible, such as 'He had a gleam in his eye', or 'Her teeth were white as pearls.'

2. If you are a Negro, try very hard to write with an eye dead on the white market – use modern stereotypes of older stereotypes – big burly Negroes, criminals, low-lifers, and prostitutes.

3. Put in a lot of profanity and as many pages as possible of near-pornography and you will be so modern you pre-date Pompei in your lonely crusade toward the best seller lists. By all means be misunderstood, unappreciated, and ahead of your time in print and out, then you can be felt-sorry-for by your own self, if not the public.

4. Never characterise characters. Just name them and then let them go for themselves. Let all of them talk the same way. If the

reader hasn't imagination enough to make something out of cardboard cut-outs, shame on him!

5. Write about China, Greece, Tibet, or the Argentine pampas – anyplace you've never seen and know nothing about. Never write about anything you know, your home town, or your home folks, or yourself.

6. Have nothing to say, but use a great many words, particularly high-sounding words, to say it.

7. If a playwright, put into your script a lot of hand-waving and spirituals, preferably the ones everybody has heard a thousand times from Marion Anderson to the Golden Gates.

8. If a poet, rhyme *June* with *moon* as often and in as many ways as possible. Also use *thee's* and *thou's* and *'tis* and *o'er*, and invert your sentences all the time. Never say, 'The sun rose, bright and shining.' But, rather, 'Bright and shining rose the sun.'

9. Pay no attention really to spelling or grammar or the neatness of the manuscript. And in writing letters, never sign your name so anyone can read it. A rapid scrawl will better indicate how important and how busy you are.

10. Drink as much liquor as possible and always write under the influence of alcohol. When you can't afford alcohol yourself, or even if you can, drink on your friends, fans, and the general public.

If you are white, there are many more things I can advise in order to be a bad writer, but since this piece is for colored writers, there are some things I know a Negro just will not do, not even for writing's sake, so there is no use mentioning them.

# ALLEN GINSBERG

Allen Ginsberg was born in 1926, in Newark, New Jersey, to a poet-teacher father and Russian emigré mother. He graduated from Columbia in 1948, despite being expelled at one point for writing obscenities on his dormitory window. He spent eight months in a New York psychiatric institute, emerging as the heart of the East Coast Beat movement before it relocated to San Francisco in the early-mid 1950s. His first publication *Howl and Other Poems* (1956) drew instant notoriety when, shortly after its publication by City Lights, it was seized by San Francisco customs and subsequently prosecuted by the Police Department on a charge of obscenity. The trial made national press and Ginsberg a star. But by the early 60s the influence of the Beat Generation would dissipate into popular culture, with *Kaddish and Other Poems* (1961) the last important literary contribution. His *Collected Poems* were published in 1984, his selected essays in 2000. He died in 1998.

Ginsberg, like Crane, saw himself as the descendant of Whitman, evoking not only the long line ('a single breath unit'), but the same 'I' of national consciousness: 'It occurs to me,' wrote Ginsberg in a 1956 poem, 'that I am America.' But his influences were also Blakean, Zen, drug-induced and promiscuously gay, and he demanded that poetic form had to be equally explorative and transcendental if it was to reflect the 'shapely' complexities of mind-body-art. Form is arbitrary, tradition disposable – all that survives is the voice from the burning bush.

# *from* 'When the Mode of the Music Changes the Walls of the City Shake'
## (1961)

### I

Trouble with conventional form (fixed line count & stanza form) is, it's too symmetrical, geometrical, numbered and pre-fixed – unlike to my own mind which has no beginning and end, nor fixed measure of thought (or speech – or writing) other than its own cornerless mystery – to transcribe the latter in a form most nearly representing its actual "occurrence" is my "method" – which requires the Skill of freedom of composition – and which will lead Poetry to the expression of the highest moments of the mind-body – mystical illumination – and its deepest emotion (through tears – love's all) – in the forms nearest to what it actually looks like (data of mystical imagery) & feels like (rhythm of actual speech & rhythm prompted by direct transcription of visual & other mental data) – plus not to

forget the sudden genius-like Imagination or fabulation of unreal &
out of this world verbal constructions which express the true gaiety
& excess of Freedom – (and also by their nature express the First
Cause of the world) by means of spontaneous irrational juxtaposi-
tion of sublimely related fact,

by the dentist drill singing against the piano music; or pure con-
struction of imaginaries, hydrogen jukeboxes, in perhaps abstract
images (made by putting together two things verbally concrete but
disparate to begin with) –

always bearing in mind, that one must verge on the unknown,
write toward the truth hitherto unrecognisable of one's own sincerity,
including the avoidable beauty of doom, shame and embarrassment,
that very area of personal self-recognition (detailed individual is
universal remember) which formal conventions, internalised, keep us
from discovering in ourselves & others – For if we write with an
eye to what the poem should be (has been), and do not get lost in it,
we will never discover anything new about ourselves in the process
of actually writing on the table, and we lose the chance to live in
our works, & make habitable the new world which every man may
discover in himself, if he lives – which is life itself, past present &
future.

Thus the mind must be trained, i.e. let loose, freed – to deal with
itself as it actually is, and not to impose on itself, or its poetic arti-
facts, an arbitrarily preconceived pattern (formal or Subject) – and
*all* patterns, unless discovered in the moment of composition – all
remembered and *applied* patterns are by their very nature arbitrarily
preconceived – no matter how wise & traditional – no matter what
sum of inherited experience they represent – The only pattern or
value of interest in poetry is the solitary, individual pattern peculiar
to the poet's moment & the poem *discovered* in the mind & in the
process of writing it out on the page, as notes, transcriptions –
reproduced in the fittest accurate form, at the time of composition.
('Time is the essence' says Kerouac.) It is this personal discovery
which is of value to the poet & to the reader – and it is of course
more, not less, communicable of actuality than a pattern chosen in
advance, with matter poured into it arbitrarily to fit, which of course
distorts & blurs the matter... Mind is shapely, art is shapely.

## II

The amount of blather & built-in misunderstanding we've en-
countered – usually in the name of good taste, moral virtue or (at
most presumptuous) civilised value – has been a revelation to me

of the absolute bankruptcy of the Academy in America today, or that which has set itself up as an academy for the conservation of literature. For the Academy has been the enemy and Philistine host itself. For my works will be taught in the schools in 20 years, or sooner – it is already being taught for that matter – after the first screams of disgruntled mediocrity, screams which lasted three years before subsiding into a raped moan.

They should treat us, the poets, on whom they make their livings, more kindly while we're around to enjoy it. After all we are poets and novelists, not Martians in disguise trying to poison man's mind with anti-earth propaganda. Tho to the more conformist of the lot this beat & Buddhist & mystic & poetic exploration may seem just that. And perhaps it is. 'Any man who does not labor to make himself obsolete is not worth his salt.' – Burroughs.

People take us too seriously & not seriously enough – nobody interested in what we mean just a lot of bad journalism about beatniks parading itself as highclass criticism in what are taken by the mob to be the great journals of the intellect.

And the ignorance of the technical accomplishment & spiritual interests is disgusting. How often have I seen my own work related to Fearing & Sandburg, proletarian literature, the 1930s by people who don't *connect* my long line with my own obvious reading: Crane's 'Atlantis', Lorca's *Poet in NY*, Biblical structures, psalms & lamentations, Shelley's high buildups, Apollinaire, Artaud, Mayakovsky, Pound, Williams & the American metrical tradition, the new tradition of measure. And Christopher Smart's *Rejoice in the Lamb*. And Melville's prose-poem *Pierre*. And finally the spirit & illumination of Rimbaud. Do I have to be stuck with Fearing (who's all right too) by phony critics whose only encounter with a long line has been anthology pieces in collections by Oscar Williams? By intellectual bastards and snobs and vulgarians and hypocrites who have never read Artaud's *Pour en finir avec le jugement de Dieu* and therefore wouldn't begin to know that this masterpiece which in 30 years will be as famous as *Anabasis* is the actual model of tone for my earlier writing? This is nothing but a raving back at the false Jews from Columbia who have lost memory of the Shekinah & are passing for middleclass. Must I be attacked and contemned by these people, I who have heard Blake's own ancient voice recite me the Sunflower a decade ago in Harlem? and who say *I* don't know about "poetic tradition"?

The only poetic tradition is the Voice out of the burning bush. The rest is trash, & will be consumed. [...]

# FRANK O'HARA

Frank O'Hara (1926-66) grew up in Grafton, Massachussetts, but it is New York with which he is strongly associated. After a spell in the US Navy and education at Harvard, where he met John Ashbery, O'Hara settled in New York and began work in the Museum of Modern Art, where he remained until his death in 1966. As part of the New York School, along with Ashbery, Kenneth Koch and James Schuyler, O'Hara perfected his version of the late 20th century urban voice in collections like *Meditations in an Emergency* (1957) and *Lunch Poems* (1964). An O'Hara poem can be literal and literate by turns, moving from the Manhattan streets and gossipy name-dropping to an exploration of linguistic equivalents to the abstract expressionists he knew and admired, in much the way Gertrude Stein applied the principles of Cubism to her writing. His casual approach to the profession of writing was evidenced by the shock with which the scale and achievement of his *Collected Poems* (1971) was greeted. His reputation and influence, correspondingly adjusted, are now considerable.

'Personism' is a prose example of O'Hara's technique: the camp dismissiveness of big macho gestures like the manifesto is offset by the emergence of a genuine aesthetic. As in the poetry, he charms the reader into constructing and questioning a decisive reading.

## Personism: A Manifesto
### (1961)

Everything is in the poems, but at the risk of sounding like the poor wealthy man's Allen Ginsberg I will write to you because I just heard that one of my fellow poets thinks that a poem of mine that can't be got at one reading is because I was confused too. Now, come on. I don't believe in god, so I don't have to make elaborately sounded structures. I hate Vachel Lindsay, always have; I don't even like rhythm, assonance, all that stuff. You just go on your nerve. If someone's chasing you down the street with a knife you just run, you don't turn around and shout, 'Give it up! I was a track star for Mineola Prep.'

That's for the writing poems part. As for their reception, suppose you're in love and someone's mistreating (*mal aimé*) you, you don't say, 'Hey, you can't hurt me this way, I *care*!' you just let all the different bodies fall where they may, and they always do may after a few months. But that's not why you fell in love in the first place, just to hang onto life, so you have to take your chances and try to avoid being logical. Pain always produces logic, which is very bad for you.

I'm not saying that I don't have practically the most lofty ideas of anyone writing today, but what difference does that make? They're just ideas. The only good thing about it is that when I get lofty enough I've stopped thinking and that's when refreshment arrives.

But how can you really care if anybody gets it, or gets what it means, or if it improves them. Improves them for what? For death? Why hurry them along? Too many poets act like a middle-aged mother trying to get her kids to eat too much cooked meat, and potatoes with drippings (tears). I don't give a damn whether they eat or not. Forced feeding leads to excessive thinness (effete). Nobody should experience anything they don't need to, if they don't need poetry bully for them. I like the movies too. And after all, only Whitman and Crane and Williams, of the American poets, are better than the movies. As for measure and other technical apparatus, that's just common sense: if you're going to buy a pair of pants you want them to be tight enough so everyone will want to go to bed with you. There's nothing metaphysical about it. Unless, of course, you flatter yourself into thinking that what you're experiencing is "yearning".

Abstraction in poetry, which Allen [Ginsberg] recently commented on in *It is*, is intriguing. I think it appears mostly in the minute particulars where decision is necessary. Abstraction (in poetry, not in painting) involves personal removal by the poet. For instance, the decision involved in the choice between 'the nostalgia of the infinite' and 'the nostalgia *for* the infinite' defines an attitude towards degree of abstraction. The nostalgia *of* the infinite representing the greater degree of abstraction, removal, and negative capability (as in Keats and Mallarmé). Personism, a movement which I recently founded and which nobody knows about, interests me a great deal, being so totally opposed to this kind of abstract removal that it is verging on a true abstraction for the first time, really, in the history of poetry. Personism is to Wallace Stevens what *la poésie pure* was to Béranger. Personism has nothing to do with philosophy, it's all art. It does not have to do with personality or intimacy, far from it! But to give you a vague idea, one of its minimal aspects is to address itself to one person (other than the poet himself), thus evoking overtones of love without destroying love's life-giving vulgarity, and sustaining the poet's feelings towards the poem while preventing love from distracting him into feeling about the person. That's part of Personism. It was founded by me after lunch with LeRoi Jones on August 27, 1959, a day in which I was in love with someone (not Roi, by the way, a blond). I went back to work and wrote a poem for this person. While I was writing

it I was realising that if I wanted to I could use the telephone instead
of writing the poem, and so Personism was born. It's a very excit-
ing movement which will undoubtedly have lots of adherents. It
puts the poem squarely between the poet and the person, Lucky
Pierre style, and the poem is correspondingly gratified. The poem is
at last between two persons instead of two pages. In all modesty, I
confess that it may be the death of literature as we know it. While
I have certain regrets, I am still glad I got there before Alain Robbe-
Grillet did. Poetry being quicker and surer than prose, it is only just
that poetry finish literature off. For a time people thought that
Artaud was going to accomplish this, but actually, for all their
magnificence, his polemical writings are not more outside literature
than Bear Mountain is outside New York State. His relation is no
more astounding than Debuffet's to painting.

What can we expect of Personism? (This is getting good, isn't it?)
Everything, but we won't get it. It is too new, too vital a move-
ment to promise anything. But it, like Africa, is on the way. The
recent propagandists for technique on the one hand, and for con-
tent on the other, had better watch out.

# AMIRI BARAKA (LEROI JONES)

Born LeRoi Jones in Newark, New Jersey, 1934, Amiri Baraka adopted his current name upon conversion to Islam in 1965. By this time he was already established as one of the foremost African-American poets of his generation, as well as founding editor of *Yugen* magazine and Totem Press. But his conversion brought new militancy to his writing, and his 1965 'State/Meant' called upon the Black Artist to aid the destruction of America and its 'White Eyes'. Around the same time, Baraka founded the Black Arts Repertory Theatre in Harlem, and his political commitments included service in the Congress of Afrikan Peoples and the short-lived National Black Political Assembly. His first collection was *Preface to a Twenty-Volume Suicide Note* (1961), and subsequent works include *The Dead Lecturer* (1964), *Black Art* (1966) and *It's Nation Time* (1970). Through the 1970s, Baraka's writing moved from black nationalism toward international Marxism, and selected editions of his poems, plays, and prose appeared in 1979.

Despite his political shifts, Baraka's formulating influences remained Modernist: Pound, Williams, 'projective verse'. Like Williams, Baraka found liberation in America's 'open' verse ('we can get nothing from England') – that 'How You Sound??' should be a reflection of content, not merely the prescription of form.

## 'How You Sound??'
### (1960)

'HOW YOU SOUND??' is what we recent fellows are up to. How *we* sound; our peculiar grasp on, say: a. Melican speech, b. Poetries of the world, c. Our selves (which is attitudes, logics, theories, jumbles of our lives, & all that), d. And the final…The Totality Of Mind: Spiritual…God?? (or you name it): Social (zeitgeist): or Heideggerian *umwelt*.

MY POETRY is whatever I think I am. (Can I be light & weightless as a sail?? Heavy & clunking like 8 black boots.) I CAN BE ANYTHING I CAN. I make a poetry with what I feel is useful & can be saved out of all the garbage of our lives. What I see, am touched by (CAN HEAR)…wives, gardens, jobs, cement yards where cats pee, all my interminable artifacts…ALL are a poetry, & nothing moves (with any grace) pried apart from these things. There cannot be closet poetry. Unless the closet be wide as God's eye.

And all that means that I *must* be completely free to do just what I want, in the poem. 'All is permitted': Ivan's crucial concept. There cannot be anything I must *fit* the poem into. Everything must be made to fit into the poem. There must not be any pre-conceived notion or *design* for what the poem ought to be. 'Who knows what a poem ought to sound? Until it's thar.' Says Charles Olson...& I follow closely with that. I'm not interested in writing sonnets, sestinas or anything...only poems. If the poem has got to be a sonnet (unlikely tho) or whatever, it'll certainly let me know. The only 'recognisable tradition' a poet need follow is himself...& with that, say, all those things out of tradition he can use, adapt, work over, into something for himself. To broaden his *own* voice with. (You have to start and finish there...your own voice...how you sound.)

For me, Lorca, Williams, Pound and Charles Olson have the greatest influence. Eliot, earlier (rhetoric can be so lovely, for a time...but only remains so for the rhetorician). And there are so many young wizards around now doing great things that everybody calling himself a poet can learn from...Whalen, Snyder, McClure, O'Hara, Loewinsohn, Wieners, Creeley, Ginsberg &c. &c. &c.

Also, all this means that we want to go into a quantitative verse ...the 'irregular foot' of Williams...the 'Projective Verse' of Olson. Accentual verse, the regular metric of rumbling iambics, is dry as slivers of sand. Nothing happens in that frame anymore. We can get nothing from England. And the diluted formalism of the academy (the formal culture of the US) is anaemic & fraught with incompetence and unreality.

# AUDRE LORDE

Born in 1934 in Harlem, New York City, Audre Lorde was educated at Hunter College and Columbia University. Following the publication of her debut collection *The First Cities* (1968) she began an academic career that would eventually lead her back to a Professorship at Hunter College. African-American, lesbian, a mother, a woman and a cancer survivor, Lorde wrote boldly of the competing identities in her life: a fusion of biography, fiction, and myth that she called 'biomythography'. Her later collections of poetry include *Coal* (1976), *The Black Unicorn* (1978), *Chosen Poems* (1982) and *Our Dead Behind Us* (1986); her essays are collected in *Sister Outsider* (1984) and *A Burst of Light* (1988). She died of cancer in 1992.

Poetry is a method of survival, Lorde believes (and here she is writing 'for each of us as women'). It mines the ancient and hidden reserves of creativity, turning hope into language, language into idea, idea into action. And in action comes the possibility of freedom – to dare to make real our inner, most intimate feelings. Poetry is of the body and the breath, the soul and the city; it is the 'skeleton architecture of our lives'.

# Poetry Is Not a Luxury
## (1977)

The quality of light by which we scrutinise our lives has direct bearing upon the product which we live, and upon the changes which we hope to bring about through those lives. It is within this light that we form those ideas by which we pursue our magic and make it realised. This is poetry as illumination, for it is through poetry that we give name to those ideas which are – until the poem – nameless and formless, about to be birthed, but already felt. That distillation of experience from which true poetry springs births thought as dream births concept, as feeling births idea, as knowledge births (precedes) understanding.

As we learn to bear the intimacy of scrutiny and to flourish within it, as we learn to use the products of that scrutiny for power within our living, those fears which rule our lives and form our silences begin to lose their control over us.

For each of us as women, there is a dark place within, where hidden and growing our true spirit rises, 'beautiful / and tough as chestnut / stanchions against (y)our nightmare of weakness /' and of impotence.

These places of possibility within ourselves are dark because they are ancient and hidden; they have survived and grown strong through that darkness. Within these deep places, each one of us holds an incredible reserve of creativity and power, of unexamined and unrecorded emotion and feeling. The woman's place of power within each of us is neither white nor surface; it is dark, it is ancient, and it is deep.

When we view living in the european mode only as a problem to be solved, we rely solely upon our ideas to make us free, for these were what the white fathers told us were precious.

But as we come more into touch with our own ancient, non-european consciousness of living as a situation to be experienced and interacted with, we learn more and more to cherish our feelings, and to respect those hidden sources of our power from where true knowledge and, therefore, lasting action comes.

At this point in time, I believe that women carry within ourselves the possibility for fusion of these two approaches so necessary for survival, and we come closest to this combination in our poetry. I speak here of poetry as a revelatory distillation of experience, not the sterile word play that, too often, the white fathers distorted the word *poetry* to mean – in order to cover a desperate wish for imagination without insight.

For women, then, poetry is not a luxury. It is a vital necessity of our existence. It forms the quality of the light within which we predicate our hopes and dreams toward survival and change, first made into language, then into idea, then into more tangible action. Poetry is the way we help give name to the nameless so it can be thought. The farthest horizons of our hopes and fears are cobbled by our poems, carved from the rock experiences of our daily lives.

As they become known to and accepted by us, our feelings and the honest exploration of them become sanctuaries and spawning grounds for the most radical and daring of ideas. They become a safe-house for that difference so necessary to change and the conceptualisation of any meaningful action. Right now, I could name at least ten ideas I would have found intolerable or incomprehensible and frightening, except as they came after dreams and poems. This is not idle fantasy, but a disciplined attention to the true meaning of "it feels right to me". We can train ourselves to respect our feelings and to transpose them into a language so they can be shared. And where that language does not yet exist, it is our poetry which helps to fashion it. Poetry is not only dream and vision; it is the skeleton architecture of our lives. It lays the foundations for a future of change, a bridge across our fears of what has never been before.

Possibility is neither forever nor instant. It is not easy to sustain belief in its efficacy. We can sometimes work long and hard to establish one beachhead of real resistance to the deaths we are expected to live, only to have that beachhead assaulted or threatened by those canards we have been socialised to fear, or by the withdrawal of those approvals that we have been warned to seek for safety. Women see ourselves diminished or softened by the falsely benign accusations of childishness, of nonuniversality, of changeability, of sensuality. And who asks the question: Am I altering your aura, your ideas, your dreams, or am I merely moving you to temporary and reactive action? And even though the latter is no mean task, it is one that must be seen within the context of a need for true alteration of the very foundations of our lives.

The white fathers told us: I think, therefore I am. The Black mother within each of us – the poet – whispers in our dreams: I feel, therefore I can be free. Poetry coins the language to express and charter this revolutionary demand, the implementation of that freedom.

However, experience has taught us that action in the now is also necessary, always. Our children cannot dream unless they live, they cannot live unless they are nourished, and who else will feed them the real food without which their dreams will be no different from ours? 'If you want us to change the world someday, we at least have to live long enough to grow up!' shouts the child.

Sometimes we drug ourselves with dreams of new ideas. The head will save us. The brain alone will set us free. But there are no new ideas still waiting in the wings to save us as women, as human. There are only old and forgotten ones, new combinations, extrapolations and recognitions from within ourselves – along with the renewed courage to try them out. And we must constantly encourage ourselves and each other to attempt the heretical actions that our dreams imply, and so many of our old ideas disparage. In the forefront of our move toward change, there is only poetry to hint at possibility made real. Our poems formulate the implications of ourselves, what we feel within and dare make real (or bring action into accordance with), our fears, our hopes, our most cherished terrors.

For within living structures defined by profit, by linear power, by institutional dehumanisation, our feelings were not meant to survive. Kept around as unavoidable adjuncts or pleasant pastimes, feelings were expected to kneel to thought as women were expected to kneel to men. But women have survived. As poets. And there are no new pains. We have felt them all already. We have hidden that fact in the same place where we have hidden our power. They surface in our dreams, and it is our dreams that point the way to freedom. Those dreams are made realisable through our poems that give us the strength and courage to see, to feel, to speak, and to dare.

If what we need to dream, to move our spirits most deeply and directly toward and through promise, is discounted as a luxury, then we give up the core – the fountain – of our power, our womanness; we give up the future of our worlds.

For there are no new ideas. There are only new ways of making them felt – of examining what those ideas feel like being lived on Sunday morning at 7 a.m., after brunch, during wild love, making war, giving birth, mourning our dead – while we suffer the old longings, battle the old warnings and fears of being silent and impotent and alone, while we taste new possibilities and strengths.

# ADRIENNE RICH

Adrienne Rich, born in 1929 in Baltimore, Maryland, is widely recognised as one of the central feminist poets in America. Her first book, *A Change of World* (1951), was selected for publication (like Ashbery's first volume) by Auden, as part of the Yale Series of Younger Poets. It is a decorous and disciplined book, unlike the passionate, rebellious voice of Rich's mature period in everything except its intense seriousness. *Necessities of Life* (1966), *Diving into the Wreck* (1973), and above all *The Dream of a Common Language* (1978), articulate the political and sexual revolution taking place in women's lives in a language both radically innovative and lyrically heightened. A spokesperson for change at a time when that change was having a profound social impact, her work is an extremely engaging testament to an era.

An essayist of equal authority, both in terms of her intellect and her experience, Rich's statement here (delivered in 1964) focuses instead on a moment of personal change which, characteristically, can now be seen to have had wider cultural consequences.

# Poetry and Experience:
## Statement at a Poetry Reading
### (1964/1973)

What a poem used to be for me, what it is today.

In the period in which my first two books were written I had a much more absolutist approach to the universe than I now have. I also felt – as many people still feel – that a poem was an arrangement of ideas and feelings, pre-determined, and it said what I had already decided it should say. There were occasional surprises, occasions of happy discovery that an unexpected turn could be taken, but control, technical mastery and intellectual clarity were the real goals, and for many reasons it was satisfying to be able to create this kind of formal order in poems.

Only gradually, within the last five or six years, did I begin to feel that these poems, even the ones I liked best and in which I felt I'd said most, were queerly limited; that in many cases I had suppressed, omitted, falsified even, certain disturbing elements, to gain that perfection of order. Perhaps this feeling began to show itself in a poem like 'Rural Reflections', in which there is an awareness already that experience is always greater and more unclassifiable than we give it credit for being.

Today, I have to say that what I know I know through making

poems. Like the novelist who finds that his characters begin to have a life of their own and to demand certain experiences, I find that I can no longer go to write a poem with a neat handful of materials and express those materials according to a prior plan: the poem itself engenders new sensations, new awareness in me as it progresses. Without for one moment turning my back on conscious choice and selection, I have been increasingly willing to let the unconscious offer its materials, to listen to more than the one voice of a single idea. Perhaps a simple way of putting it would be to say that instead of poems *about* experiences I am getting poems that *are* experiences, that contribute to my knowledge and my emotional life even while they reflect and assimilate it. In my earlier poems I told you, as precisely and eloquently as I knew how, about something; in the more recent poems something is happening, something has happened to me and, if I have been a good parent to the poem, something will happen to you who read it.

# THOM GUNN

Thom Gunn was born in 1929 in Gravesend, Kent, and educated at Cambridge. His early collections *Fighting Terms* (1954) and *A Sense of Movement* (1957) brought associations with both the Movement and the poetry of Ted Hughes, with whom he published a joint *Selected Poems* in 1961. Following his emigration to the United States in the mid-50s, Gunn's formal, metaphysical writing expanded toward Modernism – *My Sad Captains* (1961) dividing neatly his interest in both 'English' metre and 'American' syllabics. Gunn settled in San Francisco in 1961, from which date his work explores (with increasing frankness) themes of eroticism, voyeurism and homosexual desire. *The Man with the Night Sweats* (1992) and *Boss Cupid* (2000) describe the terrible devastation of AIDS; his *Collected Poems* appeared in 1993.

To write a poem, Gunn suggests, is to go where the air is thin: not a place to survive in, but the source of the mind's magical treasure. Every poem has an occasion; and if the poet is true to that occasion, then the poem becomes an incantation that will retrieve the original, lost moment.

# Writing a Poem
### (1973)

A few years ago I found myself preoccupied by certain related concepts I wanted to write about. They arose from matters real and imaginary so closely tangled with my life that it was impossible, for the time being, to isolate them as a poem. They were a familiar enough association of ideas, it's true – trust, openness, acceptance, innocence – but I felt them all the more vividly and personally the more signally I failed to get them into poems. Well, I knew by now that the thing to do was not to strain, I'd just have to go on living with the values, watering them, hardening them, getting them bushy with the detail of experience, until their flowering presented itself to me as a given fact. In what sense might you say that innocence can be repossessed, I wondered, and started on yet another sterile poem playing with the figure of a house being repossessed – and if there is one thing innocence is clearly not, it is a house. So at length I put the literary expression out of my mind and either wrote of other things or just let myself go fallow for a while, I forget which.

Then one day I was walking on a hill going down to the Pacific, which it met at a narrow, partly-sheltered beach. I came to the beach from some bushes and was confronted by a naked family – father, mother and small son. The son rushed up to me very excited, shouting 'hi there, hi there' in his shrill voice, and rushed away without waiting for an answer. I walked off and felt happy about the comeliness of the scene: it had, too, a kind of decorum that made my mind return to it several times in the next few hours. I mentioned it to some friends that evening and to others the next day, and the day after that I realised that I wanted to write a poem about the naked family. I didn't know any more than that I wanted to preserve them on paper in the best way I knew, as a kind of supersnapshot, getting my feeling for them into my description of them. It wasn't till the poem was finished that I realised I had among other things found an embodiment for my haunting cluster of concepts, though I hadn't known it at the time.

Looked at one way, idea preceded its embodiment; looked at another, particulars preceded induction. Neither process excludes the other here, because the process of writing a poem is something more comprehensive than either, and I think – in all seriousness and not as a mere playful metaphor – it is also connected with the processes of magic. It is a reaching out into the unexplained areas of the mind, in which the air is too thickly primitive or too fine for us to live continually. From that reaching I bring back loot, and don't always know at first what that loot is, except that I hope that it is of value as an understanding or as a talisman, or more likely as a combination of the two, of both rational power and irrational.

When I saw the naked family I didn't know why they satisfied me so much, why I had that strange sense of what I have called decorum. Certainly their appearance was more than a pat embodiment of innocence and its repossession, though as I have said I have come to realise that they were that too. But I did know that I had certain clear and strong feelings about them that I wanted to preserve, if possible by preserving the experience that elicited them. When I came to write the poem, it was all-important that I should be true to those feelings – even, paradoxically, at the risk of distorting the experience. And so for me the act of writing is an exploration, a reaching out, an act of trusting search for the correct incantation that will return me certain feelings whenever I want them. And of course I have never succeeded in finding the correct incantations.

# SYLVIA PLATH

Sylvia Plath wrote with a force and pain rarely matched in modern poetry, and yet only *The Colossus* (1960) and her semi-autobiographical novel *The Bell Jar* (1963) were published in her lifetime. Born in 1932 in Boston, Massachusetts, she studied at Smith College, and at Newnham, Cambridge, where in 1956 she met and married Ted Hughes. 1962 saw what Hughes called her 'curiously independent period of gestation', and following their separation in the autumn of that year came an outpouring of her most remembered and remarkable work – the *Ariel* poems (published in 1965). In the midst of an intense clinical depression, and one of the coldest winters of the century, Plath rose early on the morning of 11 February 1963 and gassed herself.

A poem, writes Plath, is a moment that changes the place of things. Like a snow-scene paperweight turned upside down and back: everything is suddenly different, never to be the same. A poem is that glimpse between the opening and closing of a door, in which we see something new about the world, something sudden but lasting: 'a garden, a person, a rainstorm, a dragonfly, a heart, a city'.

# A Comparison
## (1962)

How I envy the novelist!

I imagine him – better say her, for it is the women I look to for a parallel – I imagine her, then, pruning a rosebush with a large pair of shears, adjusting her spectacles, shuffling about among the teacups, humming, arranging ashtrays or babies, absorbing a slant of light, a fresh edge to the weather and piercing, with a kind of modest, beautiful X-ray vision, the psychic interiors of her neighbors – her neighbors on trains, in the dentist's waiting room, in the corner teashop. To her, this fortunate one, what is there that *isn't* relevant! Old shoes can be used, doorknobs, air-letters, flannel nightgowns, cathedrals, nail varnish, jet planes, rose arbors and budgerigars; little mannerisms – the sucking at a tooth, the tugging at a hemline – any weird or warty or fine or despicable thing. Not to mention emotions, motivations – those rumbling, thunderous shapes. Her business is Time, the way it shoots forward, shunts back, blooms, decays and double exposes itself. Her business is people in Time. And she, it seems to me, has all the time in the world. She can take a century if she likes, a generation, a whole summer.

I can take about a minute.

I'm not talking about epic poems. We all know how long *they* can take. I'm talking about the smallish, unofficial garden-variety poem. How shall I describe it? – a door opens, a door shuts. In between you have had a glimpse: a garden, a person, a rainstorm, a dragonfly, a heart, a city. I think of those round glass Victorian paperweights which I remember, yet can never find – a far cry from the plastic mass-productions which stud the toy counters in Woolworths. This sort of paperweight is a clear globe, self-complete, very pure, with a forest or village or family group within it. You turn it upside down, then back. It snows. Everything is changed in a minute. It will never be the same in there – not the fir trees, nor the gables, nor the faces.

So a poem takes place.

And there is really so little room! So little time! The poet becomes an expert packer of suitcases:

> The apparition of these faces in the crowd;
> Petals on a wet black bough.

There it is: the beginning and the end in one breath. How would the novelist manage that? In a paragraph? In a page? Mixing it, perhaps, like paint, with a little water, thinning it, spreading it out.

Now I am being smug, I am finding advantages.

If a poem is concentrated, a closed fist, then a novel is relaxed and expansive, an open hand; it has roads, detours, destinations; a heart line, a head line; morals and money come into it. Where the fist excludes and stuns, the open hand can touch and encompass a great deal in its travels.

I have never put a toothbrush in a poem.

I do not like to think of all the things, familiar, useful and worthy things, I have never put into a poem. I did, once, put a yew tree in. And that yew tree began, with astounding egotism, to manage and order the whole affair. It was not a yew tree by a church on a road past a house in a town where a certain woman lived...and so on, as it might have been, in a novel. Oh no. It stood squarely in the middle of my poem, manipulating its dark shades, the voices in the churchyard, the clouds, the birds, the tender melancholy with which I contemplated it – everything! I couldn't subdue it. And, in the end, my poem was a poem about a yew tree. That yew tree was just too proud to be a passing black mark in a novel.

Perhaps I shall anger some poets by implying that the *poem* is proud. The poem, too, can include everything, they will tell me. And with far more precision and power than those baggy, disheveled and undiscriminate creatures we call novels. Well, I concede these poets their steamshovels and old trousers. I really *don't* think poems should be all that chaste. I would, I think, even concede a toothbrush, if the poem was a real one. But these apparitions, these poetical toothbrushes, are rare. And when they do arrive, they are inclined, like my obstreperous yew tree, to think themselves singled out and rather special.

Not so in novels.

There the toothbrush returns to its rack with beautiful promptitude and is forgot. Time flows, eddies, meanders, and people have leisure to grow and alter before our eyes. The rich junk of life bobs all about us: bureaus, thimbles, cats, the whole much-loved, well-thumbed catalogue of the miscellaneous which the novelist wishes us to share. I do not mean that there is no pattern, no discernment, no rigorous ordering there.

I am only suggesting that perhaps the pattern does not insist so much.

The door of the novel, like the door of the poem, also shuts.

But not so fast, nor with such manic, unanswerable finality.

# STEVIE SMITH

Though born in Hull, in 1902, Stevie Smith lived all of her life in Palmers Green, London, much of it with her aunt. She rose to prominence with the publication of a novel in 1936, *Novel on Yellow Paper*, followed a year later by her first book of poems, *A Good Time Was Had by All*, and later still, *Not Waving but Drowning* (1957) and *Scorpion and Other Poems* (1972). To her admirers, Smith was a writer of touching and often very funny poems – at once idiosyncratic, celebratory, spiritual and sombre; to her detractors, she was whimsical and slight. She died in 1971 with her popularity at its zenith, but remains one of Britain's most liked and widely read poets. Her *Collected Poems* were published in 1975, her uncollected writings, *Me Again*, in 1981; Frances Spalding's biography appeared in 1988.

Poetry is 'a strong explosion in the sky' – like Smith's own writing, 'light-fingered' in touch but weighty in purpose. The muse is an angel on a strong line to Heaven (or a strong line to Hell, in her own ambivalent attraction to Christianity). The poet is merely a receiver, tuning into the cosmos for the one bright star.

# My Muse
## (1960)

My Muse is like the painting of the Court Poet and His Muse in the National Gallery; she is always howling into an indifferent ear.

It is not indifference but fear. It is the fear of a man who has a nagging wife.

It is like a coarse-grained country squire who has a fanciful wife. It is like an uneasily hearty fellow who denies his phantom. These notions of the Muse are as false as the false-hearty fellow who bites his nails because of the false picture he is making. (If he were really hearty he would not know there was anybody to listen to.)

> Why does my Muse only speak when she is unhappy?
> She does not, I only listen when I am unhappy
> When I am happy I live and despise writing
> For my Muse this cannot but be dispiriting.

This comes nearer to the truth. Here are some of the truths about poetry. She is an Angel, very strong. It is not poetry but the poet who has a feminine ending, not the Muse who is weak, but the poet. She makes a strong communication. Poetry is like a strong explosion in the sky. She makes a mushroom shape of terror and drops to the ground with a strong infection. Also she is a strong

way out. The human creature is alone in his carapace. Poetry is a
strong way out. The passage out that she blasts is often in splinters,
covered with blood; but she can come out softly. Poetry is very light-
fingered, she is like the god Hermes in my poem 'The Ambassador'
(she is very light-fingered). Also she is like the horse Hermes is
riding, this animal is dangerous.

> Underneath the broad hat is the face of the Ambassador
> He rides on a white horse through hell looking two ways.
> Doors open before him and shut when he has passed.
> He is master of the mysteries and in the market place
> He is known. He stole the trident, the girdle,
> The sword, the sceptre and many mechanical instruments.
> Thieves honour him. In the underworld he rides carelessly.
> Sometimes he rises into the air and flies silently.

Poetry does not like to be up to date, she refuses to be neat. ('Anglo-
Saxon,' wrote Gavin Bone, 'is a good language to write poetry in
because it is impossible to be neat.') All the poems Poetry writes
may be called, 'Heaven, a Detail', or 'Hell, a Detail'. (She only
writes about heaven and hell.) Poetry is like the goddess Thetis
who turned herself into a crab with silver feet, that Peleus sought
for and held. Then in his hands she became first a fire, then a
serpent, then a suffocating stench. But Peleus put sand on his
hands and wrapped his body in sodden sacking and so held her
through all her changes, till she became Thetis again, and so he
married her, and an unhappy marriage it was. Poetry is very strong
and never has any kindness at all. She is Thetis and Hermes, the
Angel, the white horse and the landscape. All Poetry has to do is
make a strong communication. All the poet has to do is to listen.
The poet is not an important fellow. There will always be another
poet.

# PHILIP LARKIN

Philip Larkin (1922-85), born in Coventry and educated in a drab post-war Oxford, peripatetic librarian till 1955, when he settled in Hull, is the archetypal poet of the English middle classes: morose, apparently misanthropic, allegedly misogynist and culturally conservative. Like his close friend Kingsley Amis, with whom he was seen as a central figure in the Movement, Larkin has constant recourse to black humour, a complex compassion for his subjects, and an effortless capacity for the memorable phrase. His mature work is confined to three collections, *The Less Deceived* (1955), *The Whitsun Weddings* (1965), and *High Windows* (1974), and the canon was not substantially augmented by the later poems added to his *Collected Poems* (1988) – not writing much being another of the identifying characteristics of the English poet he has bequeathed to his successors. But these books contain a remarkable percentage of the definitive poems of his time: rich both stanzaically and in tone, a Larkin poem projects personae of considerable subtlety not to be exhausted by his Little Englander stance.

His prose relishes the curmudgeonly posture as an appropriate shelter from which to release insights into the combination of discipline and compulsion which drove his art.

## Statement *
### (1956)

I find it hard to give any abstract views on poetry and its present condition as I find theorising on the subject no help to me as a writer. In fact it would be true to say that I make a point of not knowing what poetry is or how to read a page or about the function of myth. It is fatal to decide, intellectually, what good poetry is because you are then in honour bound to try to write it, instead of the poems that only you can write.

I write poems to preserve things I have seen/thought/felt (if I may so indicate a composite and complex experience) both for myself and for others, though I feel my prime responsibility is to the experience itself, which I am trying to keep from oblivion for its own sake. Why I should do this I have no idea, but I think that the impulse to preserve lies at the bottom of all art. Generally my poems are related, therefore, to my own personal life, but by no means always, since I can imagine horses I have never seen or the emotions of a bride without ever having been a woman or married.

As a guiding principle I believe that every poem must be its own sole freshly created universe, and therefore have no belief in "tradition" or a common myth-kitty or casual allusions in poems to other poems or poets, which last I find unpleasantly like the talk of literary understrappers letting you see they know the right people. A poet's only guide is his own judgement; if that is defective his poetry will be defective, but he had still better judge for himself than listen to anyone else. Of the contemporary scene I can say only that there are not enough poems written according to my ideas, but then if there were I should have less incentive to write myself.

**NOTE**

* When D.J. Enright was compiling *Poets of the 1950s* (published in Japan in 1956), he wrote to his contributors asking for a brief statement of their views on poetry. I assumed he would use their replies as raw material for an introduction; I was rather dashed to find them printed *verbatim*.

# TED HUGHES

Ted Hughes was born in 1930 in Mytholmroyd, West Yorkshire, and grew up in nearby Mexborough. He studied at Cambridge, where he was a contemporary of Thom Gunn, and where he would later meet Sylvia Plath (they married shortly afterwards). His first collections, *Hawk in the Rain* (1957) and *Lupercal* (1960), instantly marked him as a major, unflinching voice of a brutal natural world. Following Plath's suicide in 1963, Hughes's early, exacting poems gave way to a rhetorical, boundless quartet of mythological works – *Wodwo* (1967), *Crow* (1970, 1972), *Gaudete* (1977) and *Cave Birds* (1978) – variously, morality tales on the creation story, Original Sin, fertility and sacrifice. This same fascination with fables inspired his children's writing, *How the Whale Became* (1963), *The Iron Man* (1968) and others. His last works were his most acclaimed: *Tales from Ovid* (1997) and the bestselling *Birthday Letters* (1998) which, in describing his relationship with Plath, demonstrated for the first time her profound influence upon his own work. He was Poet Laureate from 1984 until his death in 1998.

Thematically, Hughes's work is deeply conservative: asocial and primitivist, it offers a troubling haven of violence against a debased world. Perversely, it is these very energies that lend Hughes's atavistic style such radicalism, such distinction and timelessness; as Heaney has described, his voice was simply 'longer and deeper and rougher'. In the piece here, Hughes characteristically shows words to be the tools that unlock and recover experience.

# Words and Experience
## (1967)

Sitting in a chair is simple enough, and seems to need no commentary. To see an aircraft cross the sky, while a crow flies in the opposite direction, is simple enough, and again we do not feel compelled to remark on it. To read a letter from the other side of the world, and then go and collect the debt it asks us to collect from somebody near, may not be so easy, but it needs no commentary. We do not need to describe to ourselves every step, very carefully, before we are able to take it. Words need not come into it. We imagine the whole situation, and the possible ways of dealing with it, and then proceed in the way that seems best. Our imagination works in scenes, things, little stories and people's feelings. If we imagine what someone will say, in reply to something we intend to say or do, we have first to imagine how they will feel. We are as a rule pretty confident we know how they will feel. We may be terribly wrong, of course, but at least we never doubt that it is what they feel which counts. And we can think like this without ever forming a single word in our heads. Many people, perhaps most of us, do think in words all the time, and keep a perpetual running commentary going or a mental conversation, about everything that comes under our attention or about something in the back of our minds. But it is not essential. And the people who think in dumb pictures and dim sensings seem to manage just as well. Maybe they manage even better. You can imagine who is likely to be getting most out of reading the gospels, for instance: the one who discusses every sentence word by word and argues the contradictions and questions every obscurity and challenges every absurdity, or the one who imagines, if only for a few seconds, but with the shock of full reality, just what it must have been like to be standing near when the woman touched Christ's garment and he turned round.

It is the same with all our experience of life: the actual substance of it, the material facts of it, embed themselves in us quite a long way from the world of words. It is when we set out to find words for some seemingly quite simple experience that we begin to realise what a huge gap there is between our understanding of what happens around us and inside us, and the words we have at our command to say something about it.

Words are tools, learned late and laboriously and easily forgotten, with which we try to give some part of our experience a more or less permanent shape outside ourselves. They are unnatural, in a way, and far from being ideal for their job. For one thing, a word has its own definite meanings. A word is its own little solar system of meanings. Yet we are wanting it to carry some part of our meaning, of the meaning of our experience, and the meaning of our experience is finally unfathomable, it reaches into our toes and back to before we were born and into the atom, with vague shadows and changing features, and elements that no expression of any kind can take hold of. And this is true of even the simplest experiences.

For instance, with that crow flying across, beneath the aeroplane, which I instanced as a very simple sight – how are we going to give our account of that? Forgetting for a moment the aircraft, the sky, the world beneath, and our own concerns – how are we to say what we see in the crow's flight? It is not enough to say the crow flies purposefully, or heavily, or rowingly, or whatever. There are no words to capture the infinite depth of crowiness in the crow's flight. All we can do is use a word as an indicator, or a whole bunch of words as a general directive. But the ominous thing in the crow's flight, the bare-faced, bandit thing, the tattered beggarly gipsy thing, the caressing and shaping yet slightly clumsy gesture of the downstroke, as if the wings were both too heavy and too powerful, and the headlong sort of merriment, the macabre pantomime ghoulishness and the undertaker sleekness – you could go on for a very long time with phrases of that sort and still have completely missed your instant, glimpse knowledge of the world of the crow's wingbeat. And a bookload of such descriptions is immediately rubbish when you look up and see the crow flying.

Nevertheless, there are more important things than crows to try and say something about. Yet that is an example of how words tend to shut out the simplest things we wish to say. In a way, words are continually trying to displace our experience. And in so far as they are stronger than the raw life of our experience, and full of themselves and all the dictionaries they have digested, they do displace it.

But that is enough for the moment about the wilfulness of words. What about our experience itself, the stuff we are trying to put into words – is that so easy to grasp? It may seem a strange thing to say, but do we ever know what we really do know?

A short time ago, a tramp came to our door and asked for money. I gave him something and watched him walk away. That would seem to be a simple enough experience, watching a tramp walk away. But how could I begin to describe what I saw? As with the crow, words seem suddenly a bit thin. It is not enough to say 'The tramp walked away' or even 'The tramp went away with a slinking sort of shuffle, as if he wished he were running full speed for the nearest corner.' In ordinary descriptive writing such phrases have to suffice, simply because the writer has to economise on time, and if he set down everything that is to be seen in a man's walk he would never get on to the next thing, there would not be room, he would have written a whole biography, that would be the book. And even then, again just as with the crow, he would have missed the most important factor: that what he saw, he saw and understood in one flash, a single 1,000-volt shock, that lit up everything and drove it into his bones, whereas in such words and phrases he is dribbling it out over pages in tinglings that can only just be felt.

What *do* we see in a person's walk? I have implied that we see everything, the whole biography. I believe this is in some way true. How we manage it, nobody knows. Maybe some instinctive and involuntary mimicry within us reproduces that person at first glance, imitates him so exactly that we feel at once all he feels, all that gives that particular uniqueness to the way he walks or does what he is doing. Maybe there is more to it. But however it works, we get the information.

It is one thing to get the information, and quite another to become conscious of it, to know that we have got it. In our brains there are many mansions, and most of the doors are locked, with the keys inside. Usually, from our first meeting with a person, we get some single main impression, of like or dislike, confidence or distrust, reality or artificiality, or some single, vivid something that we cannot pin down in more than a tentative, vague phrase. That little phrase is like the visible moving fin of a great fish in a dark pool: we can see only the fin: we cannot see the fish, let alone catch or lift it out. Or usually we cannot. Sometimes we can. And some people have a regular gift for it.

I remember reading that the novelist H.E. Bates was in the habit of inventing quick brief biographies or adventures for people he met or saw who struck his imagination. Some of these little fantasies he noted down, to use in his stories. But as time passed, he discovered that these so-called fantasies were occasionally literal and accurate accounts of the lives of those very individuals he had seen. The odd thing about this, is that when he first invented them, he had thought it was all just imagination, that he was making it all up. In other words, he had received somehow or other accurate information, in great detail, by just looking – but hadn't recognised it for what it was. He had simply found it lying there in his mind, at that moment, unlabelled.

The great Swiss psychoanalyst Jung describes something similar in his autobiography. During a certain conversation, he wanted to illustrate some general point he was trying to make, and so just for an example he invented a fictitious character and set him in a fictitious situation and described his probable actions – all to illustrate his point. The man to whom he was speaking, somebody he had never met before, became terribly upset, and Jung could not understand why, until later, when he learned that the little story he had invented had been in fact a detailed circumstantial account of that man's own private life. Somehow or other, as they talked, Jung had picked it up – but without recognising it. He had simply found it when he reached into his imagination for any odd materials that would make up a story of the kind he wanted.

Neither of these two men would have realised what they had learned if they had not both had occasion to invent stories on the spot, and if they had not by chance discovered later that what had seemed to them pure imagination had also somehow been fact. Neither had recognised their own experience. Neither had known what they really knew.

There are records of individuals who have the gift to recognise their experience at once, when it is of this sort. At first meeting with a stranger, such people sometimes see his whole life in a few seconds, like a film reeling past, in clear pictures. When this happens, they cannot help it. They simply see it, and know at once that it belongs to this person in front of them. Jung and Bates also saw it, but did not know – and they saw it only in an odd way, when they compelled themselves to produce a story at that very moment. And I believe we all share this sort of reception, this sort of experience, to some degree.

There are other individuals who have the gift to recognise in themselves not simply experience of this sort, but even a similar insight into the past lives and adventures of objects. Such people are known as psychometrists, and have been used by the police. From some weapon or tool used in a crime, they can as it were read off a description of the criminal and often a great deal about him. They are not infallible. But the best of them have amazing records of successes. They take hold of the particular object and the knowledge they are after flashes across their imaginations. Again, it is said by some that this is a gift we all share, potentially, that it is simply one of the characteristics of being alive in these mysterious electrical bodies of ours, and the difficult thing is not to pick up the information but to recognise it – to accept it into our consciousness. But this is not surprising. Most of us find it difficult to know what we are feeling about anything. In any situation, it is almost impossible to know what is really happening to us. This is one of the penalties of being human and having a brain so swarming with interesting suggestions and ideas and self-distrust.

And so with my tramp, I was aware of a strong impression all right, which disturbed me for a long time after he had gone. But what exactly had I learned? And how could I begin to delve into the tangled, rather painful mass of whatever it was that stirred in my mind as I watched him go away?

And watching a tramp go away, even if you have just been subliminally burdened with his entire biography, is a slight experience compared to the events that are developing in us all the time, as our private history and our personal make-up and hour by hour biological changes and our present immediate circumstances and all that we know, in fact, struggle together, trying to make sense of themselves in our single life, trying to work out exactly what is going on in and around us, and exactly what we are or could be, what we ought and ought not to do, and what exactly did happen in those situations which though we lived through them long since still go on inside us as if time could only make things fresher.

And all this is our experience. It is the final facts, as they are registered on this particular human measuring instrument. I have tried to suggest how infinitely beyond our ordinary notions of what we know our real knowledge, the real facts for us, really is. And to live removed from this inner universe of experience is also to live removed from ourself, banished from ourself and our real life. The struggle truly to possess his own experience, in other words to regain his genuine self, has been man's principal occupation, wherever he could find leisure for it, ever since he first grew this enormous surplus of brain. Men have invented religion to do this for others. But to do it for themselves, they have invented art – music, painting, dancing, sculpture, and the activity that includes all these, which is poetry.

Because it is occasionally possible, just for brief moments, to find the words that will unlock the doors of all those many mansions inside the head and express something – perhaps not much, just something – of the crush of information that presses in on us from the way a crow flies over and the way a man walks and the look of a street and from what we did one day a dozen years ago. Words that will express something of the deep complexity that makes us precisely the way we are, from the momentary effect of the barometer to the force that created men distinct from trees. Something of the inaudible music that moves us along in our bodies from moment to moment like water in a river. Something of the spirit of the snowflake in the water of the river. Something of the duplicity and the relativity and the merely fleeting quality of all this. Something of the almighty importance of it and something of the utter meaninglessness. And when words can manage something of this, and manage it in a moment of time, and in that same moment make out of it all the vital signature of a human being – not of an atom, or of a geometrical diagram, or of a heap of lenses, but a human being – we call it poetry.

# SEAMUS HEANEY

Born in 1939 into a Catholic farming family in Mossbawn, Co. Derry, Seamus Heaney read (and later taught) English at Queen's University, Belfast. In 1972 he moved south into the Republic of Ireland, where he still lives, dividing his time between Dublin and a professorship at Harvard. He was Oxford Professor of Poetry from 1989 to 1994, and winner of the Nobel Prize for Literature in 1995. His early collections *Death of a Naturalist* (1966) and *Door into the Dark* (1969) expressed a physical, rural lyricism, touched by Kavanagh and his friend Ted Hughes. The tightly wrought style of *Wintering Out* (1972) and his most politically confrontational work *North* (1975) gradually loosens in his later works, becoming more allegorical along the way. But his concerns for the land, language and troubled history of Ireland run throughout his work, as does a profound quest for balance: the need to reflect his origins without becoming a simple propagandist. His selected edition *Opened Ground: Poems 1966-1996* appeared in 1998, and was followed by his bestselling translation of *Beowulf* (1999).

'Craft and Technique' is the author's own edited version of his 1974 lecture 'Feelings into Words', and expresses his conviction that a poet's technique reflects not only a particular way with words but the writer's very perception of life.

# Craft and Technique
## (1974/2000)

'Are your praties dry
And are they fit for digging?'
'Put in your spade and try,'
Says Dirty-Faced McGuigan.

CHILDHOOD RHYME

I think technique is different from craft. Craft is what you can learn from other verse. Craft is the skill of making. It wins competitions in the *Irish Times* or the *New Statesman*. It can be deployed without reference to the feelings or the self. It knows how to keep up a capable verbal athletic display; it can be content to be *vox et praeterea nihil* – all voice and nothing else – but not voice as in 'finding a voice'. Learning the craft is learning to turn the windlass at the well of poetry. Usually you begin by dropping the bucket halfway down the shaft and winding up a taking of air. You are miming the real thing until one day the chain draws unexpectedly tight and you have dipped into waters that will continue to entice you back. You'll have broken the skin on the pool of yourself. Your praties will be 'fit for digging'.

At that point it becomes appropriate to speak of technique rather than craft. Technique, as I would define it, involves not only a poet's way with words, his management of metre, rhythm and verbal texture; it involves also a definition of his stance towards life, a definition of his own reality. It involves the discovery of ways to go out of his normal cognitive bounds and raid the inarticulate: a dynamic alertness that mediates between the origins of feeling in memory and experience and the formal ploys that express these in a work of art. Technique entails the watermarking of your essential patterns of perception, voice and thought into the touch and texture of your lines; it is that whole creative effort of the mind's and body's resources to bring the meaning of experience within the jurisdiction of form. Technique is what turns, in Yeats's phrase, 'the bundle of accident and incoherence that sits down to breakfast' into 'an idea, something intended, complete'.

It is indeed conceivable that a poet could have a real technique and a wobbly craft – I think this was true of Alun Lewis and Patrick Kavanagh – but more often it is a case of a sure enough craft and a failure of technique. And if I were asked for a figure who represents pure technique, I would say a water diviner. You can't learn the craft of dowsing or divining – it is a gift for being in touch with what is there, hidden and real, a gift for mediating between the latent resource and the community that wants it current and released.

Technique is what allows that first stirring of the mind round a word or an image or a memory to grow towards articulation: articulation not necessarily in terms of argument or explication but in terms of its own potential for harmonious self-reproduction. The seminal excitement has to be granted conditions in which, in Hopkins's words, it 'selves, goes itself...crying / What I do is me, for that I came'. Technique ensures that the first gleam attains its proper effulgence. And I don't just mean a felicity in the choice of words to flesh the theme – that is a problem also but it is not so critical. A poem can survive stylistic blemishes but it cannot survive a stillbirth. The crucial action is pre-verbal, to be able to allow the first alertness or come-hither, sensed in a blurred or incomplete way, to dilate and approach as a thought or a theme or a phrase. Robert Frost put it this way: 'a poem begins as a lump in the throat, a homesickness, a lovesickness. It finds the thought and the thought finds the words.' As far as I am concerned, technique is more vitally and sensitively connected with that first activity where the 'lump in the throat' finds 'the thought' than with 'the thought' finding 'the words'. That first emergence involves the divining, vatic, oracular function; the second, the making function. To say, as Auden did, that a poem is a 'verbal contraption' is to keep one or two tricks up your sleeve.

# TONY HARRISON

Tony Harrison was born in Leeds in 1937, and educated at Leeds University where he read Classics. His first collection *The Loiners* (1970) established his ease with a public, declaratory poetry and was a frank treatment of class, power and exclusion in language. The television broadcast of his controversial, landmark poem *v.* (1985), written during the Miners' Strike, produced a hysterical response in the right-wing press, and secured the work a notoriety not seen since Ginsberg's *Howl* (1956). Harrison's pursuit of different literary forms has delivered theatrical translations of Molière, Racine and Aeschylus, and a number of film and television works, and is part of a project to widen the scope and audience of 'a public poetry'. His belief that language should communicate 'directly and immediately' stems from his desire to speak (and he insists that his poetry is speech) directly to and for his working-class background. Yet Harrison's work shows an acute awareness that his ability to articulate on behalf of his class is also what divides him from it; especially in *The School of Eloquence*, the continuing sonnet sequence he first collected in 1978 and expanded through later books (*Continuous*, 1981; *Selected Poems*, 1984, 1987; *The Gaze of the Gorgon*, 1992). His most recent collection is *Laureate's Block* (2000).

## 'Poetry is all I write'
### (1987)

Poetry is all I write, whether for books, or readings, or for the National Theatre, or for the opera house and concert hall, or even for TV. All these activities are part of the same quest for a public poetry, though in that word "public" I would never want to exclude inwardness. I think how Milton's sonnets range from the directly outward to the tenderly inward, and how the public address of the one makes a clearing for the shared privacy of the other. In the same way I sometimes think that my dramatic poetry has made a clearing for my other poems. I sometimes work with ancient originals written at times when poetry had the range and ambition to net everything, but if I go to them for courage to take on the breadth and complexity of the world, my upbringing among so-called "inarticulate" people has given me a passion for language that communicates directly and immediately. I prefer the idea of men speaking to men to a man speaking to god, or even worse to Oxford's anointed. And books are only a part of what I see as poetry. It seems to me no accident that some of the best poetry in the world is in some of its drama from the Greeks onwards. In it I find a reaffirmation of the power of the word, eroded by other media and by some of the speechless events of our worst century. Sometimes, despite the fact that the range of poetry has been diminished by the apparently effortless way that the mass media seem to depict reality, I believe that, maybe, poetry, the word at its most eloquent, is one medium which could concentrate our attention on our worst experiences without leaving us with the feeling, as other media can, that life in this century has had its affirmative spirit burnt out.

# DOUGLAS DUNN

Douglas Dunn was born in 1942 in Renfrewshire and worked as a librarian in Hull under an acknowledged influence, Philip Larkin. His first book, *Terry Street* (1969) marked him out as a "northern", but not necessarily Scottish voice. Successive collections demonstrated his formal acuities and distinctive tone, politically sharp and wittily disgruntled, capable of a highly sensual celebration; but it was not until *Barbarians* (1979) and *St Kilda's Parliament* (1981) that these acquired the historically and culturally distinct dimensions that are associated with his mature voice. *Elegies* (1985), about the untimely death of his first wife, found a wide audience, and *Northlight* (1988) continued his conscious relocation within the 'estuarial republic' of small-town Scotland, also explored in two volumes of short stories. He teaches at St Andrews University where he is a Professor in the School of English. Recent collections include *Dante's Drum-kit* (1993), *The Year's Afternoon* (2000) and his long poem, *The Donkey's Ears* (2000). His role is assured as one of the decentred masters – along with Heaney, Harrison, Murray and Walcott – of contemporary poetry.

# A Difficult, Simple Art
(2000)

Seamus Heaney probably reflects the innermost convictions of most contemporary poets when he states that poetry follows its own pretexts. However, adverse political and private circumstances in which any poet can find himself or herself during the course of a lifetime, usually more than once, provides occasions when sheer delight in the freedom of aesthetic choice as superior to any other kind of decision feels indulgent or a case of special pleading. But in answering to the topical or immediate as well as the timeless, a poet might be doing nothing more or less than being faithful to the impulses of experience. Poetry can be seen as a contest between the desire to celebrate and preserve the better events and people of a life and its experiences, and the need also to record, reflect or meditate on the negative or painful or repulsive. It can be seen as a struggle between the lyrical and the satirical, between acceptance and rejection. To a large extent this might always have been the case but it appears especially prominent in poetry written since the Great War, if, that is, we concentrate – I hope momentarily – on the pressures which history and society and private life can exert on the art of poetry. Such pressures can oblige poetry to follow what can seem to be pretexts other than its own.

A poet as assailed and victimised by history as Osip Mandelstam could triumph over his misfortunes – and the victory is that of poetry – by writing:

> Into the distance go the mounds of people's heads.
> I am growing smaller here – no one notices me any more,
> but in caressing books and children's games
> I will rise from the dead to say the sun is shining.
>
> (trans. David McDuff)

It is appallingly instructive. Although I love these lines and what I understand by them, then, like most poets of my generation in the British islands, and those younger, they tell me that I don't know the half of suffering. As for "suffering for my art", then such examples as Mandelstam, and too many others, turn that syndrome into a bad joke.

Still, all countries have their different political circumstances. Comparatively speaking, and despite the casualties they have caused, the social and cultural stuntedness which they continue to perpetuate, in the British islands we have been fortunate in even the worst of our governments. Even so, the political and topical can offer a poet an arid language, a reliance on political or ideological attitudes, as well as the blandishments of populism. Many, if not all poets, realise that it is necessary to create a Shakespearean freedom of decision when it comes to the imaginative investigation of political life and ideals. It is not always possible, even in great talents. W.H. Auden, for example, exemplifies, almost classically, topicality and statement that have to be revised or removed subsequently, or, in the case of Pound and Eliot, which are later criticised for mistaken dabbling in the bad beliefs of their times, such as fascism and anti-Semitism. Just as bad (or so I would claim), in a culture which has come to be intimately associated with commerce and dependent on publicity, poets could be anxious to court popularity and "reputation" at the expense of what is more profoundly known as poetry.

All poets are real in the sense that they are at least the equals of others alive at the same time, in terms of their rights as citizens if not always in poetic achievements. Philosophically, and psychologically, however, it is possible to confuse oneself with reality. That is, it is possible for a poet to see the self as equal to what it is not – a self-evidently multiple, various and larger range of persons, experiences and things than can be contained within any one individual. The mistake to which this can lead is that in writing self-consciously about or from oneself then the subject is reality. It is not the same phenomenon as writing "*from* experience". What the poet needs to learn is how to avoid the delusion or hubris that experience is the equal of reality instead of merely one of many threads that connects the poet with others.

Many poets come to learn that lesson. They establish as instinctive enough of an independent humility to encourage original observation and imagery. It also leads to the creation of what the French thinker Gaston Bachelard (although in a different context) called 'a non-I which belongs to the I'. I want to understand that as a fluid, a non-egotistical first-person singular, a poetic I. Indeed, my inclination is to believe that much poetry depends on what I call 'the quality of the first-person singular', and which, I suggest, is the *artistic* quality of a poet's personality instead of a reliance on the autobiographical merely. Outside of the *Sonnets*, in Shakespeare's massive array of characters and what they do and say, his first-person singular can seem invisible or unvoiced, but it is present in his exploitation of conventions and his examination of them, within his apparent convictions. Likewise, Milton's personality is unobtrusive in *Paradise Lost*, with the exception of his invocation to his Muse Urania at the beginning of Book VII. In some of his sonnets his 'I' is personal and plangent, perhaps even more than John Donne's, or the equal of Ben Jonson's in his poem on the death of his son.

Testimony is not, of course, a primary goal of poetry. It is something that occurs from time to time in some poets, and most of the time in those for whom their gift is almost entirely lyrical. While its effacement by dramatic poets such as Browning was influential on the first modernists (Pound especially), it could be best (or at least arguable) to understand such a move away from the lyrical first-person singular as an attempt to enlarge the imaginative franchise through the adoption of a "persona". Self-annihilation and "impersonality", however, have become chimeras after which some poets choose to hunt. In recent years it has been surrounded by a miasmic quasi-scientificism – misty, indeed, because its practitioners would seem as "literary" as other poets, and their attitudes of science adopted rather than learned in laboratories. In other words, and with a few exceptions (the late Miroslav Holub, for example, David Morley, or Iain Bamforth), they are scientists only in a similar way as "Scientologists" or Christian Scientists.

Poetry is resistant to innovation or radical change in its principles and procedures. Although embedded in the ethical, it can at times be an exercise of or in the irrational and predisposed to recognise or discover but not to fabricate the mysterious, that dimension of life and mind perhaps best described as spiritual.

While not based on the primacy of reason to the same extent as other human activities, the self-aware artistry of ordered verse promotes an illusion of rationality – a constructive, enabling and ironic illusion when artistry is seen to convey disordered thoughts and feelings and the attempt to make sense of them.

All this would seem to stem from the poetic imagination's ability sometimes to release itself from the restraints of reason while refusing to abandon analytical intelligence altogether, and, indeed, often to serve it, as if from another direction. Poetry, however, is not a substitute for religion. It is too secular, captivated as it is by phenomena and by the erotic, by the plurality and divergences of life. It is *like* a religion in the sense that it is a devotion for its practitioners: it is a theology without a God. Instead, a poet aspires to obey what is nebulously, numinously and sometimes ruinously called a Muse. It is the *anima* of poetry, its sensuousness, its feelingness, its desire to live daringly, that promises (although it does not always produce) its honesty in a world when words are so often of the weasel variety and not always to be trusted. Similarly, through an ambiguous relationship with reason and a willingness to encourage chance and daring, a poet has to feel able to shed the "grammar gods" of schooling and education while at the same time plundering the memory for erudition and learning. In poetry, learning, and the academic, are the fall-backs of dunces. Poetry exists in a lived vernacular crossed with the discoveries of a vivid observation and imagination. A poet learns the contemporary language and its literary version through being alive, meeting people, loving them, learning what it is about some of them that is to be disliked or distrusted, by sheer amusement, entertainment in people and phenomena, by sheer sorrow, by laughter, tears, by wonderment, puzzlement, by repulsion, by immersion in existence.

What I am saying is that the best passages of poetry are involuntary even when their artistry has been mastered through years of severe rehearsal and concentration. Poetry appears to exist in all languages, cultures and societies. It is heartening to suppose that it does. If nothing else, it would seem to justify a life squandered in a devotion to an arduous, satisfying, lonely, disillusioned, grievous, joyful, difficult and simple art.

# DEREK WALCOTT

Derek Walcott was born in 1930 in St Lucia, and was educated in the West Indies. He founded the Trinidad Theatre Workshop in 1959, which has prem- ièred many of his own plays, including *Dream on Monkey Mountain* in 1967, *The Joker of Seville* (1974) and *O Babylon!* (1976). But he is predominantly known as a poet who, though publishing through the 1960s, made his break- through with *Another Life* in 1973 and also *Seagrapes* (1976). Walcott pub- lished his *Collected Poems* in 1986, followed by *The Arkansas Testament* (1987), the Homeric *Omeros* (1990), *The Bounty* (1997) and *Tiepolo's Hound* (2000), reflecting his tireless pursuit of identity in Caribbean culture, the legacy of European colonialism, and the expression of Creole vocabulary and calypso rhythms. He was awarded the Nobel Prize for Literature in 1992, and divides his time between his home island of St Lucia, New York City, and a teaching post at Boston University. His essays are collected in *What the Twilight Says* (1998).

Walcott chose not to write a statement for this book but agreed, instead, to outline his reservations verbally, and the following is a complete transcription of a conversation with Matthew Hollis recorded on 11 December 1999. (Walcott refers in passing to Keats' famous line 'Beauty is truth, truth beauty' in 'Ode on a Grecian Urn'.)

# In Conversation
### (2000)

**MH:** How much does it matter what poets say about their art?

**DW:** If the poet describes what he or she is trying to do then to me that's another voice that shouldn't be there – that should be a sort of self appointed critic, generally congratulatory about the writer's work. When poets write about other poets they're interesting though – in fact I find that very interesting to read: what poets as critics say about other writers.

**MH:** And yet you think to write about your own work is actually essentially less interesting?

**DW:** Well, I don't see the point. I think if you're writing about your own work, pointing out either the struggle you had in trying to resolve something or what you intended – I mean, nobody thumps their chest and says, 'I achieved this', you know, some people might, *but.* What you explain is less important than what you have done, the explanation serves either as an excuse or as an extension of what you *have* done, and I don't see the point of that.

MH: Do you think explication is actually *against* the very fabric of poetry?

DW: The ethic to be simultaneous, the ethic to be both creator and explainer, seems to me contradictory. There are passages in Eliot in which he is obviously pointing out, and you can see a model, you can take all the essays he's written as sort of drafts of what he intends to do with his own poetry, but it's never really a direct "chest thump" that says this is my marker and this is what my goal is. But the most self-explaining poet we have is Whitman, so that all the intention of Whitman is *already* in the poetry, even a line like, 'Do I contradict myself? Very well, I contradict myself' is contained in the sub-criticism or phrase that is there in the statements made by Whitman. So that I don't mind: I don't mind autobiographical, even vain or pseudo-humble, or remaining presentations of one's own work. But it's the other thing that I find rather secondary.

MH: Can a manifesto explore what an artist thinks is important in their art, rather than simply describe how they came to write a poem?

DW: A manifesto stating the general atmosphere? – say, a black writer, for instance, in America explaining what the black writer is trying to do, and involving history and race, etc etc?

MH: For example.

DW: Yes I can understand it. But I'm just saying it's another department. It's sort of like moral history – another kind of aesthetic that gets involved here in terms of dragging history into things. We all know certain poets in certain phases in history or time have written manifestos of what poetry needs to become – Pound is the best example we have recently of that, and what Pound said in terms of contemporary poetry is extremely valuable. I'm not sure that Pound, though, addresses his own work in that respect. In other words, the Pound that is there, intending what he wanted to do, as in the *Pisan Cantos* or something else, it's already in the poetry. I'm really talking about another shape – I'm talking about the prose shape that becomes a shadow over the completed poem.

MH: So if it's only in *poetry* that a poet speaks, and not in writing *about* poetry, then a poem must be distinct, in your mind, to other forms of writing?

DW: Oh, absolutely. I don't believe in the prose poem, I don't think there's such an animal, except really Rimbaud and to a degree Borges and Baudelaire, but I don't think it works in English, for instance, it's just not in the spirit of the language. The payback is too pathetic, I think, the prose poem in English.

MH: When you're writing does some part of you remain necessarily unconscious? Is that part of the resistance to articulating what's explicit in a poem?

DW: Yes, you've described it much more precisely than I have. The process that made the poem is not the process that made the manifesto. It's a different process: a process that in a way is a kind of propaganda that the poet may think necessary, and it may be necessary, perhaps, for the poet to express himself or herself at that time through some kind of manifesto. But the manifestos vanish: the manifestos go away and the poetry remains. To include the manifesto in the poem, there's nothing wrong with that, I'm talking about something treated separately. I think that's a *secondary* inspiration – if it's an inspiration at all.

MH: So it's the art that remains? And not what's written about it?

DW: Even by the maker of the art.

MH: So does a poet have responsibilities?

DW: Yes, tremendous responsibilities. Everything. The primary responsibility is honesty to his craft, and not to lie. And I think those of us who write verse spend most of the time gliding on a kind of a lie that we accept about ourselves, even if that lie is melodramatic and self-critical. We're not always in key – we're very very rarely in key – with the truth of what one wants to say. And I think that is what Keats meant: simply *that*, I think, that in terms of the responsibility to *that* truth. I think that takes in the entire world, it takes in all of living: it takes in politics, the lie that is inherent in most political activity which is a sham; the lie that is there in human relationships or love; there may even be a lie that is death, maybe death is a lie, and that's the examination of a reality that is the responsibility of the poet.

MH: And is it that truth, that search for truth, that has seen you writing poems now for 50 years – for I wonder what is it about a poem, or poetry, that so keeps you coming back?

DW: I don't want to put myself up in a category where I'm made a knight in some kind of super quest – no, I don't think of that, and I don't think any writer thinks of that, you know, undertaking the journey that is going to take me to the Grail, and at the end of it is going to be some kind of illumination and the Heavenly Father. I don't think that. I think the daily thing is that the practice of the craft involves such punishing honesty that most of the time we kind of evade it *by* craft, and that's the difficulty, because we become very crafted, very adept in technique, style; and even with reputation, what should happen is that every time one attempts to write a poem reputation is cancelled and one has to begin again. In fact that's what one tries to do. The 50 years is nothing compared to beginning again.

MH: But any poetics should always remain firmly within the lines of a poem? And the poem is enough? The poem is everything?

DW: I'm trying to think of places where poets have written about their craft and what they have said. They're generally not analytical in terms of what they're trying to do – if one *can* make a metrical idea out of the technique of poetry and whether one is interested in doing that in writing at all. There are lots of things said about poetry by poets in terms of the craft, such as you know, 'The lyf so short, the craft so long to lerne', and other things that are there in poets from Chaucer to Pound – in Wordsworth, even. But in terms of addressing the manner in which we write, I think maybe that's a very modern thing because after all it doesn't require the presentation of the ego – and I don't know when that's all been done but certainly it's 20th century to describe what one is doing as if the daily occupation of the poet were of interest to a public, however small. We acquire some kind of identity that gets in the way of the creation of the poem. If you look at how many forms and conflicting theories there are in terms of 20th century poetry, especially in America, in a way it becomes amusing that there should be so many formulas for making poems, and some of them extremely emphatic – belligerent, in fact – in the insistence of 'this is the way, the only way, that one can write'. And that creates a lot of manifestos. And the manifestos create a kind of poetry that really isn't poetry at all – it's really a rhythmical manifesto.

MH: So the poem needs to remain free from that level of explication or manifesto to attain a good level of poetry?

DW: I think so. I think that we have done that, the recent 20th century writers who have formed different schools – whether it's the Black Mountain *this*, or the Syllabic *that* – all the different labels and names have formed little schools. But it's not even an urban thing, anyway, it's a metropolitan thing: they don't really affect people outside the metropolis. But that's what the metropolis is from the outside, a lot of little gangs of people stating their manifestos very emphatically and writing poems that will demonstrate those manifestos.

MH: Whereas what will actually survive in the end is the poem?

DW: You see, in painting you can't do it. You can't paint and say, 'this is what I'm trying to do here, as theory'. You can't paint theory. Because it's language you can do all sorts of things that make the reputation out of the poetry expand. But painting's one of the crafts in which you can't. I don't think you can do it in music either, to say, 'this is what I'm stating'. I'm not saying that you cannot have a general idea, like you might be a revolutionary and think, well, this music is revolutionary and that's why it's there. But in terms of simultaneously having an explication of what you're intending to do, which is what we have so much of in terms of poetry, such writing *about* poetry...

MH: And yet Yeats has also said that all writers have had some philosophy, some criticism of their art, and actually that criticism has sometimes shown the best illumination of that poet's work.

DW: But Yeats was talking about larger things. I don't think he has any predilections to saying 'look what I'm doing here'. He does have texts in which he says, 'what I'm trying to do is $x$ or $y$', but those texts are larger issues in the technique of poetry. I'm talking about people writing about their technique, and that is what we have a lot of, and that's what I'm against, that's what I won't try. I'm not talking about larger issues. If I had to say anything about Caribbean history, for instance, it would be very much in a pamphlet against things that have happened. But if I want to put it, as I have, in the work that I've written about Caribbean history then all the vehemence, perhaps even the manner of expression, is self-contained in the poem's style or even content. That's what I'm saying: it's in the poem.

# PAUL MULDOON

Paul Muldoon was born in 1951 in Portadown, Co. Armagh, and studied at Queen's University, Belfast. He published *New Weather* (1973) when he was just 21, and his subsequent collections, *Mules* (1977), *Why Brownlee Left* (1980) and *Quoof* (1983) established him as one of the most influential poets of his generation. Formally dazzling and a skilled exponent of rhyme (Muldoon is sometimes said to be the only poet capable of rhyming 'cat' with 'dog'), his poetry is punning, ironic, allusive, mischievous, and intimately bound-up with Irish language and custom. His later collections include *Madoc – A Mystery* (1990), *The Annals of Chile* (1994) and *Hay* (1998), as well as several books for children. A *Collected Poems* is forthcoming, and he has edited *The Faber Book of Contemporary Irish Verse* (1988) and *The Faber Book of Beasts* (1997). In 1999 he was appointed Oxford Professor of Poetry, and his first critical book, *To Ireland, I* (2000), is a provocative A-Z of Irish literature. He lives and teaches in Princeton. 'Go Figure' is his selection from his 1998 lecture 'Getting Round'.

# Go Figure
## (1998/2000)

So. What can I tell you?

You have before you a person who:

(1) argues for the primacy of unknowing yet insists on almost total knowingness on the part of the poet as first reader;

(2) accepts that a poet is necessarily a product of his or her time, someone trying to make sense of him or herself in their time, through whom the time may best be told, yet, largely because of that, insists on the freedom not to espouse directly any political position;

(3) recognises that a poem must necessarily effect a change in the world but accepts, both reluctantly and with a sense of relief, that such a change can only ever be slight and;

(4) is tempted by the post-Romantic urge expressed by Keats, in 'Sleep and Poetry', when he describes 'the great end / Of poesy, that it should be a friend / To soothe the cares, and lift the thoughts of man', yet quite disavows the notion of poetry as a moral force, offering respite or retribution.

To those of you whom I hear mutter, 'Get over yourself', I can merely suggest, however feeble it sounds, that it is partly out of this muddle of contradictions that I continue to try to make '*a ware*', as Frost's speaker would have it in 'The Silken Tent'.

Go figure.

# TOM PAULIN

Tom Paulin is the leading Northern Irish poet-critic. He was born in Leeds in 1949, brought up in Belfast, and was educated at Hull and Oxford where he now teaches. His first collection, *A State of Justice* (1977), was unflinching in its treatment of Ulster and the Protestant condition. But his subsequent work, *The Strange Museum* (1980), *Liberty Tree* (1983) and *Fivemiletown* (1987), shows an increasingly complex employment of politics. His *Selected Poems* appeared in 1993 and his most recent collection is *The Wind Dog* (1999). He has published three books of essays, *Ireland & the English Crisis* (1984), *Minotaur* (1992) and *Writing to the Moment* (1996); a study of William Hazlitt, *The Day-Star of Liberty* (1998); and two anthologies, *The Faber Book of Political Verse* (1986) and *The Faber Book of Vernacular Verse* (1990), from which he has drawn his statement here.

# Tracking *The Wind Dog*
### (1990/2000)

(*Vernacular Verse* was a protest against the then Tory government's insistence on the need for Standard English. With hindsight I can see I was tracking *The Wind Dog*, but I didn't know it then.)

John Clare's oral writings issue from the experience of a kind of internal colonialism – Enclosure – which traumatised him and led him to reject Anglicanism and become a Ranter. Clare felt robbed of his language and complained that 'grammer in learning is like Tyranny in government'. His publisher, John Taylor, urged him to get rid of oral 'provincialisms' in his poetry – for example to substitute 'gush'd' for 'gulsh'd' or drop 'himsen'. Taylor edited, reshaped and sometimes rewrote Clare's unpunctuated poems so that Clare felt robbed of his ties to the land and to his native speech-community. The restored texts of the poems embody an alternative social idea. With their lack of punctuation, freedom from standard spelling and charged demotic ripples, they become a form of Nation Language that rejects the polished urbanity of Official Standard. They are communal speech – the speech of the Northamptonshire peasantry – vulnerable before the all-powerful language of aristocratic politicians and the printed language of parliamentary statutes.

Clare's biblical Protestantism, his Ranter's sense of being trapped within an unjust society and an authoritarian language, show in this letter he wrote from Northampton General Lunatic Asylum:

> this is the English Bastile a government Prison where harmless people
> are trapped & tortured till they die – English priestcraft & english
> bondage more severe then the slavery of Egypt & Affrica

In his anguished madness, Clare dramatises his experience of the
class system and its codified language as exile and imprisonment
in Babylon.

The voice of Babylon speaks in this contemporary review of
Clare's *The Shepherd's Calendar*:

> We had not, however, perused many pages before we discovered that
> our suspicions were wholly groundless. Wretched taste, poverty of
> thought, and unintelligible phraseology, for some time appeared its
> only characteristics. There was nothing, perhaps, which more pro-
> voked our spleen than the want of a glossary; for, without such assist-
> ance, how could we perceive the fitness and beauty of such words as –
> *crizzling – sliveth – whinneys – greening – tootles – croodling – hings –
> progged – spindling – siling – struttles* &c. &c.

The italicised words each have that unique, one-off, familial rareness
Muldoon celebrates in 'Quoof', but here they enter the language
only to be expelled by the uptight efficient voice of Official Standard.
These are homeless, evicted words powerlessly falling through a
social void. And in 'The Lament of Swordy Well' the common land
protests against this type of violent social and linguistic engineering.
Many of Clare's poems are pitched against the Lockean idea of
individualism, personal property, the view that words are merely
flat functional signs. It's as if Clare, like a native American, believes
the land owns the people, instead of being owned by certain indi-
viduals.

Printed language is alien, inauthentic and cruelly powerful. Print
is a form of violence, its signs are like that 'curious T' which Pip's
brain-damaged sister chalks on her slate in *Great Expectations*. In
Dickens's novel, the letter *T*, a leg-iron and hammer are identified
– the *T* signifies Orlick who has felled Mrs Gargery with the leg-
iron that clamped Magwitch's ankle. Dickens shows how the oral
community which Mrs Gargery, Joe, Magwitch and initially Pip
belong to is powerless before the force of print, the legal system,
male violence and gentility.

Pip, like Clare, moves out of the oral community into the literate
and hostile public world:

> 'MI DEER JO I OPE U R KR WITE WELL I OPE I SHAL SON B
> HABELL 4 2 TEEDGE U JO AN THEN WE SHORL B SO GLODD AN
> WEN I M PRENGTD 2 U JO WOT LARX AN BLEVE ME INF XN PIP.'

Pip's inscribed speech is poignant because it contains the threat of
future alienation – Pip will one day become a chill and educated

gentleman who snobbishly looks down on the illiterate Joe. Now, in the moment of the hearth's warmth, Joe doesn't understand that Pip will write himself out of their Edenic oral world. The hearth is covered with all the letters of the alphabet – death's signs have infiltrated the house. And even though it's a statement of his bond of love with Joe, Pip's slate symbolises the decomposition of paradisal speech, the beginning of the Fall.

I have no wish to sentimentalise orality, only to notice that the vernacular imagination distrusts print in the way that most of us dislike legal documents. That imagination expresses itself in speech and feels trammelled by the monolithic simplicities of print, by the formulaic monotonies which distort the spirit of the living language. When I consider this – consider the way in which print-culture overrides local differences of speech and vocabulary – I recall a moment when that imagination spoke directly to me. I was out in a boat, lazily fishing for mackerel with a man I was fond of, an merchant seaman from Islandmagee in Co. Antrim. He nodded up at the rainwashed blue sky and said, 'D'you see thon wind-dog?' I looked up and saw a broken bit of rainbow and thought how rare and new 'wind-dog' seemed, how dull and beaten thin 'rainbow' was. It was MacDiarmid's 'chitterin' licht' of the watergaw just happening as he spoke.

From an early age I became immersed in the wild dash and wit and loving playfulness of Northern Irish speech, a speech that is celebrated in Sally Belfrage's *The Crack*: 'You know what yer mon's like; like.' – 'Och aye. Not a titter of wit.' 'Did you get the sausingers but?' – 'I'm only after goin' til the shop so.'

In Robert Frost's terms, this is a speech packed with 'sentence sounds', sounds which writers gather 'by the ear from the vernacular'. Listening to a vocal phrase like 'Go you on back now' or 'I'll be with you in a minute but' or 'D'you see thon wind-dog?', I'm returned to Frost's aesthetic of the spoken word, to Huck's listening to those voices on the ferry landing, to these lines from a favourite Belfast street-song:

> my Aunt Jane has a bell on the door
> a white stone step and a clean swept floor
> candy apples    hard green pears
> conversation lozengers
> candy apples    hard green pears
> conversation lozengers

The lovely packed stresses – a whíte stóne stép and a cléan swépt flóor – have an ecstatic tribal innocence that suddenly breaks the surface-rhythm like a shoal of fry. And deep down I hear a phrase in another stanza – 'three black lumps' – as '*th-hee* black lumps'. For a moment, Belfast's Ormeau Road is the omphalos of the universe, then those doubts some navel-gazers are prone to intervene …might a poem by Betjeman not be having the same effect elsewhere?

But in that moment what I discover is an entrance to that wild and perfect garden which is celebrated in naive or primitive art. That art was a powerful influence on Elizabeth Bishop's writing, and her cherishing vernacular affirms its value in 'Crusoe in England' when Crusoe exclaims, 'Home-made, home-made!', and then adds, 'But aren't we all?'

# CRAIG RAINE

Craig Raine was born in 1944 in Shildon, Co. Durham. He studied at Oxford, where he now teaches, was poetry editor at Faber and Faber through the 1980s, and founded *Areté* magazine in 1999. His first collections of poems, *The Onion, Memory* (1978) and *A Martian Sends a Postcard Home* (1979), established what James Fenton coined the 'Martian' school of poetry, with its slightly surreal (and slightly Modernist) look at the business of the everyday. *A Free Translation* (1981) and *Rich* (1984) followed, as have two stage adaptions, a libretto, a version of Racine's *Andromaque*, and his epic verse novel *History: the Home Movie* (1994). *À La Recherche du Temps Perdu*, a long poem, was published in 2000.

# Babylonish Dialects
### (1984)

1. How do we think? Consider Nabokov on the stream of consciousness in *Ulysses*: 'it exaggerates the verbal side of thought. Man thinks not always in words but also in images, whereas the stream of consciousness presupposes a flow of words that can be notated: it is difficult, however, to believe that Bloom was continually talking to himself.'

2. How do I refute Nabokov? By saying this is true, but only because we are not always thinking while we are conscious? By offering up Wordsworth on his couch, in vacant or in pensive mood?

3. What about the other mental phenomena which inhabit Wordsworth's vacancy – the dreams, the emotions, those daffodils? They cannot be verbalised, though they undoubtedly exist.

4. I see the current Oxford Professor of Poetry in the street and E.P. Thompson on the train. Both are talking to themselves. They are thinking aloud. If I was closer, I could bathe in their stream of consciousness, hear their words. For a second, I see myself with my trousers rolled up: is this a thought or a picture?

5. 'How can I tell what I think till I see what I say?' asks E.M. Forster. This implies that all thinking is verbal, that without language we cannot think. This is what happens to Ralph in *Lord of the Flies*: 'he lost himself in a maze of thoughts that were rendered vague by his lack of words to express them'.

6. On the other hand, Forster is also saying that we cannot articulate thought without using language. True. But that still leaves inarticulate thought, Ralph's 'maze of thoughts' in which he is lost.

7. Wittgenstein is masturbating. His mind is continuously occupied for five minutes, shall we say, by a series of obscene pictures – not by the words 'tit' and 'bum'. This is a thought process even though it is unrelated to language.

8. Music is a language to which we listen in order to experience a distinct penumbra we could not describe. Much poetry initially works in this way, too. 'Genuine poetry,' said Eliot, 'can communicate before it is understood.' A philosopher might retort: 'for people who cannot think, this passes for thought.'

9. But most of the time, we are at the mercy of language. If we introspect, we see in our minds the words, 'if we introspect'. And surely we can be misled by language, as Wittgenstein explains metaphorically: 'philosophers often behave like little children who scribble marks on a piece of paper at random and then ask the grown-up "What's that?" It happened like this: the grown-up had drawn pictures for the child several times and said: "this is a man", "this is a house", etc. And then the child makes some marks too and asks: "what's *this* then?"'

10. Often language tells us what to think. Poetry, though, can use language to help us escape this tyranny of language. T.S. Eliot said of Edward Lear's poetry that it was not nonsense but a parody of sense. As readers, we are like Wittgenstein's child, but from deliberate choice. We hear the language and, while we know there is no sense to it, we experience the sensation of thought. The mind is Pavlovian: it salivates at the sound of a word, as if there was here real food for thought. The nebulous effect corresponds to something within our minds before we have said what we think.

11. Poetry written in dialect belongs to the world of non-sense and the world of sense – depending on how familiar you are with the dialect.

12. All great poetry is written in dialect. This is Johnson on Milton: 'through all his greater works there prevails an uniform peculiarity of *Diction*, a mode and cast of expression which bears little resemblance to that of any other former writer, and which is so far removed from common use, that an unlearned reader, when he first opens his book, finds himself surprised by a new language...Of him, at last, may be said what Jonson says of Spenser, that *he wrote no language*, but has formed what Butler calls a *Babylonish dialect...*'

13. It follows that if all great poetry is written in dialect, then it is all poised between sense and non-sense – which seems unlikely until you consider, say, Southey's reaction to the 'Ancient Mariner' ('many of the stanzas are laboriously beautiful, but in connection they are absurd or unintelligible') and Wordsworth's insistence that

new art must create the taste by which it is to be enjoyed.

14. Most bad poetry is written in the dialect of the previous age. Some bad poetry is written in the dialect of no particular age – only the dialect of poetry. But if language dates, no language dates quicker than the self-consciously timeless, which is already dated.

15. Wordsworth's dialect, Hopkins's complicated dialect, Frost's simple American dialect – we have mastered them all. The task is to invent a new dialect or even dialects.

16. Why? There are two reasons. We become so familiar with a dialect that we no longer hear its individuality. Or the dialect becomes in time more and more difficult: presumably some such thought is behind A.L. Rowse's scheme to render *Romeo and Juliet* into modern English.

17. And there is a further reason. The advantage of dialect is this: if nonsense poetry can create in us the sensation of thought, then dialect can create in us different thoughts. Alter the language and you alter thought. Our ways of thinking are renewed.

18. Why should we want to do this? Let me quote Wittgenstein again: 'the idea is worn out by now and no longer usable...Like silver paper, which can never be quite smoothed out again once it has been crumpled. Nearly all my ideas are a bit crumpled.' Good: let us have some uncrumpled ideas, if not some new ones; let us change the language.

19. The bonus of dialect is easy to see. 'Wee, sleeket, cowran, tim'rous beastie' alters our thought, our perception, gives us a clearer idea of the mouse than standard English. Everything vivid here would cloud at the mere approach of A.L. Rowse.

20. Hopkins wrote to Robert Bridges that he had been reading *Two Years Before the Mast*: 'all true, but bristling with technicality – seamanship – which I most carefully go over and even enjoy but cannot understand...' This is true of any dialect: we enjoy without at first fully understanding. But what is the nature of the enjoyment? Compare the opening of the *Tempest*: 'Down with the topmast! Yare! lower, lower! Bring her to try with main-course.'

Quite. Shakespeare is bluffing. He is adding spices to his recipe. Neither he nor we may know exactly what they are, but we can taste the tiny, authentic explosions. They give us the sensation of thought by their confident, but ultimately opaque, particularity.

21. In *Riddley Walker*, Russell Hoban uses language like Molesworth in *Down with Skool*:

> She said, 'Its some kynd of thing it aint us but yet its in us. Its looking out thru our eye hoals. May be you dont take no noatis of it only some times. Say you get woak up suddn in the middl of the nite. 1 minim

youre a sleep and the nex youre on your feet with a spear in your han.
Wel it wernt you put that spear in your han it wer that other thing
whats looking out thru your eye hoals. It aint you nor it dont even
know your name. Its in us lorn and loan and sheltering how it can.'

One is immediately struck by the way Hoban completely escapes
the comedy implicit in the Molesworth idiom, then by how little
has been changed – the odd spelling, haphazard punctuation. Yet
the effect is enormous: the change in the language has actually
changed the thought. The woman is discussing the soul, but much
more vividly than if Hoban had confined her to that word. The
concept is renewed.

22. In the same way, MacDiarmid's poem, 'The Bonnie Broukit
Bairn', renews our acquaintance with the stars after centuries of
stale classical mythologising:

> Mars is braw in crammasy,
> Venus in a green silk goun...

They are no longer simply stars, but aristocrats in a laird's hall. The
metaphor on its own would take us this far, but the dialect brings
with it an implicit sense of class awareness: we are underlings of
no importance and what is true of the earth is also true of man's
place in the universe. Both are fixed systems.

23. In *The Inheritors*, Golding invents a dialect for his neander-
thal people. Again, the language employed alters our perception of
even the simplest things, like a bow and arrow: 'the stick began to
grow shorter at both ends. Then it shot to full length again.' Or an
echo: 'their words had flown away from them like a flock of birds
that circled and multiplied mysteriously.' In both these examples,
Golding refuses the easy noun ('he writes in no language') and with
it the easy thought. The initial obscurity, the moment of non-sense,
puts us in touch with our non-verbal thoughts, or their simulacrum.
And even after the necessary translation is effected, the strangeness
lingers.

24. Nothing is more difficult than being open-minded. The mind
is a vast country whose borders are closed. We know less than we
think about its economy. It is teeming with peasants, productive
souls, who are hard-working but mute. There are elections, about
which we hear. Language is the prime minister who tells us the
results, like a spokesman reading quite confidently from a brief he
was handed in the dark, or simply found in his inside pocket.

25.

26. 'TIT'?

27. '*BUM*'.

28.

# ANNE STEVENSON

Born in Cambridge in 1933 of American parentage, Anne Stevenson was educated at Michigan University. Her first collection, *Correspondences* (1974), established her concern for the breakdown of puritanical American morals and a sharp observation of human behaviour. Her work also shows an appreciation of Elizabeth Bishop (about whom she has written two studies), although it was Sylvia Plath who would be the subject of her controversial biography, *Bitter Fame* (1989). Her *Collected Poems 1955-1995* appeared in 1996, *Granny Scarecrow* in 2000; her critical essays are published in *Between the Iceberg and the Ship* (1998). Contrary to the prevailing optimism, Stevenson warns here that poetry is in fact 'in pieces', having become saturated with the literary and cultural themes of the present. Echoing Pound's vision of a century ago, she looks forward to the poetry to come: original yet informed by its past, expressive not partisan; voicing a critical need to return the poet to the 'weird tyranny' of the poem.

# A Few Words for the New Century
## (2000)

Like it or not, the turn of the millennium finds most of us at the mercy of technology and in thrall to the media. Poetry, like other humanist arts, is in pieces. Those who care about it are proportionally few, and those who seek to perpetuate it as an art form, fewer still. Nevertheless, in England, as in the States, poets proliferate under pressure to please a specialist clientele. Writing poems (not reading or reciting them) has become an approved communal activity, creative writing classes providing more and more people every year with friends and a sense of individual purpose or with a gratifying and comparatively easy escape route from personal frustrations. Nothing wrong there; indeed, there's a great deal to be said for any counter-cultural movement that encourages people to turn off the television, ignore the simpering pornography of the magazine racks and forget for a few hours every week that they live in a consumer society.

Just the same, human beings crave nourishment from art – I mean the art that we're constantly reminded of by the crowds that queue to attend every major production of Shakespeare, every performance of "classical music" from Bach to Stravinsky, every exhibition of Old Masters mounted by the Royal Academy or the National Gallery – sometimes even by the Tate. Does the drawing

power of "dead" or "hothouse art" in our demotic society suggest
that our children, reared on junk-culture and television silliness,
will mill in, once they've grown up, with the crowds that throng
London's galleries and concert halls? I wish I could think a pref-
erence for the best over the fashionable could be acquired so easily.
Since my subject is poetry, let me say outright that I think it does
harm – to art, to literature and to the people who flock to writing
courses as to beacons in a dark age – to make either the writing or
the understanding of poetry easy. Easy, as any musician or athlete
will tell you, does not make happy and does not make good. Easy
means self-indulgence, laziness when faced with a challenge, and a
cowardly unwillingness to hurt people by telling them the truth or
upsetting the status quo. Easy means accepting art's least common
denominator and spreading about the rumour that anything that
suits most people must be OK.

That doesn't mean we should make poetry more difficult by
injecting it with theories. What a lot of yammering we hear as post-
modernism tries to make it newer and newer. The notion that art
"progresses" in the way science does has led to hideously destructive
misunderstandings. For while it is possible to demonstrate that in
chemistry, for example, centuries of experiment and deduction have
rendered the magical formulae of the alchemists redundant, no
one could seriously propose that the plays of Shakespeare be per-
manently replaced by the "more valid" dramas of Harold Pinter.
In the perspective of "deep time", say the geologists, human civil-
isation is a mere blink of time's eye. If we were to plot our cul-
tural achievements on a spread sheet drawn to the scale of human
time, the graph would show western architecture maybe at a peak
in Greece in the 5th and 4th century BC, western music up with
the spheres in the 18th and early 19th centuries AD, literature
beginning at a high with Homer eight centuries before the Christian
era. In so far as western art moved forward in the last (short) cen-
tury, it did so mainly by backing away from the established styles
of an exhausted culture while finding inspiration in foreign, exotic,
very often defeated traditions: jazz, African sculpture, aboriginal
painting, Indian or Indonesian music. Yet modern composers who
reject classical harmony are not "better" than Bach and Beethoven;
it is probable that they will never enjoy a like following. And though
Eliot and Pound dethroned Milton to put Dante in his place, and
Philip Larkin looked askance at the *vers libre* of the modernists to
find a model in Thomas Hardy, no justification by faith or politi-
cal opinion can prove that either Larkin or the modernists were
"right".

So much strong feeling goes into shifts of direction or fashion in the arts that it is easy to forget that no one time or culture has ever had a monopoly on excellence. We can't possibly know what future readers will make of late 20th century poetry, but I think we who are writing now should think of ourselves as having come to the end of the period we call modernist. Postmodernism is a weak coda to a turbulent movement that in itself was a coda to romanticism. To truly make it new, we must look around for constants that transcend fashion and the human itch to experiment; instead we should ask ourselves what poetry is. Why do we care for it? How does it affect or help us? By constants I mean those elements common to the best poetry of all times: speech sounds and rhythmic patterns derived from rhythms of heartbeat and footsteps, verbal images derived from things we can see, the unforced expression of emotion and above all compassion, a more than common psychological perceptiveness, a more than common instinct for matching subject-matter with form. In my book, the ideal poem of the next century will not be a game of hunt the references. It will not be a furious tirade, or an in-depth self-interview, or a river of tears that floods its banks with self-pity. It will not mistake novelty for originality. It will not be afraid of learning from the poetry of the past, but it will not be imitative either. For a while it may not win poetry prizes, for it won't be written with "promotion" in mind. Nor will it be written by a culture, a gender, a race, a nation, a political party or a creative writing group. Although many such influences may flow into the writing of it, in the end it will be written by a very rare person – a poet who is in thrall to nothing but poetry's weird tyranny and ungovernable need to exist.

# C.K. WILLIAMS

C.K. Williams was born in 1936 in Newark, New Jersey and divides his time between Paris and the US, where he teaches at Princeton University. His experimental work of the 1960s and 1970s has moved toward a longer, Whitmanesque engagement with 'what is really in the world' as he puts it here. He frequently addresses themes of neglect and exclusion, committed to the belief that it is the task of the poem to 'sing' the evidence of such experiences and desires. His *New and Selected Poems* appeared in 1995, *The Vigil* in 1997, and a book of essays, *Poetry and Consciousness*, in 1998. *Repair* (1999) won the Pulitzer Prize for Poetry, and was followed by *Misgivings,* a book of autobiographical meditation, and *Love Poems and Poems About Love.*

# Contexts: An Essay on Intentions
## (1983)

I think that the primary business of poetry in our time – or at least poetry as I conceive it – is to offer evidence. We have to know what is there before us, we have to have the facts, and to get them straight, because without a clear and at least relatively detailed knowledge of our condition and the condition of our world, how can we expect to accomplish what are our obvious tasks: to confront, to cure or comfort, solace or succor, to change, correct, resolve, take into account, come to terms with, redeem, surmount, transfigure or transform? How will we save ourselves and save this vulnerable world that so desperately seems to need to be protected from its protectors?

Because our capacity for blindness, for forgetfulness and for distortion is so limitless, we have to be reminded again and again of what is really in the world, or what is there before our eyes and what is within us – those double theaters offering us their tragedies and comedies, their grand guignol and slapstick – and we have to be recalled again and again to the difficult knowledge that not only are there two theaters, but that each of us is at once the tormented and exalted and valiant hero, the rapacious and licentious villain, and the spear-bearer in the dumbshow chorus, and that each of us is in some undeniable sense responsible for all the identities of all our fellows.

We have to know again and again what our tasks are and what our capacities are, because despite our best intentions, and despite the fact that we all think we nobly and incessantly attempt all we can, we still manage to omit so unconscionably much of what implores us or hints almost invisibly to us of the necessity of our intervention. Our shortcomings, our unfulfilled potentials, our desires, acknowledged or agonisingly private, our ability to think like angels and to gibber like hyenas, the splendors of our ideals and the paucity of the means we have developed to implement these ideals, our overcomings and our capitulations, our willingness to confront our false fantasies and our weary wishes, and our submission to our incessant and erratic and wistful and impotent longings for something we are not and are not even able to specify very clearly – it is perhaps all of this that poetry must take into account now, and what is most astonishing, as always, is that poetry is not merely to offer evidence for all of this, but to sing that evidence.

It is within this apparent contradiction, this clearly unresolvable but ever-vibrant paradox that poetry exists. The poem, every poem, is to confront our two theaters, or our many theaters, or the endless bits of seemingly random information that flutter before us, and still do these two things at once: mean, and sing.

The language of poetry is narcissism itself. It calls attention to itself at every possible opportunity. It is as vain and self-conscious and as tensioned and competitive as an adolescent. It wishes all eyes to be on it: we are to hear its voice only, to love only it and to spurn its competition, although this competition is life, is everything else in reality, everything that has not yet been transfigured not only into language but into the particular language and the particular music of this poem. The language of the poem desires to be opaque: nothing is to pass through it. The subject is utterly incidental to it. We are to be conscious only of it, of its inexhaustible capacity for energy and play, of the delight it can offer even in the most dire recitation, of harmony and counterpoint, elegant association and brutal, lovely disjunction. And, further, in our age, in the epoch of the democratic, the language of poetry also wants us to know how it loves us: we are to be aware of how deeply poetry can delve into the language of our every speaking, thinking moment and still recover and display the poetry that is there, muffled in guises of function or of commerce or of chat. We are to know that we are musicians in our speech: our poems convince us that we are geniuses of music even in the most abashed recitations of ourselves.

The paradox of course is that at the same time the subject of the poem, whatever it is, flower or star, love or war or scrap of lost ambition, also makes clear and absolute demands. The subject is jealous of us: it, too, requires all of our attention, we are to bring upon it all that we possess: our language, our emotions, our most acute mental discrimination, even our passions, even our most banal experience; all is to be committed to doing justice to what is under consideration. The poem makes enormous demands: we are to be confronted with all our inattention, with how small mind we pay to what is offered us. We are to become aware of how little we have allowed experience actually to touch us, and at the same time we are to face the responsibilities implied in our awareness of that experience.

Consciousness by definition desires freedom for itself before all else, because consciousness by definition is freedom. But we also sadly know that consciousness has the uncanny and unpredictable gift of weaving veils before us, veils of habit, of inertia, of indolence and fear – there is even a veil of love that is the most touching of all. The poem is song and play and evidence, and the process of our interaction with it is also a stripping away of what is between ourselves and the realities that sorrow so for our engagement with them, and in this sense the language of the poem and even the poem itself seem to want not to exist at all. The poem is in the deepest sense to be a medium through which our attention flows, uncolored by any necessity whatsoever.

The essential mystery of poetry is that these two disparate elements, so contradictory, somehow intensify each other, when by any logical reasoning they should be distracting and subtracting from each other. Perhaps it is this paradox that makes poetry so forbidding, so "difficult" for many of the otherwise fine minds of our time. Or perhaps it is because poetry has assumed for itself – and all of us don't know this yet, don't understand what's at stake – many of the passions and concerns and quandaries that have traditionally been the realm of religion or moral or social philosophy, but which the withdrawal of God from our active affairs, or our exorcism of him, or our dedication to the realisation of human promise, have redistributed through the continents of consciousness and of art. Or perhaps it is because at the same time that all this has occurred, the means of poetry, and the nature of poetry, have not changed and probably cannot and should not change very radically. Poetry is always being seduced to become what it is not: to be philosophy or fiction, theosophy or myth, but all of these quickly become mere means for the essential activity of poetry; they are means and moments, of no more urgency than anything else. There is that in the human which apparently always wishes to be what it is not: we are all in our souls young gods, dedicated only to what is most pure and profound in the universes of our existence, but if it is one thing that life actually and truly and undeceivedly teaches us it is that it is always the day to day, the lover's smile, the friend's death, the evident suffering of the stranger, or the scent of morning air, that determines who we really are in relation to everything else: to God, to our consciousness and our community, to the very notion of our essence. If poems are written that are not overtly committed to the quotidian, no poem can afford not to take it into account, and if those to whom poetry is a foreign language find that often it chooses apparently inconsequential strips of reality to brood or to reflect upon, poetry knows that this apparent inconsequence is not the question, it is rather our so-called deeper, or higher, or broader visions that are most susceptible to processes of selection, of abstraction, of generalisation, of false raptures of transcendence.

Our poetry will paint the stripes on the tulip, this is its limitation and its glory, but as we paint the stripe we will also know and tell who owns the garden in which the tulip grows, and where the bulb came from and under what condition it was brought to us and who shovelled the manure upon its root and who picked and vased it on their shelf...and even perhaps what that room looks like and where the person who lives there is going out tonight, and how much they might know of all of this.

And we also probably have to know, we of the poem, how conscious that poem has been of itself, how much it has been forced to omit or elide, to avoid or evade or skip or skim because of the exigencies of structure or of form, or of that glorious song. For the form of the poem, and the quality and intensity of its song, is a part, and not a small part, of the evidence.

# ELAINE FEINSTEIN

Elaine Feinstein was born in 1930, and studied at Cambridge University and trained for the bar. Her early writing was closely connected to American Modernism (notably, William Carlos Williams and Wallace Stevens), and her interest in Modernist poetics solicited Charles Olson's much quoted 'Letter to Elaine Feinstein' of 1959. Her translation of the Russian poet Marina Tsvetaeva has been through multiple editions (*Selected Poems*, 1971, 1981, 1986, 1993, 1999) and has been a profound inspiration to Feinstein's own writing, which includes nine novels and six collections of poetry, beginning with *In a Green Eye* (1966) and extending up to *Gold* (2000).

# A Question of Voice
## (2000)

It's easy to see why I turned towards American lyricism when I first began to write poetry in the 50s. I was looking for a tradition that could accommodate the voice of an outsider. As I was born in Liverpool, into a family of Jewish immigrants from Odessa, and moreover a woman, perhaps that was hardly surprising.

Not that you can find the landscape of Liverpool, or even the Midlands where I grew up, in my poetry. The fenland and shallow rivers of Cambridge, or the streets of London have been my territory. But the gibing lilt of the Liverpool voice filled my childhood ears and insinuated a number of things: notably a sceptical dislike of the pretentious. Perhaps that is why I've never liked obscurity in my poems, and make little use of metaphor. Whatever the reason, I work most of all for directness and lucidity, and still profoundly distrust a music that drowns the pressure of what has been felt.

The cautious, ironic tone of the new Movement did not excite me. It was so smugly self-protective, so determined not to expose the indignities of feeling. In any case, I was not part of it. Indeed, I have never been conscious of being part of any particular grouping, since the *English Intelligencer* poets who followed Jeremy Prynne came and sat on my Trumpington floor in the 60s, and I'm not sure how much I shared with them even then. I relished their lyric voice, their quiet cadences, and their ear for syllables, and we shared an admiration for Charles Olson. But their passion for geography and local history asserted an Englishness as insistent as the Movement itself.

It was the great Russian poet Marina Tsvetaeva who proved to be the most important single influence on my own work. Technically,

she taught me how intensity of passion creates a strong rhythm that
will flow down a page even when held in stanzas. After working on
my versions of her poems, I began to see poetry as a matter of the
spoken voice pushing against the shape of the verses on the page.
After that, I rarely used completely open forms. But perhaps there
was another link that was even more important.

Donald Davie pointed out long ago that I recognised myself in
her, even though my own life was not marked by the tragedies of
loss and exile that tormented hers. I was drawn to her wish for
abandonment, and also to her ruthless insistence that writing poetry
took priority over other responsibilities. She was a dangerous example,
since in both of us domestic impracticality meant the usual tensions
of wife, mother and poet were written horrifyingly large.

Tsvetaeva's vision of womanhood was altogether different from
that of the great female poets I looked to on both sides of the
Atlantic. In poverty and neglect, she put herself in harness for
two children and a sick husband, and survived with little support
and reassurance. Her stamina recalled the women in my father's
family, one of whom ran a wood shop. Untouched by any reading
acquaintance with feminism, they too were the living exponents of
an independence which – in their case – presumably went back to
the old *stetl* world where women ran the shop while their husbands
pored over holy books.

Some five years ago, reflecting on the way I found my own poems
had become bonier and more bare as I got older, I remarked that
I had no ambition to write a long poem. So much for statements
of poets' intentions: now I have done so, though I have tried to
retain the local pleasures of lyric verse. *Gold* is written in the
voice of Lorenzo da Ponte, Mozart's librettist, whose adventures
took him from a Ceneda ghetto to the Imperial Court in Vienna,
while he was never allowed to forget his origins, for all the genius
he brought to the despised art of librettist. I chose da Ponte as I
might have chosen a character for one of my novels. Historical
personages allow poets to go outside autobiography, without for-
feiting the colour of their own concerns.

There is a marvellous poem of Joseph Brodsky, in which he talks
about imprisonment and exile, and being thrown out of two countries
and how nevertheless his primary emotion was gratitude for the great
privilege of being alive. I think that's the central emotion I wanted
to come out of da Ponte's story. The poets of the past I most read
for pleasure – Wyatt, George Herbert, Wordsworth, Lawrence,
Charles Reznikoff, Ted Hughes – always renew my alertness to
the world around me. Poetry remains a way of feeling more alive.

# EDWIN MORGAN

Edwin Morgan was born in Glasgow in 1920, and has always lived in the city with which his work is strongly associated. He learned Russian whilst studying at the University, initiating a lifelong interest in translation from a host of languages gathered in several volumes, including *Rites of Passage* (1976) and *Collected Translations* (1996). During the Second World War, like his predecessor, MacDiarmid, he served in the Medical Corps, and his experiences in North Africa found delayed expression in *The New Divan* (1977). He taught at the University of Glasgow in the English Department until his retirement in 1980, since when he has continued to pursue a very active writing career. The key to Morgan's work is diversity: after a late flowering in the late 60s, partly inspired by the Beats, his frequent volumes have moved restlessly between formal poetry, free verse, sound and concrete poetry, embracing the mainstream and experimentation with equal energy. Key volumes include *The Second Life* (1968), *From Glasgow to Saturn* (1973) and *Themes on a Variation* (1988). His *Collected Poems* (originally *Poems of Thirty Years*) appeared in 1990, as did his essays in *Crossing the Border*. He is the central modern influence after MacDiarmid on younger Scots poets.

## Roof of Fireflies
### (1999)

I am not sure that I believe in the old adage that 'the unexamined life is not worth having', the sources of whatever power one has are not too fond of being poked and prodded to see how they are doing, and may withdraw their cooperation. A few years ago I visited the Waitomo underground caves in New Zealand, where you descend by a series of roughly cut staircases to a large underground lake and are taken in boats over the dark still waters, gliding in silence so that no conversation or other noise will disturb the thousands of fireflies shining in the roof of the cavern. It is a remarkable and beautiful sight, and like any other visitor I found it thrilling, but somehow it was more than thrilling, it was moving, it was saying things that only things can say, and my mind kept recurring to it for days and months afterwards, and I can feel a tingling even while I write about it now. But if what it said could be put in a letter, I was not going to open the envelope. I have not written a poem about it, though it might well come into a poem if it could do so unawares, with no tedious moralising or clumsy piling of analogies (Charon's ferry or Auden's limestone or whatever). The subterraneanness, both physical and mental, enfolds its value, as a geode its flash, and that is where this visitor at least is going to leave it.

With that proviso, I have to say that I felt I must ask myself, and did ask myself, why I was not writing poetry about the Second World War at the time when I was engaged in it, as a private soldier in the Royal Army Medical Corps in various parts of the Middle East. If Owen and Rosenberg, whom I much admired, could do it in the First War, why could I not do it in the Second? I knew the situations were different, both because the apocalyptic surprise and horror of trench warfare in France, with its intense emotional involvement, could not be matched in the African desert campaign of the 1940s, and also because I belonged to a hospital unit which by its nature had to be some distance behind the front line. For all that, I felt guilty, and angry with myself, at least during the times when I had leisure to reflect. Did something tell me, or was something trying to tell me, that it didn't matter? That there is no pattern in the poetic life which decrees one must write about the immediacy of forceful or strident events? I didn't even keep a journal, which doesn't mean I didn't think the things that were happening around me and to me weren't important, but that possibly my instinct about subterranean workings preferred to leave them in the limbo of memory. A risky pool to leave prized things swimming in! Would I live long enough for the right moment to come for fishing them out? It turned out in fact that the images and incidents of that time and place remained fresh and vigorous 30 years later, when I cast my mind back and wrote my hundred-poem sequence *The New Divan*, embedding long-belated war poems in a geographically horizontal and historically vertical panorama of the Middle East where Hafiz and Sindbad and Scheherazade could watch as tutelary spirits over 'the thud of land-mines'. (It is my hidden poem, which no one ever writes about!) While it is tempting to say therefore that nothing is lost, I would have to admit to myself that that sequence would not have been instigated if the Middle East had not been again so much in the news in the 1970s, driving my mind through memorial labyrinths that were almost labyrinths of witness. – To which I add a sudden lateral thought: what sort of inevitability was it that sent me to the Middle East in the first place, since at school I had been strongly attracted by Egypt and Mesopotamia and not at all by the classical world of Greece and Rome?

Relating art to life may be dodgy at the best of times, but I would have almost too many, certainly not too few, reasons why I found the 60s such a productive period that it seemed to have lifted me totally out of the slough of self-doubt I was in some danger of creeping about in during the aftermath of the war. I daresay some backlash against that remarkable decade was bound to come, but I would never find myself subscribing to the down-grading it has received in would-be virtuous quarters. The unex-amined life in me – let us bring it back – does not know whether the decade was waiting for me or I was waiting for the decade. Do I want to know? I don't think so! I was in love, and that casts a light and a glow that transform everything else. But without that I would still have thrilled to the new music, to the exploration of space, to the exploratory international poetries, beat, concrete, aural, oral, to the political and sexual radicalisms that were at last putting their heads above the parapet. I was at the same time, and without any sense of strain or strangeness, writing love poems, space poems, verbally experimental poems, and poems about social con-ditions in a Glasgow poised between grimness and potential renewal. Looking back, I would find it hard to scrub any of these interests, or to say that whatever it was I had to do in poetry was harmed by the diversity. I knew that it was not my job to 'find my own voice', as reviewers are always encouraging young writers to do. That is one kind of poetry, which is not mine. Good luck to Seamus Heaney, but I pushed out, and continue to push out, a different boat. What about a boat that is itself a shape-shifter: the nuclear-powered icebreaker is now a light white felucca triangle fading in the heat-haze and then a bathyscaphe goggling at black smokers and it emerges as an oily junk on the contraband run and before you know it it is a ship of space out there up there riding the solar wind.

Poets of many voices – Dunbar, Blake, Khlebnikov, Voznesensky, Weöres, Prigov – have therefore always exerted an appeal that I am aware of and acknowledge. I liked to see exploration, divergence, risk-taking. I liked the idea of an avant-garde, and the common assumption that *The Iliad*, to say nothing of the much older *Gilga-mesh*, had not been "beaten" by anything later and greater did not seem to me to validate an anti-evolutionary view of art. Biodiversity, whether vegetal, animal, human, geophysical, or astrophysical, is surely the key. The range of poetries has grown enormously and continues to grow. Unknown territories beckon. Alien territories beckon. I recall the military origin of the term avant-garde, the band of scouts who went ahead of the main troop, not out of bravado or to gain kudos but in order to facilitate or encourage a general advance. In this sense, both Whitman and Hopkins were a true avant-garde of their times. The extreme dislocations of the 20th century have naturally manipulated the use of the term, sharpening or roughening it according to one's point of view, but certainly allowing it to problematise the idea of trailblazing. Dmitry Prigov (*b.* 1940), arch-perestroikist and deconstructor of Soviet social realities, has used an enormous variety of forms to roll back what he saw as the timorous traditionalism and incipient sentimentalism of Russian lyric poetry, and he has made a large impact. I sense a kinship with his work, and yet I also realise that his task cannot be the same as mine. He has said: 'I don't deal with human emotions directly, neither am I able to identify myself with any individual feeling or idea.' I, on the contrary, don't find in myself the either/or of the personal and the impersonal, the direct or the deconstructional. I have poems in invented languages; poems with compressed or dislocated syntax; permutational poems; simulated computer poems; poems in code; poems of one word, and even of one letter. But the pleasure of writing such poems, of making something meaningful out of something very new, the pleasure in language itself, its malleability, its untapped potential, is not enough. I need, with another part of me, the very things Prigov is suspicious of: a direct poetry of human relationships, friends, lovers, family, a poetry of vulnerabilities, desires, losses, encounters missed and encounters won. This being so, who would not be impatient of categories?

An English astronomer was interviewed recently about the severe problems being undergone by the Russian space station Mir, including problems that might involve the actual survival of the astronauts. He scarcely disguised his belief that the whole operation was little better than a waste of valuable resources and time. Why risk men's lives when machines could do everything we wanted? Space telescopes, space probes, as automated as technology can provide, that was the cleancut way to do things, no crewmen fumbling and bumbling about among the – oops – cables. Cut to his American counterpart at NASA: no sir, we have to go up there; we have already learned good lessons from the troubles in Mir; everything we do is a step forward, not a setback; even disasters don't stop what is a matter of destiny. Needless to say, I rejoiced in the positiveness of the second interview after being depressed (though it was a familiar pattern) by the first. Poetry, just like Mir and the greater space stations which are planned as launchpads for planetary exploration, seems to me to want to take its human load wherever it is possible for that human load to go. When Gagarin first saw the blue glow round the globe of the earth, he commented on its beauty in a way no machine would be able to do. What good is beauty? We don't know. But if we sense it, we ought to record it. Words go with everything human. Poetry is a brilliant vibrating interface between the human and the non-human. A gutter in Calcutta or a rille on the moon, we're there, and if we're not there, push us, drive us! And don't try to tell us that the gutters of Calcutta will run with milk and honey if we dismantle the space programme; they won't, the world is not like that. *Medécins sans frontières – oui, assurement! Astronautes sans frontières – naturellement! Poètes sans frontières – pourquoi pas?*

As I write this, Scotland has voted to have its own parliament, with law-making and tax-varying powers and a fair measure of autonomy, though still within the United Kingdom. As a member of the universe, Scotland does seem to be twinkling, however faintly. It is my place, and I shall continue to write about it as occasion arises. Its fate, as an entity, haunts me, and will not haunt me the less if I stand on a hill in Glasgow and look up on a clear night at a dash of stars.

# TOM LEONARD

Tom Leonard is a distinctly Glaswegian writer. Born in 1944, educated and living there, much of his most significant work is written in his native dialect, and reproduces the sounds, syncopations and gestures of the city in his highly original address of class politics and power. *Intimate Voices* (1984) is an important selection of his work between 1965 and 1983, and records his affinity with William Carlos Williams and a poetry to reflect the world as heard, listened to, and spoken of. Leonard's quest is an ultimately democratic one, and his introduction to *Radical Renfrew* (1989), extracted here by himself, rallies against the "coding" of literature by schools and academies, and demands a poetry that is 'the voice of ordinary discourse'.

# From the Introduction to *Radical Renfrew*
## (1989)

Any society is a society in conflict, and any anthology of a society's poetry that does not reflect this, is a lie. But poetry has been so defined in the public mind as usually to exclude the possibility of social conflicts appearing. The belief is widespread that poetry is not about the expression of opinion, not about "politics", not about employment, not about what people actually do with their time between waking up and falling asleep each day; not about what they eat, not about how much the food costs. It is not in the voice of ordinary discourse, contains nothing anyone anywhere could find offensive, above all contains nothing that will interfere with the lawful exercise of an English teacher going about his or her duty in a classroom.

To an extent the connection between poetry and school has been the problem. It is not that teachers deserve any less respect than anyone else out working for a living; the trouble lies in the notion that poetry has to be "taught" in the first place, and that there is a professional caste of people best equipped so to do. For to be "taught" poetry has meant to be given guidance in a classroom as to how best ultimately to pass exams about it. This has had the effect of installing in people's minds certain basic ideas:

1. A "real" poem is one that an English teacher would approve for use in an English class.
2. A "real" poem requires some explanation and guidance as to interpretation, by an English teacher.

3. The best poems come to be set in the exams.

4. The people best able to pass these exams will be the people best able to understand and to write poetry.

The roots of all this pernicious nonsense about what a poem isn't and what it is, can be traced back to the 19th century invention of Literature as a "subject" in schools. This invention was based on certain specific principles:

1. The creation of a "canon" of Literature, the new subject's "set books" as it were.

2. The establishment of that canon – to be overseen by Her Majesty's Inspectorate for Schools – on the premise that Literature is a *code* embodying desirable social, moral and political values.

3. The exclusion from that canon of works that did not recognise this code, or did not see Literature as a code in the first place.

4. The exclusion from that canon of works whose main focus was thought properly to be that of another "subject" in the curriculum.

The important word is *code*. To understand Literature is to understand a code, and the teacher is the person trained to possess the code that Literature is in. This has to be accepted unconditionally, as it is the sole basis of the teacher's power to grade pupils' responses. A piece of writing that does not acknowledge the code that the teacher has been trained to possess, can not be accepted as Literature: for such writing deprives the teacher of the only basis of his power of assessment. This applies even when the "canon" has been enlarged to "allow" some writing about, for instance, working-class lives. The teacher's right to grade the pupils' responses must never be threatened; therefore the writing must never be such as might give the pupils the right to challenge the teacher's claim to possess it.

Literature shrinks to Teachable Literature. Taking a fairly mild and non-poetic example, the excellent prose work Winwood Reade's *The Martyrdom of Man* is considered far too "literary" to be History, and far too historical to be Literature; even more damaging, it is thought far too heretical of orthodox beliefs to be thought an appropriate object for pupils' potential approval. And so it can not as the phrase goes "enter the canon".

In fact the spread of education as a right to the mass of people has paradoxically led to the deprivation, from them, of much they once held to be valid literature. Generation after generation has been "taught" that a poem itself has as it were to pass an exam before it can earn the right to be called a poem in the first place;

but only those people who have passed exams about poems, can
give a new would-be poem the new exam necessary to decide
whether it is a poem or not. The "subject" has functioned to assure
the mass of people that until they have a licence to prove other-
wise, they have no public right to make, criticise, or even claim to
understand, anything that might seriously be called Literature.
This is a serious matter, and raises the question of what is meant
by democracy.

# FLEUR ADCOCK

Conversational and urbane, and keenly perceptive of personal relationships, Fleur Adcock is one of this country's leading women poets. She was born in 1934 in Auckland, New Zealand, and settled in London in 1963. Her collections include *High Tide in the Garden* (1971), *The Scenic Route* (1974), *The Incident Book* (1986), *Time-Zones* (1991) and *Looking Back* (1997), most of the poems from which are included in her *Poems 1960-2000*. She is editor of *The Oxford Book of Contemporary New Zealand Poetry* (1982) and *The Faber Book of Twentieth Century Women's Poetry* (1987). In her contribution here, she goes some way to outlining her approach to poetry, but attaches a note of caution: that a poem is vulnerable to fashion – the more modish it is, the more likely to become an 'ex-poem'.

# Not Quite a Statement
(2000)

Forty years ago I'd have been entranced by the idea of contributing to a collection of statements about poetry. Twenty or thirty years ago I'd still have been interested. But more recently I've developed a great aversion to theory and definitions. I long since decided that a poem is simply a piece of writing which, when I read it, I recognise as a poem and not just as something pretending to be one. What is the difference between poetry and prose? Prose fills the page-width; a poem has white space around it. ('Art's whatever you choose to frame,' as I found myself writing at the end of a poem about how looking at paintings in a gallery changes one's view of the world outside.)

So there are poems and non-poems. But there is also a third category: ex-poems. Never underestimate the dread influence of fashion – look at back numbers of literary magazines, or faded volumes in libraries: ex-poems everywhere. They were poetry when the editors accepted them, but they've died. (This makes it hard for an anthologist to be dispassionate when surveying, for example, the 1940s.)

In the full awareness that such of my productions as managed to achieve poem-status are probably even now on the way to becoming ex-poems, I'll offer some comments on how they came into being. The following is extracted from a piece I wrote in 1989 for a series of lectures at the Manchester Poetry Centre:

I'll begin with the question of rhythm, because this is the one crucial factor which distinguishes poetry from other forms of writing. It was rhythm that seduced me into liking poetry in the beginning: clearly identifiable rhythms at first, in my early childhood, when I fell for nursery rhymes and Sunday school hymns and the Georgian poets my mother read to me at bedtime; and then, in my teens, the more subtle rhythms of poets I was taught at school or discovered for myself: Milton, Donne, Blake, Eliot. (It's sometimes hard to separate rhythm from tone, in its effects. I remember being transported, at about fourteen, by the poignancy of Blake's line in *The Book of Thel*: 'Art thou a Worm? Image of weakness, art thou but a Worm?' I'd repeat it to myself until it seemed to be nothing *but* rhythm; but perhaps it was the tender, pitying tone that so appealed to me. To talk of one element in isolation is always a little risky.)

In my own writing I'm always conscious of the rhythm, without always being in control of it; quite often my feeling is that a poem is being dictated to me, rather than by me, particularly in the early stages. What seems to happen is this: a phrase arrives in my head, usually when I'm in a relaxed dreamy state – quite commonly when I'm about to fall asleep or have just woken up, times when the barriers between the conscious and the unconscious mind are at their most permeable. This "given" phrase (which almost always turns out to be the first line of the poem, but can occasionally end up elsewhere) contains, as it were, a genetic fingerprint of what is to follow: the rhythm of the phrase indicates the rhythm and to some extent the tone, shape, texture, and even the length of the finished poem; these qualities are all wrapped up in those few initial words, as the embryo of a plant is wrapped up in a seed, and it is my job to nurture and encourage the seed until it expands into its final form.

Free verse seems to me the purest type of verse, in that its rhythms are entirely innate and inherent in the phrases that make it up. It has no rules by which to adjust them. I find it extremely difficult to write, because you can never be reassured by external considerations that you've got it right. This may be why very few of my poems avoid falling into stanzas of some kind, or taking on a pattern of more or less regularly stressed lines. The few which manage to be entirely "free" are usually short, reflecting my difficulty in sustaining the impulse, and tend to be haunted, middle-of-the-night pieces, arising directly from the subconscious.

I suppose it's becoming obvious that I believe strongly in the authority of the voice inside my head (which is an aspect of my own physical voice, although it takes on other personae and accents). On the whole the voice speaks colloquial English of the age I live in. This affects the rhythmical structure of what I write, even when I'm using a strict metrical form. More often it dictates a looser, more flexible type of verse, based on stress rhythms, with lines of roughly equal lengths, usually divided in stanzas of anything from two to eight lines. Sometimes these are self-contained and sometimes not, and there are other possible variations, such as the presence or absence of rhyme.

On the whole I write in normal sentences, with normal grammar and syntax and, as a rule, normal punctuation...The tone I feel at home in is one in which I can address people without embarrassing or alarming them; I should like them to relax and listen as if to an intimate conversation (or, to be honest, an intimate monologue) rather than to an operatic aria. This doesn't mean that there are no shocks in store for them, but I tend to avoid the deliberately eccentric...

I could, and did, go on; but much of what I've said is far from unique to me. I'd rather people just read the poems.

# LES MURRAY

Born in 1938 in New South Wales, Les Murray is widely considered Australia's leading poet. He studied at Sydney University (although he left without taking a degree) and lives on a 40-acre farm in Bunyah, where he grew up. His first volume of poems (*The Ilex Tree*) was published in 1965 and his work (*Collected* in 1998) is a lavish, lyrical response to the vast territory of the Bush and the legacy of the pioneer settlers. Murray has also been an extremely influential editor at home, and his works in include *The New Oxford Book of Australian Verse* (1996). Rather than respond in prose, 'The Instrument' was chosen by Murray for *Strong Words* as, with characteristic modesty, 'the little I know about poetry'.

# The Instrument
## (1999)

Who reads poetry? Not our intellectuals;
they want to control it. Not lovers, not the combative,
not examinees. They too skim it for bouquets
and magic trump cards. Not poor schoolkids
furtively farting as they get immunised against it.

Poetry is read by the lovers of poetry
and heard by some more they coax to the café
or the district library for a bifocal reading.
Lovers of poetry may total a million people
on the whole planet. Fewer than the players of *skat*.

What gives them delight is a never-murderous skim
distilled, to verse mainly, and suspended in rapt
calm on the surface of paper. The rest of poetry
to which this was once integral still rules
the continents, as it always did. But on condition now

that its true name is never spoken. This, feral poetry,
the opposite but also the secret of the rational,
who reads that? Ah, the lovers, the schoolkids,
debaters, generals, crime-lords, everybody reads it:
Porsche, lift-off, Gaia, Cool, patriarchy.

Among the feral stanzas are many that demand your flesh
to embody themselves. Only completed art
free of obedience to its time can pirouette you
through and athwart the larger poems you are in.
Being outside all poetry is an unreachable void.

Why write poetry? For the weird unemployment.
For the painless headaches, that must be tapped to strike
down along your writing arm at the accumulated moment.
For the adjustments after, aligning facets in a verb
before the trance leaves you. For working always beyond

your own intelligence. For not needing to rise
and betray the poor to do it. For a non-devouring fame.
Little in politics resembles it: perhaps
the Australian colonists' re-inventing of the snide
far-adopted secret ballot, in which deflation could hide

and, as a welfare bringer, shame the mass-grave Revolutions,
so axe-edged, so lictor-y.
Was that moral cowardice's one shining world victory?
Breathing in dream-rhythm when awake and far from bed
evinces the gift. Being tragic with a book on your head.

# JOHN KINSELLA

John Kinsella was born in 1963 in Perth, Australia, and attended the University of Western Australia. His father managed a farm in the northern wheatlands, a landscape that dominates Kinsella's at times 'anti-pastoral' work. *The Frozen Sea* was published in 1983, followed by his first full-length collection, *Night Parrots*, in 1989, and a dozen subsequent books of poetry – notably, *The Silo: A Pastoral Symphony* (1995, 1997), *The Hunt* and *Poems 1980-1994* (both 1998) – all of which testify to Kinsella's experimental range and versatility. He also edits the international magazines *Salt* (with Tracy Ryan) and *Stand* (with Michael Hulse), and is a Fellow of Churchill College, Cambridge, dividing his time between Britain and Australia. His most recent books include *Visitants* (1999) and *The Hierarchy of Sheep* (2000), his anthology *Landbridge: Contemporary Australian Poetry* (1999), and a two-poet collection shared with Dorothy Hewett, *Wheatlands* (2000).

# Almost a Dialogue with Lyn Hejinian: Quotations and Phantom Limbs...
## (2000)

Lyn Hejinian, in a recent e-mail written in response to a poem entitled 'Insides', which I had dedicated to her, asked: 'Do you think poetry is physiological?' I'm still to reply in full – and maybe this is my answer. I dedicated the poem 'Insides' to Lyn because many years earlier she'd told me about attending autopsies. Back then I'd written the following:

In the dissection
of the corpse of this poem
I recall Lyn Hejinian
telling me how she'd gone to watch
autopsies with Mike Patton,
the lead singer of Faith No More.
I wouldn't have mentioned Mike but his music
has always interested me & if he hadn't been
on world tour I'd have tried to solicit
material for the literary journal I edit.
Lyn said
that in this de-sensitised environment
(actually that's my word, I can't remember
what she said specifically but its effect
on me was to suggest this) the body
wasn't that frightening.
I think she held a liver.

I asked if it was like a collection of artefacts
being removed carefully from a tomb.
I think she laughed.
But it might not have
been a comfortable laugh.

This is an extract from a long poem, 'Nature Morte: Oh, Rhetoric'. The poem is a kind of poetics. An Ars Poetica? What is experienced is lost with words, but is also reinvented by words. Words make it a new, or at least different, experience. Words create a new kind of emotion, they negotiate the gaps between the moment itself and the vicarious "re-experiencing" that comes with the telling or the reading of the interpretation of that moment through poetry. I'm talking about poetry specifically. The compactness and intensity – capturing the unsayable, giving the reader space/latitude – or enough rope. But there's something disingenuous in this. I'm constantly reiterating the death of the author, but not of the subject. But the word is its own subject. Yes, but the word is more than that. The body being dissected and disseminated by words, by both obfuscations of parataxis AND neat renderings – ironic or "sincere" – with metrics and rhyme, is not the body that was once living. It has been embalmed, preserved as something it wasn't. The corpse has no emotions – we take (or leave) our emotions to an autopsy. They are not stored latent in the necrotic flesh, the functionless organs. I say this with suspicious certainty. Never trust the convinced...?

Maybe this is what allows us to disassociate ourselves from the horror of the war or famine or epidemic the newspapers hand us. Media images become steadily more confronting, but so does our ability to receive these images. The girl burnt by napalm "falling" towards the camera – as if compelled, as if the camera were her destiny, as if it was always meant to be there; the officer shooting the prisoner through the temple, and any of the other "images that defined the time" that was the Vietnam era, when our "desensitisation" developed a life of its own. Shocking at first, and then part of our mental archives of what's negotiable. Or how about the staged flag call of the US marines at Iwo Jima? The propaganda image that lifted the morale of a nation. And the clinically terrifying images of "smart weapons" finding their targets in the "CNN wars". No, we know about context and can take a step back. But this isn't what deconstruction is supposed to do – it isn't "supposed" to desensitise, but to make us aware.

Poetry, of course, isn't like that...it actually sensitises...heightens awareness. Worked via the poem, words live multiple lives. They can't be pinned down. Even the most formulaic poem lives outside

its own conventions. But for me poems are above all else moral –
they work through and against conventions, they are constantly
grappling with responsibility and rebellion. They lust, they fear,
they operate clinically and subjectively. They are Deleuze's and
Guattari's bodies without organs, waiting to be filled by the reader.
For the poet, they are his or her phantom limb or third eye. The
gaps between the physical and perceived world are blurred. It's a
liminal space. Frames, borders, constraints, and yet elasticity; these
are the things that aesthetically interest me.

I'm (also) interested in collaborative writing. I've said enough
about the defects of the "lyrical I" to revisit that denuded ground.
The lyric is back, with a vengeance. Damaged eyes can be corrected
by lasers now. They grow lenses in pigs to replace lenses in humans.
They gene-search and delete genetic imperfections. My child's child
won't be of my flesh. Paternity is not the poem, and never was.
Back to the borders. To Hejinian. I did a virtual discussion project
for the Bath Literature Festival recently – with John Burnside and
George Szirtes. This is one of my commentaries:

> Maybe I can pick up tangentially through mentioning a seminar Rod
> Mengham and I gave today on the poetry of Lyn Hejinian and Jennifer
> Moxley. I quoted a couple of paragraphs from Hejinian's essay 'La
> Faustienne' (*Knowledge Poetics Journal*, 10) with regard to the liminal:
>
> 'Current literary interest in knowledge – and its implicit questions
> with regard to both literary devices (details) and literary method (address
> from and to the world) – finds itself in what social theory might call a
> liminal period – at a threshold or, to enlarge the metaphorical landscape,
> along a border. The question of boundaries, of possible shifts or dis-
> placements along them, and the question of what is being bounded (or
> unbounded) are pre-eminent ones. If we are indeed in a liminal period,
> then the border is not out there somewhere at the edge of the frame
> but rather it is here, at zero degree, where the X and Y co-ordinates
> meet. It is a site of encounter, a point of transition. The marginal is all
> around. The transgressivity, sometimes overt, sometimes implicit, that
> motivates certain strategies in much current work, is meaningful *only*
> in liminal situations.'

Hejinian has a long history of collaborating with other poets. The
antiphonal shifts between voice that are at once mediated by the
word itself, and "persona", identity or signature, provide a con-
versational tension. But I'm most interested where voice blurs, and
identity of the individual author is lost to the collaborative piece.
Where meaning exists on both sides of the border, and also is
absent. E-mail and web collaborative projects abound. They are
something that attract me. Quickfire interactions on discussion lists
– projects with "the list" as author, which may consist of a couple
of hundred people. Of course, collected for book publication, the

editorial voice operates loudly, despite any claims to the contrary. An interesting example of this has been the Interactive Geographies projects on Poetryetc – basically the creation of a large prose poem on the notion of "place". A spatial project, a mapping of virtual and "real" places. Here are the guidelines issued for the first GEO project:

> ...like to invite Poetryetc participants to assist in the creation of a geo-text. The aim is to break down territories, boundaries, demarcation lines etc by creating an interactive regionalism. If people would send to the list responses to their immediate surroundings – responses to location, demographics, spiritual signifiers, gender, and so on – I'll work the collective effort into a single text and publish it as a *Salt* pamphlet in a few weeks. Your responses should be without punctuation and in continuous text – no line breaks. You will be appropriated, altered and mixed. So, maybe Douglas could begin with "Paris", or maybe it's the Alberta Douglas, or maybe Alison in Melbourne, or someone who lives purely in cyberspace. Deserts, oceans, and the maps of circuit boards all welcome. Interact away!

The possibility – no, the inevitability of crossover and encounter in what appear to be different geographies on the surface – proved fascinating. Be it different locations on the maps, or different states of mind – the mapping process linked the project together. The texts flowed through each other. Editing it became an exercise in cartography – reminding one of recent claims that the coast of Western Australia is a ripe location for orientating *Gulliver's Travels*. The net forms its own tribal groupings. There are those who enter discussion lists with the sole intent of dismantling discussion and list integrity. On an experimental list they'll post formal poems; on a formalist list, encrypt the villanelles of others. As long as it doesn't get personal or abusive, I welcome this. It's another face of hybridising. It's a liminal process.

So, that's what I have to say about my work. My body? Well, I could refer to a recent discussion on Poetryetc about body-types and the repetitions of certain letters in names, but if people are interested they can search the Poetryetc archives. I guess they'll then need my body, or at least a picture of it. Or maybe they could read my poetry instead. Or somebody else's. That would do fine. Yes, as they say, maybe I'm present in absence. I do know that my state of health is directly linked to what I write. I know that the psychological and the physical are inseparable. I know the field of the page is the map of my body, of our bodies. As a kid I was fascinated by the plastic overlays of the body in the *World Book Encyclopaedia* – a weird pleasure not so easily replicated in the non-tactile (challenge this!) virtual world of the net. Anyway, this poem is about bodies – not mine. Everybody's? Or just about the word *body* itself? Maybe...

# Insides
### *for Lyn Hejinian*

The layout...formatting
within the body cavity,
and how, if you think
about it, things will stop:
not quite adding up,
so vulnerable.

Taking the corpse
of a still-warm rabbit
and opening it:
skin peeled back
to bone-joint,
insides flicked
into a bucket, mixed
with the insides
of other rabbits – the bits
that made them work
now pig-feed. Or sheep
strung up, headless
sacks, guts gathered
in barrows below.
Fly-thick, dogs
frantic, pig-feed.

We can't look at
each other like that...
so easily unravelled,
come unstuck.

Held close by a loved one,
nurturing and knowing;
plastic models in biology
class – the liver
fitting there
and the heart
locked up tight.
The plastic overlays
in encyclopaedias – this organ
on that, clear cut.

Forget about it –
it works even when
you sleep.

# U.A. FANTHORPE

Born in Kent in 1929, U.A. Fanthorpe studied at Oxford and the London Institute of Education, and was Head of English at Cheltenham Ladies' College and a hospital clerk in Bristol. With the publication of *Side Effects* (1978), *Standing To* (1982) and *Voices Off* (1984), Fanthorpe achieved popularity as an astute observer of the people and places of the everyday, a collage of the ordinary rather than the expressly political; and it is in this spirit that she writes here for 'the not-yet-poets of Iraq, Bosnia' and elsewhere. Her *Selected Poems* appeared in 1986; her most recent collection is *Consequences* (2000).

# War, Poetry, the Child
## (2000)

The war was World War Two, which began officially in 1939. The child was me; I was nine, and chiefly preoccupied with the spelling of Czechoslovakia, which seemed to be a matter of national importance. War was much less interesting than the novels of Sir Walter Scott, which engrossed me at the time. Poetry was a sort of frill to English lessons, and mostly written by the other Walter, de la Mare. I didn't feel deeply involved, though late on Friday afternoons there was a certain creepy charm to him.

The war put an end to this innocent life. My war was domestic. It happened in England. It involved evacuation, dog-fights over the garden, whines, thuds, gutted houses, not being told things (when people we knew were killed, or about the defeat at Dunkirk and how close the enemy was). It also involved being told things one didn't want to hear: my mother had a way of endlessly reciting the provisions made for my brother and me when anything happened to Them, which was difficult to forget. It never occurred to me that this might be a subject of poetry too.

One thinks of one's childhood as normal, as being the sort of childhood everyone else has. It didn't occur to me to think otherwise until a friend in Lancashire said to me out of the blue years later, 'Of course you're like me – you had a wartime education.' What is a wartime education? For me it consisted very largely of silence. We were constantly being warned that Careless Talk Costs Lives – all the posters and newspapers said so. This encouraged a habit of taciturnity. In addition, it was difficult to know whose side one was on. Watching a dog-fight above our house between a Spitfire and a Messerschmitt, it was hard not to sympathise with the loser. But it was unsafe to speak one's feelings aloud: the first time I did this I was assured that the Messerschmitt's intention had been to kill me. I lacked the courage of the infant Fleur Adcock ('Loving Hitler'), who 'came out with it':

'I love Hitler.'
They turned on me: 'You can't love Hitler!
Dreadful, wicked – ' (mutter, mutter,
the shocked voices buzzing together) –
'Don't be silly. You don't mean it.'

We discovered we lived in 'Bomb Alley', so called because it was the route for German bombers into and out of London; we were also near Biggin Hill, which was the fighter pilots' HQ. All schools in the area were closed instantly. I never saw any of my friends again. I somehow never found compensation for this utter and sudden loss (some were killed in raids, some were sent elsewhere; all were lost to me). My parents despatched my brother and me to Surrey, which was supposed to be safer. I arrived three weeks after term had started (always a fatal thing to do) and hated all my fellow-pupils on sight. It was quite obvious to the unhappy ones among us that we couldn't tell our parents how wretched we were – ill-fed, cold, neglected. Things were clearly much worse for them: they were fighting, or else engaged in that mysterious thing 'war-work', or, like my mother, wrestling at home with blast damage and shortages. What got me through the war was reading, and while my contemporaries were all apparently content with Georgette Heyer and Mazo de la Roche, I became as highbrow as the not very ambitious school library would let me. My chief discoveries were *The Waste Land*, *The Sword in the Stone*, and Plato's *Republic*. In English lessons I sat at the back and read under my desk lid. Despite this, one or two pieces of greatness filtered through, like 'The Forsaken Merman' (with whom I identified passionately) and the more melancholy border ballads.

After nine years of solitary dissidence, while my school contemporaries were filing off to RADA and various colleges of music, I at last got into Oxford, and thought I'd found my different world. The war was over, Oxford would be full of answers to questions, and the sort of friends I'd missed for so long. Having got there, I went to ground among the Anglo-Saxons, the Metaphysicals, the *DNB* and the *OED*, all safely removed in time and space. As far as friends were concerned, Oxford was full of ex-service men and women, who were older, and whose lives had been hard and challenging. These were the sort of people tutors wanted to talk to; they had something to say. I had something to say, too, but I didn't find out what it was until years later. I had had long experience at

silence, and I needed no persuasion to go on with it. At that time,
Sir Walter Scott still strong in me, I supposed that the proper sub-
ject for a writer was heroism, things achieved, Everest climbed, and
so on. It seemed to me in the company of such noble ex-service
spirits that I had nothing to write about.

After Oxford, I got a job, and did it. The only interesting thing
about this ignoble saga is that, throughout it all, I wanted to write.
But in one way or another war had muffled me.

In middle age I found my voice among the sad little individual
wars of a neuro-psychiatric hospital. Only poetry could deal with this
matter. At last the distress I encountered there seemed to liberate
my vocation: I began by writing about the damaged. The war came
back to me much later, in 1991, when the Gulf War started. It was
like the war I'd known, in that we could see on television, and imagine
as well, the civilian suffering, could hear the bombs, the whining
aircraft, the missiles, the sirens, could see the crumbling walls, the
clouds of dust, the dead. There was a new, distasteful vocabulary
of war which somehow made it worse. I was distressed, more than
I could account for, and found myself in the middle of a poem I
couldn't remember starting, called 'Collateral Damage'. Then it all
became clear. I had in a way been there; I was part of the damage.

Why write about all this now? Because it took so long to dis-
entangle the unconscious process. Since this has been a century of
war and dispossession, many people in the future may find their
mouths blocked as mine was. I'd like them to know that they can
retrieve and use their silence.

So I write this for the not-yet-poets of Iraq, Bosnia, Kosova,
Chechnya, Croatia, Rwanda, Palestine, Northern Ireland, Tibet; the
places where war is, or was, not over there, but here, at home. You
will have so much to write about, but it may need to be suppressed
for years before you can deal with it justly. Don't worry. The great
thing about poetry is that it will wait till you're ready. And when
you are ready, you will be summoned, as the great Russian poet
Anna Akhmatova was. During the Stalinist terror, she was waiting
in a line outside the Leningrad prison where her son was detained.

> A woman with blue lips standing behind me...suddenly woke out of
> the benumbed condition in which we all found ourselves at that time
> and whispered in my ear (in those days we all spoke in a whisper):
> – Can you put this into words?
> And I said:
> – I can.

We all have to be ready for the moment when that woman with
blue lips turns to us.

# GRACE NICHOLS

Grace Nichols was born in Guyana in 1950 and moved to Britain in her 20s. From her first collection, *I is a Long Memoried Woman* (1983), Nichols's tough and often stinging wit has brought a considerable audience to her treatment of race, womanhood, and residency in Britain. She has published three other collections of poetry (*The Fat Black Woman's Poems*, 1984; *Lazy Thoughts of a Lazy Woman*, 1989; *Sunris*, 1996), some children's writing and a novel, *Whole of a Morning Sky* (1986). Her statement here connects, intimately, her poetry with the landscape of her upbringing.

## 'The poetry I feel closest to'
### (2000)

The poetry I feel closest to has always been the kind that also keeps an eye on the landscape and has within it enough space for the elements to move. Although poetry is first and foremost an act of language it seems to me that rhythm is affected by the broader rhythm of the living landscape. Not surprisingly a sense of place has always been important to me as a writer.

I don't know whether it's wishful thinking on my part, but I believe I owe the fact that I write at all to the village along the Atlantic coast in Guyana where I spent my small-girl days, stealing down to the shore with my sisters and brother to catch crabs just before dawn; catching fish in old baskets and tins in our own backyard whenever there was a flood. To this day I have this image of myself around the age of six, standing in rippling brown water lit by the sun and watching the shapes of fish going by below the surface. It's an enduring picture of myself caught in an innocent kind of cosmic bliss.

As a symbol, an image, the fish has a lot of significance for me, in some strange way it seems that my creativity is linked to the place and the act of catching fish in itself. In the same way that fish inhabit the sea and are brought up to the surface, similarly I think, that the seeds and ideas for poems and books also inhabit our subconscious, our inner sea, that whole area of our emotions, memory shadowy thoughts, and what we do as writers is to fish them up, infuse them and bring them into some kind of living form or shape. Of course every poet works differently and the sources of inspirations are as many as they're varied.

As a child I read a lot and loved reading in bed, which is prob-
ably one of the nicest ways of reading, with its cradling memory,
especially poetry, indolently alert, absorbing yourself in the music
and images that come to mind. The two elements of sound and
image are probably the two most essential qualities in poetry for
me and the ones that give me the most pleasure. I love the image-
making power of poetry and am still literally bowled over when I
come across a particularly striking image such as Derek Walcott's,
'nail holes of stars in the sky roof' (from his 'Schooner *Flight*') or
Sylvia Plath's wind, 'Slapping its phantom laundry in my face'
('Blackberrying'). The pleasure derived from both images, Walcott's
with his West Indian cadence, lies not only in the exhilaration they
arouse but also in the fact that we recognise them in a flash, they
carry through and ring true, apart from their freshness and that's
where the genius lie. Sometimes it takes just one particular image
for me to love a poem, sometimes it's the resonance that the poem
leaves.

In the act of writing a poem you're working to satisfy a lot of
deep things, you want your ideas and feelings to come out but in
a way that's memorable and pleasurable to, so all your feelers
are out, musical and otherwise, as ideas leap across and link in a
process that's intuitive. Your inner ear is attuned to the underlying
rhythm and the actual sounds of words and in a way you're like a
musical composer also, creating almost unconsciously your own
harmony.

A poem lives with the life you put into it and the "success" of
a poem at times has more to do with the degree of energy, passion
or fascination you bring to it rather than formal poetic rules.

# BRENDAN KENNELLY

Brendan Kennelly was born in 1936 in Ballylongford, Co. Kerry, and educated at Trinity College, Dublin where he would later become Professor of Modern English Literature. *My Dark Fathers* (1964) established Kennelly as an important lyrical voice, but his profile was transformed by the success of the best-selling *Cromwell* (1983), a weighty exploration of Ireland's relationship with its historical oppressor. His recent publications include a new selected (*A Time for Voices*, 1990), *The Book of Judas* (1991), *Poetry My Arse* (1995), *The Man Made of Rain* (1998) and *Begin* (1999). He edited *The Penguin Book of Irish Verse* (1970/1981), and his critical essays are collected in *Journey into Joy* (1994). 'Voices', as he states here, are critical to his work – not only the dual tongues talking English and Irish, but giving expression to the silenced in history. A surrender to voice is an assault upon intolerance, and marks poetry as both 'ongoing revolution and ultimate democracy'.

# Voices

## (2000)

To sit alone in a dark room and to listen imaginatively and openly to the voices of living and dead is a revealing and challenging experience. The absence of the need to communicate creates new presences. Solitude can be an act of private mastery or an act of calm surrender. To live in Ireland is to live with slogans such as 'No Surrender!', banging from one end of the island to the other, truculently and predictably asserting themselves in the face of difference. Poetry is both a continuing revolution and ultimate democracy because it is forever both questioning these voices I mentioned and also creating for them the kind of space which may become the scene of the overthrow of the inherited values of the poet-questioner himself or herself. The culture of No Surrender is deep, constant and strong and is embedded in people who sometimes pride themselves on their tolerance and liberalism. I see poetry as a conscious attack on the notion of No Surrender. Eliot's line, 'the awful daring of a moment's surrender' has often come into my head when I am trying to work on the notion that poetry is an attacking force born of a state of conscious surrender. For me, this surrender is made possible by listening to voices, letting them speak, especially if these voices are of those who are outcasts in history and myth, reviled, damned, and not worth a second thought. Poetry is born of second thoughts when these second thoughts are surrendered to, allowed to question the mind that relegated them to the status of "second thoughts" in the first place. So a poem can be an act of rebellion against the poet himself, because a second thought can go on to generate third and fourth thoughts, fifth and sixth thoughts, until the poor devil of a poet begins to wonder what it is he appears to have unleashed, or what he has sent out on parole from the prison of himself.

If there are two languages knocking about in your head from the start (in my case Irish and English), you develop a special relationship with voices. The voice talking Irish and the voice talking English belonging to the same person is not one voice but two. Two-voiced individuals have, or sound as if they have, two minds. This is not simply ambiguity, this is a double-voiced state of linguistic possibilities which can be, on the one hand, eloquently cunning and evasive and, on the other, brutally candid and direct. Irish and English, like England and Ireland, are in many ways quite remote from each other, but they are also, in the areas of language and thinking, more entangled in each other than either seems prepared to acknowledge. There is a process of cross-fertilisation at work, a richness born of tension, a fertility rooted in old antagonisms. This double-voiced fertility is at least partially responsible for my attempts to let voices be heard, especially the voices of those whom my culture would dismiss or damn forever to arid silence. I'm thinking of Cromwell, for example, about whom it is a sin (or was when I was growing up) to say a good word, or even to begin to try to understand as a complex human being. This giving-a-voice in poetry is like giving such a man a licence to exist, to be, where previously his name was a spit in the street, a black, horrible curse in the night, a maligned monster in a nowhere desert.

Because I believe in, and practise, this giving-a-voice in poetry, I spent the best part of eight years writing *The Book of Judas*. I realised the poem had achieved something of its own reality when a man said to me one day that I should be hanged for writing it.

Surrendering to an outcast voice means that one surrenders to complexities of history, religion, geography, memory, language, family, streetlife, journalism, gossip, scandal, education, politics (including the politics of poetry), notions of success and failure and swirling concepts of post-colonialism. No Surrender, like hatred, makes one assured, justified and strong. Hatred, like No Surrender, asks no questions since it has all the answers. Surrender turns the whole self into a river of uncertainties. These uncertainties demand to be uttered in all their challenging, disruptive force.

That is what I try to do, anyway.

# EAVAN BOLAND

Born in Dublin in 1944, Eavan Boland grew up in London and New York.
She now divides her time between Dublin and Stanford, California, where
she is Professor of English and Director of the Creative Writing Program.
Her most recent book is *The Lost Land*. She is co-editor with Mark Strand
of *The Making of a Poem: A Norton Anthology of Poetic Forms*, and her work
has often shown a fascination with the role of the poet in the making of poetry.
She has also written powerfully on aspects of womanhood, Irish history and
domesticity, and her *Collected Poems* were published in 1995. In her statement
below, she outlines the anti-popular turn that poetry took into modernism – a
turn that all but abandoned the reader, and condemned poetry into the margins
of daily relevance.

# The Wrong Way
### (2000)

In the first years of the 19th century, so the story goes, Lord Byron
and Tom Moore were sitting together on the banks of the Thames.
A boat went by, crowded with holiday-makers, all of them singing
one of Moore's melodies. When they had passed, Byron turned to
Moore. 'Ah, Tom,' he said, 'that's fame.'

Small as the story is, apocryphal as it may be, it works well as
either fiction or fact. It signals the wry, affectionate respect of a
canonical poet for a song-maker. It suggests the dependence of one
on the other, the nourishment of one by the other. It reminds us
that the dialect of poetic Romanticism could honour the powerful
vernacular of popular joy and memory – enough in fact to suggest
that they were neither separated nor separable.

I am writing this to propose that 20th century poetry took a
wrong turning: that the living proof of this is that the dialect and
vernacular have not only separated, but that they were in fact –
with hindsight and understanding – deliberately sundered. That the
consequences have been damaging, far-reaching and surprisingly
unquestioned. That we have been far slower, as poets, to do what
other practitioners in music, art and fiction have done – that is,
look at our household gods in the cold light of day and consider
their purposes and powers. But what households? What gods? In
order to continue this argument I will take it for a moment from
the general and frame it in the personal and particular.

I began to write and publish in the decade after the mid-century.

It was a calm, magisterial, eerily unquestioning time. To start with, Dublin was still a town, with all the amenities of the pre-urban moment. The coffee bars had strong tea, brown scones and peaty fires. The pubs were full of wild conversation. Lights burned late. Arguments continued into the small hours. These were the early 60s and poetry – as passion, as pursuit – seemed to be at the centre of this small city, sheltered by its histories and misfortunes from a wider world.

But this was deceptive. The 20th century ethos, with its travel, its free exchange of cultures and examples, had made sure that no poetry world could ever again secede from a so-called mainstream. In the universities, almost by stealth, a new set of pieties was moving into place. Almost without our noticing or understanding it, a new way of configuring both the poem and the idea of the poet – we now call it high modernism – had become the mainstream culture of poetry. Yeats, Eliot, Pound, Stevens were not only held up as examples. They were also simplified, pulled out of shape, reduced from the awkward, luminous spirits they were, to suit a new hieratic code that fitted suspiciously well into the ambitions of a post-war academy. Suddenly, high modernism was not simply a moment in poetry. It had become, as if by mandate, its manifest destiny.

When I look back, I see that moment – that mid-century hubristic time – as deeply authoritarian. Ideas and interpretations were being handed down as tables of the law. Young poets were allowed to listen but not to question. They were to be ready to consider the greatness of the past, but not its flaws. Ready to assume that everything had led inevitably to high modernism and that high modernism would inevitably ordain its own succession.

It would take me years to unlearn these first impressions. But I did. I stumbled, almost without knowing it, into the life of a woman. I married. I moved to a suburb. Gradually it all looked different. The making of the poetic past, which once I thought every young poet should be part of, was now I realised, an act of power and exclusion which I needed to reflect on. It was not simply that the canon was obstinately, endlessly male. It was also that its self-inventions seemed to me, increasingly, destructive of that wonderful spirit in which Byron had turned, so easily and graciously, to Tom Moore. It was not simply that readers were haemorrhaging away from poetry. It was also that those readers – with their lives, with their ordinary actions that I could see from my house and enact within it – were ceasing to matter to poetry. Poetry was learning a new, infinitely more exclusive speech. And therefore a thoroughly toxic one. But what had happened? If my own answers to this seem abrasive, the truth is we are still, as poets, only beginning to search for them.

Modernism had two great projects. We have lived, as poets and readers, in the light of the first and the shadow of the second for almost 80 years. The first project cannot be contested. It was to re-make the poem so that it could converse with the world it came from; and therefore with the past. So that its language and form and, finally, its elusive energies might be adequate to the experiences beyond it. This project involved poets like Pound, Eliot and Yeats – and later others – in an epic struggle of will and conscience and courage so that they could undo the false bonds between the poem and a decorum which had begun to choke it.

The second project, however, was catastrophic. It was to re-make, not the poem this time, but the reader of the poem. This was essential to what it saw as its radicalisation of poetic form and history. This – as the statements and arguments of modernist advocates began to make clear – meant cutting the reader off from the old popular expectations of the poem and the historic popular audience.

This in turn meant requiring a readership to forget a vast, sun-splashed hinterland where the troubadours had sung and the balladeer had shaped the day's events. It meant forgetting the rooms where poems were recited, couplets remembered, quatrains thrown whole into a group of people who could finish them. It meant, above all, compelling the reader – if they were to be true adherents of the new poetry – to sacrifice an ancient and communal contract between poet and audience for a newer, narrower interpretation of both poem and reader.

In trying to pre-judge, re-make, re-train the poetry reader away from the old joys of memory and sentiment and song, the secondary modernist project cut deep into the root and sap of the art. Frost's dictum about a poem – 'it begins in delight and ends in wisdom' – was put at risk in an entirely new way. And Frost's other dictum – 'no tears in the writer, no tears in the reader' – began to look all too true. As one American critic put it, 'There is some truth in the argument…that high Modernist art was not simply unpopular, as any new art may be for a while, but antipopular.'

I am one of the poets who believes the losses in all of this have been incalculable. A centuries-old, bright partnership between poet and reader has been injured. An ancient trust has been hurt. Poetry which once followed a man or woman through life, whispering in their ear from their first infatuation to their final sickness, which was at the centre of a society's self-definition, is now defensive and on the margins. Any comparison between the currency of poetry today and that of a hundred years ago shows a staggering loss of purpose and centrality. And far too little contemporary poetry criticism is willing to call a mistake by its proper name.

The only consolation may be that all this has made clearer the crucial difference between the canon and the tradition. The canon, always valuable and illuminating in what it includes, is almost worthless in the rhetoric and restriction it uses to exclude. But the tradition provides a counter-argument: it is to be found in those lines, fragments, cadences, pieces of language which readers take from their private reading. Which they store in their solitary memory and hand on, burnished and freighted, to one another. It is to be found in odd places. In the subway, in the office, in a moment of talk. Or in a boat full of song, going down a summer river.

# MEDBH McGUCKIAN

Medbh McGuckian was born in 1950 in Belfast, where she still lives. She studied at Queen's College, Belfast, and was the first woman to be writer-in-residence there. Winner of 1979 National Poetry Award, she published three collections of poetry with OUP, all since reissued in revised editions by Gallery Press, along with her five later books, including *Selected Poems 1978-1994* (1997). Her poetry is steeped in imagery that she has described as belonging to a 'feminine subconscious' (in particular the motifs of shadows, rivers and flowers), and is by turns playful, inventive, encrypted, eerie and disarming. She is currently writer-in-residence at Trinity College Dublin.

# And Cry Jesus to the Mice
### (2000)

'Statement' sounds like something taken from you, and it is. To be listed like solemn prophets in the Old and New Testaments. I am not strong enough to be 'among the English poets' *before* my death? Rilke says the world is less and less visible, we depend on the past's superior visibility to project what's left. Is this what Lawrence means: 'The passionate dead act within us and with us... of the dead who really live, we know their hush...they look on and *help*.' Virginia says (I am sticking to what the superior past says) poetry is just a question of what we now call 'space' and literary awards, of speaking your mind and leaving out half of what you would normally put in a novel called *Life's Adventure*. In a hundred years everyone will be humming under their breath at luncheon parties.

Why is it you can use both tooth and brush but not together, poems do now, wittily. The English language, as far as Irish poets go, which is to America, is only over a century old, we still relish its freshness as Shakespeare, or at least respect its Old Frenchness. Heaney's line in *Beowulf* about a daughter, a queen, 'a balm in bed for the battle-scarred Swede', enjoys the way things used to be before aromatherapy, when you hardly got a scratch on you. 'And, oh! she was the Sunday in every week' type of thing, except Sundays nowadays.

Of all the voices represented here the one I'm fondest of is Dylan Thomas. Bert Trick (sic) wrote of him in November 1934 (in November one will write anything): 'Modern poetry is roughly divided into two schools: that which works *towards* words and that which works *from* words. The latter is abstract and purely intellectual in its appeal. Mr Thomas is its best exponent...Each line is so impregnated with images, allusion, antithesis, that it becomes a poem within the poem. Words are treated like vials, new meaning being poured into them.'

Oh, Mr Thomas, your vials and your pouring. I don't agree with it being purely intellectual, but with each line being a poem, yes, so people can't read it quickly and yet still come away with something even if they only read the title. Dylan says himself he likes things 'that are difficult to write and difficult to understand', though for me it's more a case, or it was, of being misunderstood by the wrong people, as under Stalin. For different reasons I suppose I like 'redeeming the contraries with secretive images', contradicting 'my' images, saying two things at once in one word, four in two and one in six. (The hard bit is one in six, or any thing at all, as here, in five hundred.) Poetry should, when he and I write it, not everybody, mind, work from words, 'from the substance of words and the rhythm of substantial words set together, not towards words'.

One can't have every word substantial (none of these are at all) but as many as all telegraph pole and no wire – 'tread bejumpered (over) (the) sheepy fields.' Naturally the result is 'I am getting more obscure day by day', 'I shall never be understood', (bliss), 'I think I shall send no more poetry away but write stories alone.'

Dylan despairingly explains his anguish over one line, not a very good example, since it's not a very good line, which really accounts for the anguish: 'I try to drag out, from the whirlpooling words around my everlasting ideas of the importance of death on the living, some connected words that will explain how the starry system of the dead is seen, ordered as in the grave's sky, along the orbit of a foot or a flower. But when the words do come, I pick them so thoroughly of their live associations that only the death in the words remains...a line of mine is seen naked on paper and seen to be as meaningless as a Sanskrit limerick. Nothing but their barbaric sounds remained. Or if I did write a line, "My dead upon the orbit of a rose", I saw that "dead" did not mean "dead", "orbit" not "orbit", and "rose" most certainly not "rose", no, indeed, Gertrude. Even "upon" a syllable too many, lengthened for the inhibited reason of rhythm. My lines, all my lines, are of the tenth intensity (not of the thirtieth, like homeopathic remedies?). They are not the words that express what I want to express: they are the only words I can find that come near to expressing a half.'

A half though seems a lot better than a tenth. I understand something of his frustration with words on their own, the limits of single words. Groups of words are more likely to reproduce. Constantine Fitzgibbon in 1965 suggested, 'What he was trying to express in his poems was a view of the world for which the English language failed to provide the words, let alone the syntax.' (Would the Welsh language one wonders, have provided a more suitable medium? Vernon Watkins believes that the strict *cynghanedd* rules of Welsh verse would have cramped him.) Yet he was determined to achieve the near impossible, and he forced himself as he forced the words. At the same time James Joyce was doing much the same in *Finnegans Wake*.

There are so many languages possible in the English language, even Irish, I struggle with it, but as long as it continues to be printed in books and not just web-sites I imagine it failing only with my eyesight. Poetry is very much a luxury, because a book is costly, because work is never anything to do with it. When I am unhappy the Muse does not speak. She is always happy and I can only listen when I am. Nothing about me dispirits her. It comes back down to the importance again of life on the dead. As St Teresa writes, 'There is nothing we can do about them; we cannot see more or less of them at will, and we can neither call them up nor banish them by our own efforts.'

# BERNARD O'DONOGHUE

Bernard O'Donoghue was born in 1945 in Cullen, Co. Cork, and now teaches
medieval English at Wadham College, Oxford. His collections of poetry – *The
Weakness* (1991), *Gunpowder* (1995) and *Here Nor There* (1999) – have been
much praised for their gentle and evocative lyricism, and indeed the middle
of the three won the Whitbread Prize for Poetry. He believes profoundly in
the social role of poetry, and 'poetry's concern' is a commitment to look out
at the world, even if that begins from a particular, localised experience.

## Poetry's Concern
### (2000)

What poetry *mustn't* do is talk to itself. Nothing is easier than to
get a gathering of poets to extol the value and insight of poetry
and to lament its marginalisation. Apart from the warm glow that
this confers, it doesn't achieve very much. A convention of beer-
drinkers or foxhunters would claim as much. But the danger of
introversion is particularly acute in the case of poetry, a verbal art
which uses as its medium the terms that people employ in all their
acts of communication. The poet borrows the currency of general
exchange and must spend it productively; otherwise the loan is
abused. The users of the language as a whole are entitled to an
opinion on how it is used in poetry. As it happens, despite a lot of
complaining by poets about the slighting of poetry, people in gen-
eral are curiously respectful of it: more than it deserves, I often
think. If someone makes out they are a poet, then they have to
answer to the responsibilities as well as claiming the considerable
privileges and kudos. The fact is that poetry mostly manages to
maintain its social status without making much social return.

This is a delicate business, of course. It has to be decided what
society the poet writes out of, and to. When Antoine Raftery wrote
his great lament for 'Anach Chuan' about a multiple drowning in
Lough Corrib in the 1820s, the constituency was clear enough. As
proof of its aptness, his poem is still sung in the locality two cen-
turies later, in Irish and English. But when Andrew Motion, with
commendable generosity of spirit, wrote a poem for the TUC Con-
ference, it was not so clear that he was writing for a constituency
he belonged to. There is something satisfyingly profound about
the twist by which the singer of 'I belong to Glasgow' finds that

when he has 'a couple of pints on a Saturday, Glasgow belongs to' him. It is true; you can tell by the accent he sings in.

The point here, I suppose, is that it is much easier to be a local poet than a national one. That is, it is much clearer what poetry is *for* locally than nationally. What *is* the national poet to do, to repay the debt to the society which recognises him/her? The least they can do, it might be thought, is to take society and its politics seriously. But the problem is that there is a strong bias against political poetry in English, at least on the home front. We are much more ready to admire political poetry in the distance: distance either of place – like Eastern Europe – or time – like the First World War. This was interestingly borne out by the coldness which greeted Tony Harrison's *Guardian* poems during the Gulf War. It was striking that the objection mostly took a familiar disingenuous form: a pretence that what was being objected to was the *formal* quality of the political poem. Harrison's powerful and bitterly vivid poems were said to fall short in prosody. Likewise, Seamus Heaney's more declaredly political poems were greeted with more unease than most of his writing, even it sometimes seemed by the poet himself. The obvious case was Heaney's light-hearted murmur of protest against his inclusion under the heading 'British' in the Motion-Morrison Penguin anthology in 1982. People kept saying: 'he can say what he likes. But it's not very well *written*, is it?'

In these cases, it is clear that those objecting to public pronouncement in poetry – what Yeats deplored as 'opinion' – are reluctant to descend to public statement themselves, even in criticism. They want the debate to proceed in mannerly formal terms, in commentary as in poetry. The issue in Heaney's case arose again last year when much of the public comment in England failed to see that he couldn't possibly become the Poet Laureate even if his Northern Irish birth entitled him to British citizenship. How on earth could a Dublin-based poet of Northern Irish Catholic origins, however well-disposed, take on a role that implied that he should write paeans for the British Royal family? And how on earth could some parts of the English poetic world have thought that he might? It was another example of failing to locate poetry in a public context.

Heaney, as it happens, is a complex case. He has always spoken for a very wide constituency, and he takes his responsibilities towards poetry at least as seriously as those towards the public world. One of his most important books is *The Government of the Tongue* where he says 'poetry can be as potentially redemptive and possibly as illusory as love.' But what he yearns is that the poet's tongue should be liberated from the tyranny of having been 'governed for so long in the social sphere by considerations of tact and fidelity, by nice obeisances to one's origin within the minority or the majority.' Repeatedly he has said 'poetry has its own jurisdiction' (or words to that effect), not in itself governed by the laws of 'the minority or the majority', the local or the national.

I am not so sure. Wilfred Owen is much quoted for saying: 'Above all, I am not concerned with poetry.' The conditions in which Owen was writing were especially terrible ones in which a primary concern for poetry might seem crass. But we could do worse than keep Owen's dictum in mind in all circumstances. It is tempting to say that anybody who thinks poetry is the most serious thing will not be capable of writing serious poetry because they cannot see what things are *really* serious.

This will all sound very churlish, coming from someone who has, I think, had more recognition from the poetic world than I have earned. In an age of mindless materialism (which is of course how writers have always characterised their own, unappreciative times), it will seem to be weighing in on the wrong side of the scale. But of course it is not that I am *against* poetry or writing or art. They are the things that mean most to me professionally, by definition; indeed I have no remaining aspirations beyond involvement with literature and the arts. Everyone, however slight their practice of poetry, understands the observation of Patrick Kavanagh: that he started to toy with verse and woke one day to find that it had become his life. But that doesn't exempt us from trying to say anew in every generation *why* poetry is important: why it warrants the exalted status accorded to it. We no longer, I trust, claim anything as grand as vatic insight or as insignificant as private solace ('I write for myself'). In the end, the answer is that poetry means something different in every generation and an important part of the poet's duty is to find out what its meaning is for their own time. The Northern Irish critic Edna Longley says that every poem worth its salt is in part about poetry. I think this is absolutely right. Moreover, poetry has to be redefined not only in time but also in place. We can't rest on shared laurels and say: 'Poetry is what Dante and Shakespeare wrote; I am a poet, so let's have a bit of respect.'

As it happens, I find myself writing repeatedly about the same place, the part of Ireland I come from, which is a still a relatively hermetically sealed community with active interest in language, history and archaeology, and a musical tradition which can only be called classical. It is a very easy community to write out of. The most obvious form to write back to it in is elegy. But that is all local, writing for the minority. Like Auden's valley cheese, 'local, but prized elsewhere', such writing is very fortunate if it appeals to any kind of appetite in a wider world. It is a kind of talking to yourself which must try to be alert to the context in which it is over-heard. And it must be equally grateful to the world that provides its material and the busy world of communication that pauses to listen.

# DAVID CONSTANTINE

David Constantine was born in 1944 in Salford, and lectured in German at Durham and Oxford from 1969 to 2000; he is now a freelance writer and translator. His first collection was *A Brightness to Cast Shadows* (1980), and a *Selected Poems* appeared in 1991. His latest poetry books are *Caspar Hauser* (1994) and *The Pelt of Wasps* (1998). He published a critical study of Hölderlin in 1988, and his *Selected Poems* (1990/1996) of Hölderlin won the European Poetry Translation Prize in 1997; and he shares many of the German poet's romantic and classical expression of tenderness, longing and anxiety. Indeed his statement here reflects some of the same drive for harmony. Poetry, he outlines, uses the peculiar (the individual moment and motive of writing) to express commonality (the shared experience, the link through history), and in so doing may represent an evasion of death.

## Common and Peculiar
(2000)

Poetry is common. The stuff of it is common, even commonplace. Poetry comes from what we as human beings have in common. It puts us in living touch with our shared realities. And it can extend and increase the things we share. This needs insisting on because too many people assume that poetry is not for them. They think it has nothing to say to them. But in fact the stuff of poetry is the stuff of ordinary lives. Much of what poetry tells us we know already, but not well enough, not keenly enough, not so that it matters. Poetry helps us realise common things better.

At the same time, poetry is peculiar. This also needs insisting on, not just conceding. Unlike music, poetry has as its medium something which is in common use for other purposes. Its medium is language. For that reason – because language mostly serves other non-poetic and indeed often very *un*-poetic purposes – poetic language has to be other and peculiar. Myself, I feel it to be *quite* peculiar, and not just at one end of a linguistic spectrum or continuum whose other end is functional prose. And yet the actual words in use might be the same. The hundred or so words of a sonnet written today might all be dispersed back into the common language and not be noticed there. The peculiarity of poetry is not just linguistic, but still we can say that poetry must signal its peculiarity, its otherness, by the means and the medium of its very existence: by language. Many poets nowadays make a virtue of only using the words that everybody uses. In so doing they counter older and wholly discredited notions that some words are poetic and others aren't. Words are what we do with them. They become poetic by their rhythm, by how they consort.

The risk in removing the language of poetry too far from that of common speech is obvious. You lose touch. Readers will not be able to see what that sort of language has in common with the lives they lead. But there is also a risk in coming too close to common speech. If the poetic line comes so close to the spoken and written sentences of everyday that it merges with them, it will lose its purchase on the realities of everyday, it will have no slant or hold on them, be powerless to affect them. This is by far the greater risk of verse today. And knowingness is no safeguard. Irony and parody are necessary strategies, no doubt, but employ them constantly and your language will merge with the language you are ironising and parodying, and so lose all purchase and have no good effect.

The purpose of maintaining a decided otherness in poetic language – neither too far away from nor too close to common speech – is to return us to what as human beings we have in common. The common, the commonplace, will only be brought home to us by means of a language beautifully and intriguingly and shockingly estranging it. The conditions of modern life are taking us further and further out of community and reality, into isolation and the merely virtual; actually into insensateness. Poetry is a way of countering that.

A poem is quite peculiar to the person writing it in a particular time and place. And yet it transcends – or, better, it dissolves – that particularity in an act of empathy, a quickening of interest and involvement, across any amount of time and space. It can induce us to care about Hecuba. Poetry then, made of words, engenders a condition in which the single personality dissolves and we enter into other lives, other possibilities of being human. That seems to me the chief moral effect of poetry. An effect without the intention. I don't think the writer can consciously aim for it. His or her concern must be to attend as closely as possible to real present circumstances, to the real and particular and perhaps even unique conditions of the project in hand. Poetry can only generalise through the particular. It affirms and extends community by being true to what is individual and peculiar. Its politics, you might say, are ideally democratic.

I had a consoling thought about poetry the other day. I was watching a film about some musicians who had got together again after a gap of half a century. There they were, all old people, making

music. A man in his 90s was singing love songs. My thought was:
It's for someone else. And likewise poetry, perhaps even more so.
Poetry is for someone else. Of course when I write it, it is for me,
here and now. It is for whomever I might address a particular
poem to. But manifestly – ever more manifestly the nearer the
writer gets to death – the poem is over and beyond its author and
the people he or she loves, for someone else. And I don't mean
that poets are aiming at survival. Again, it is an effect without an
intention. It is a quality, a sort of generosity, an unselfishness, a
leaving behind of selfishness, a conversion of the biographical self
into other people's lives, which is inherent in every successful
poem. And that inherent generosity is the chief deed of poetry
against the fact of death. Every line of verse is doing its best to
wriggle free of death. The whole achieved poem is a deed of life,
in the face, in the teeth of death. Poetics is the devising of strat-
egies, a reflection on the practice of a deed of life against all death
in life, against the numerous forms of living death, and against the
fact and reality of death itself.

# HUGO WILLIAMS

Hugo Williams was born in Windsor in 1942, son of the actor Hugh Williams, and was educated at Eton. His first collection *Symptoms of Loss* was published in 1965, but it is his later work that has reached its widest audience: *Writing Home* (1985), *Self-Portrait with a Slide* (1990), *Dock Leaves* (1994) and *Billy's Rain* (1999, and winner of the T.S. Eliot Prize). He has published two volumes of travel writing, and his columns for the *Times Literary Supplement* appeared as *Freelancing: Adventures of a Poet* in 1995. A *Selected Poems* was published in 1989. Poignant and disarming, Williams's often bittersweet poems play the downtrodden hero to a tee, mixing confession and a melancholic humour. His statement here expresses an idea so characteristic of his work: an affection for simplicity and a plainness that 'operates without the safety net of the poetical'.

# Leaping Versus Blabbing
## (2000)

Keep it simple and make it visual seems to be the best idea. 'Cult-ivate simplicity, Coleridge,' wrote Charles Lamb to the poet on the publication of his first book, 'or rather, I should say, banish elaborateness; for simplicity springs spontaneous from the heart, and carries into daylight its own modest buds and genuine, sweet and clear flowers of expression. I allow no hot-beds in the Garden of Parnassus.' And Coleridge himself had some equally good advice for Thomas Poole: 'I could inform the dullest author how he might write an interesting book – let him relate the events of his own life with honesty – not disguising the feelings that accompanied them.'

Why is it that surfaces go so deep in writing? I sometimes think there are two separate English languages, one made up of visible things, the other of invisible, and there can be no doubt that the former is better for poetry. 'In the amorous realm,' wrote Roland Barthes, 'the most painful wounds are inflicted more often by what one sees than by what one knows.' Given that poems themselves are metaphors, I find overt metaphors more and more embarrass-ing in poems. The trouble seems to start when you find yourself lying to make an effect. For instance, 'Every week we put up the Christmas decorations' might seem at first to be a good way of describing the speeded up passage of time as we get older, but it isn't any good because it isn't true.

I like what Andrew Motion once said about writing poetry. 'What I try to do is lean two things up against each other and see what

happens.' He went on to say that the two things might be a public
and a private element, which would operate as metaphors for each
other, as in his poem 'The Letter'. 'But the only technique that
matters,' said F.R. Leavis, 'is that which compels words to express
an intensely personal way of feeling, so that the reader responds,
not in a general way that he knows beforehand to be "poetical",
but in a precise, particular way that no frequenting of the Oxford
Book could have made familiar to him.'

I once had a copy of Robert Bly's magazine *The Sixties*, in which
he put forward the concept of 'leaping' in poetry – that poets were
lightning conductors, leaping between images, or that they were
guides leading the reader across the pond of the page on which
the stepping stones of the images were just under the water. It
was all a matter of trust. I remember his example of an old chapel
and a howling dog. I thought I could see the connection and felt
proud that I had passed the test. In fact, it was just another version
of surrealism, of South American 'hot' surrealism as Bly called it,
as opposed to the 'cold' French surrealism of André Breton and
Marcel Duchamp, whose umbrella and sewing machine met (list-
lessly, surely) on an operating table. Personally, I could do without
either. Surrealism is hell, the epitome of self-licensing artiness,
which beats readers away with sticks. Coleridge called the method
'Fancy': 'arbitrary connections wittily made', as opposed to the
Imagination which was 'a synthesis bringing the poem into the
depths of the real'. Whatever that means. Lovers of surrealism tend
to claim that the surreal exists in the everyday, but they traduce
and degrade the ordinary with their over-excited attentions, like
slumming tourists.

When I mentioned to Michael Hofmann how much I longed for
a high style in poetry, he looked at me as if I were mad. 'Surely
not?' he said. 'Low, low.' And I agree with him now that the low
road is the only way, the lower the better in fact, since those roads
aren't on the maps. The high style is necessarily a pastiche of past
dictions, a pumping up of old generalities, as in neo-surrealists John
Ashbery, Jeremy Prynne and their followers. When I read the
counterfeit madness of these poetries I can't help thinking of the
struggle of John Clare in his asylum, seeking and finding lucidity in
his real madness. The thought of those tongue-in-cheek hipsters
playing the cross-eyed loon to impressionable academics isn't a
pretty one.

Towards the end of his life, the Japanese poet Basho cautioned
fellow poets to rid their minds of superficiality by means of *karumi*
(lightness), the artistic expression of non-attachment. In his view,

a good poem was one in which the form of the verse and the join-
ing of its two parts seemed light as a shallow river flowing over its
sandy bed. His style is known for two other aesthetic ideals, *sabi*,
contented solitariness, and *wabi*, the spirit of poverty, an appreci-
ation of the commonplace. I feel sure that Basho would have got on
with Patrick Kavanagh, although Kavanagh's love of the ordinary
had a more democratic slant: 'There is nothing as dead and damned
as an important thing. The things that really matter are casual,
insignificant little things, things you would be ashamed to talk about
publicly. You are ashamed and then after years someone blabs and
you find that you are in the secret majority.' I love that word 'blabs'
there. He blabbed. She blabbed. I can't think of a better word for
good writing. Kavanagh was a friend of John Betjeman, who put it
more contentiously: 'There is nothing so unimportant as the News.'

I was looking through an old *London Magazine* poetry question-
naire from 1962 in the hope of finding some perception from my
19-year-old self that would be worth replaying, but without suc-
cess. Only one of my sentences seems to be in English. On the
subject of poetry's duty to take up the big issues, I agree with
everyone else: 'Such things have always been implicit in certain
personal conflicts.' Sylvia Plath said it better: 'My poems do not
turn out to be about Hiroshima, but about a child forming itself
finger by finger in the dark. They are not about the terrors of
mass extinction, but about the bleakness of the moon over a yew
tree in a neighbouring graveyard. Not about the testaments of tor-
tured Algerians, but about the night thoughts of a tired surgeon.'
That was exactly a year before she died.

When you are young and drunk with words you want to read
someone who is drunk with words too, and so you read Shelley,
Hopkins, Dylan Thomas, Sylvia Plath. I still feel a dizzy kind of
nostalgia for the sub-Thomasian poems of Laurie Lee, which I
used to copy out at school: 'Such a moment it is when love / leans
through geranium windows / and calls with a cockerel's tongue'.
Later on you want something less heated, less decorative. When I
was in my 20s I was mad about the word-drunk late T'ang poet
Li Ho (791-817), a sort of quasi-precursor of Keats, Baudelaire
and Trakl. I wrote to his editor, J.D. Frodsham, who was teaching
Chinese literature at the University of Dar es Salaam, asking if I
could put some of his Li Ho translations in a magazine I was trying
to get off the ground. Frodsham wrote back saying he was working
on the later Sung Dynasty now (960-1279) and enclosing some Sung
poems, which, in my naivety, I found disappointing. 'Sung dynasty
verse is like tea,' explained Frodsham in a later letter. 'T'ang verse

is like wine. One needs both. One couldn't live at Li Ho's pitch of intensity continually.' Well, I must have been trying to at the time. Now, in my tea-drinking 50s, it seems to me that there is more, not less intensity in plainness, because simple stuff operates without the safety net of the poetical.

'To make verse speak the language of prose, without being prosaic,' wrote William Cowper, 'to marshal the words of it in such an order as they might naturally take in falling from the lips of an extemporary speaker, yet without meanness, harmoniously, and without seeming to displace a syllable for the sake of rhyme, is one of the most arduous tasks a poet can undertake.' Yes indeed. But he didn't say it as well as Fred Astaire: 'If it doesn't look easy, you aren't working hard enough.'

# ANDREW MOTION

Poet Laureate, critic, biographer, Professor of Creative Writing, Andrew
Motion is the quintessential man of letters. Born in London in 1952, he was
educated at Oxford and published his first collection, *The Pleasure Steamers*, in
1978. His poetry combines narrative and lyricism, although some of his con-
cerns are distinctly postmodern. His *Selected Poems 1976-1997* (1998) replaces
the earlier *Dangerous Play* (1985). He has written biographies of Philip Larkin
(1993) and Keats (1997), and co-edited the formative *Penguin Book of Contem-
porary British Poetry* (1982) with Blake Morrison. Following the death of Ted
Hughes, he was appointed Poet Laureate in 1999 (from which point on his
work has shown an ever increasing turn toward 'public poetry'), and he con-
tinues to teach at the University of East Anglia.

# Yes and No
## (2000)

Poetic manifestos invariably say 'yes' and 'no', but poetry itself
'maybe' and 'perhaps'.

Public poetry must address occasions squarely, but look beneath
and beyond them. Personal poetry must register ambiguities and
paradoxes. In doing so, both find their own ways of saying 'yes'
and 'no' – 'yes' to risk, chance, elusiveness; 'no' to having too pal-
pable a design on us.

In either event, poetry discovers its peculiar kind of intelligence
– not inevitably the intelligence of analysis and exegesis, but the
intelligence of feeling things upon our pulses.

Not that we always expect the meanings of poetry to come clear
at the front of our minds. With music, with cadence, with form,
poetry speaks for what cannot be spoken, as well as what can. It
does not baffle or confound the due process of thought, but opens
a corridor between head and heart.

In this respect, the appeal of poetry is visceral and primitive, no
matter how shrewd and watchful it might be. Also in this respect,
and in others, poetry is hindered as well as helped by manifestos.
Public or personal, satirical or lyrical, trumpeting or softly-spoken,
true poems retain their independence at all costs. They must be
against-the-grain, even subversive, to create whatever sympathy
they intend.

# CIARAN CARSON

Ciaran Carson was born in 1948 in Belfast, where he attended Queen's University. His books of poetry include *The New Estate* (1976), *The Irish for No* (1987), *Belfast Confetti* (1989), *First Language* (1993), *Opera Et Cetera* (1996) and *The Twelfth of Never* (1999). His prose works include *Last Night's Fun* (1996), a memoir of Irish traditional music, and *The Star Factory* (1998), a memoir of Belfast. Among the many awards he has won are the *Irish Times* Literature Prize and the T.S. Eliot Prize. He also plays the Irish traditional flute, and lives in Belfast with his wife, the fiddle player Deirdre Shannon, and their three children. Carson's work, often expressed in long formal lines, considers the constantly evolving identities of language and map-making in his native city – the movement between places and tongues; between Irish and English; between absence and presence.

# The Other
## (2000)

What is poetry? 'I don't know what it is, but I know it when I see it.' Or, 'I know it when I hear it.' Poetry takes place in books, and in the ear. Let me turn to someone else for another reply, which perhaps engages both vision and hearing. The someone is the Irish poet Seán Ó Ríordáin (1916-77), who wrote in his second language, Irish. I have translated this passage before, sometimes in print, sometimes mentally, so this is yet another version. It comes from the Preface (or, rather, Foreword, *Réamhrá*) to his first collection, *Eireaball Spideoige* (*A Robin's Tail*), published in 1952.

> What is poetry? The mind of a child? Imagine two people in a room, a child and his father, and a horse clopping in the street outside. The father looks out and says, 'There's Mary's horse going by.' That's a statement. It seems the father has lost the horse because he remains outside it. Say a horse is a disease. The father doesn't catch this disease. The horse does not enrich the father's life. But as for the child, he feels the sound of the horse in his bones. He licks his lips with the sound of the horse. He listens to the sound getting dimmer and dimmer, till it fades at last into silence. To him, both sound and silence are full of wonder. He re-imagines the horse's hooves, and ponders their antique authority. The world then blooms with horsiness, and the magic of reins. It's like – it's like having another head. And that, I think, is poetry.

As it happens, I was reared bilingually: for my parents, Irish was a second language, which they spoke exclusively at home. So I think Irish was my first language, by a short head. I remember, or think I remember, lying awake at night as a child, and hearing a horse and cart going by on the street outside; this was Belfast in the early 50s, and such things – milk-carts, coal-carts, brewer's drays – were perfectly feasible. I would say the word *horse* over and over to myself; then the Irish word, *capall*, which seemed more onomatopoeically equine, yet with its ghost of English *cobble*, and then I'd mentally feel the bumps of the cobblestoned street. The more I'd say the word into myself, the more its meaning faded, reiterated into nonsense by the time I fell asleep.

Thinking now about those slate-blue cobbles, *cobalt* comes to mind, from the German *Kobold*, a demon, for this deep blue substance was supposed by German miners to be a mischievous and hurtful metal. Cobalt-60 is a radioactive isotope. I remember cold-war talk of cobalt bombs. The word creates a fall-out.

You can see I use dictionaries. The language is too big for me, and I've come to realise more and more my ignorance of it. If language is a mirror, I look up *mirror*, and discover it to be, among other things, 'a small glass formerly worn in the hat by men and at the girdle by women'; it is 'the speculum of a bird's wing'. I use thesauruses, those treasuries or temples of words, for the English language in particular seems littered with near-synonyms, each expressing different weights and shades of meaning. Rhyming dictionaries throw up bizarre combinations of word-neighbours: *Cleopatra, Sinatra, et cetera.*

But is this poetry? I don't know, but I do know that anything I've written under the auspices of poetry involves a word-search, an exploration; and I don't know what I'll say, until it's said. It's a discovery. In poetry, the destination of the journey should remain unknown until one arrives. Then one is pleasantly surprised. 'Poetry is what gets lost in translation.' Perhaps; but poetry is itself translation, carrying a burden of meaning from one place to another, feeling it change in shape and weight as it travels. Words are a shifty business. Ó Ríordáin's horse vanishes over the horizon, leaving the echo of its presence behind: a kind of Pegasus, endowed with Keats's 'viewless wings of poesy'.

I write in English, but the ghost of Irish hovers behind it; and English itself is full of ghostly presences, of others who wrote before you, and of words as yet unknown to you. Poetry's a kind of dream-world. It is *other*, a word that the *American Heritage Dictionary* refers to the Indo-European root *al-*: important derivatives are *alarm, alert, ultimate, else, alien, alter, alias, alibi, allegory, parallel,* and *eldritch*, that eerie, otherworldly word. All these words will do for now. Poetry has many heads.

# SEAN O'BRIEN

Born in London in 1952, Sean O'Brien grew up in Hull; he now lives in Newcastle and teaches writing at Sheffield Hallam University. He studied at Cambridge, Birmingham and Hull, and his early poetry (*The Indoor Park*, 1983) showed connections to the Humberside of Douglas Dunn and Philip Larkin. O'Brien is among the most expressly political of contemporary poets, and his work often reflects the fierce regional inequalities stoked-up under Thatcherism – at times with anger, at times with satirical or piquant wit. His subsequent collections are *The Frighteners* (1987), *HMS Glasshouse* (1991) and the Forward Prize-winning *Ghost Train* (1995); a new collection, *Downriver*, is due in 2001. His most recent books consider the condition of England through a mixture of history and narrative fantasy. A regular poetry reviewer for the *Sunday Times*, he is an impressive and important surveyor of the contemporary scene, as his study *The Deregulated Muse: Essays on Contemporary British & Irish Poetry* and his anthology *The Firebox: Poetry in Britain and Ireland after 1945* (both 1998) testify.

## Proceedings in Palmersville
(2000)

Break with the tendency before encountering it.

\*

What do you mean you're surprised by the self-righteousness of parasites?

\*

Millenarian Update. Sooner or later the Devil comes round in his speedboat. Only then will poets learn again what the material is in which they've been swimming so freely.

\*

One plank of the manifesto: that manifestos are what planks have.

\*

Don't forget to exhaust your early promise in the repetition of the same few mannered tropes.

\*

The avant garde imagines, and the mainstream regrets, that it exists. If you chuck The Grand Wazoo's COLLECTED in the river, it doesn't sink. Analogies for this phenomenon.

\*

Bernstein. That would be Elmer, right? Jackson Mac Low Yo Yo. Rae Armantroutmaskreplica. Les Filles de Sillimanjaro. High and Low could coexist peacefully, were it not for Lower Middle, which sponsors Low and must seek to destroy High. As Adorno puts it: 'The culture industry intentionally integrates its consumers from above. To the detriment of both it forces together the spheres of high and low art...The seriousness of high art is destroyed in speculation about its efficacy; the seriousness of the lower vanishes with the constraints imposed on the rebellious resistance inherent within it.'

*

Work? We have John Kinsella to do that for us.

*

Location. Location. Location.

*

Has poetry learned how to behave in public, in restaurants, palaces, corridors, vestibules, anterooms, courtyards, crypts, mausolea, Admiralty yards and so on? Then it had better forget. Forget how to turn up and sit politely while an actor reads *poytri* aloud "properly" in his/her beautiful voice, not noticing that he/she's got two stanzas in the wrong order on his photocopy, then smirking as if this were the poem's fault and proved something known about it "in the real world".

*

Not institutions. Not "understandings". Not "your place". Certainly not mine.

*

'Whoever speaks of culture speaks of administration – whether that is his intention or not...At the same time, however...culture is opposed to administration.' – Adorno.

*

*Trahison des berks.* You tell me that you don't want to like tell people what to do and that it's all up to the individual because like everybody has like a different point of like view. That's not a manifesto, that's a sicknote.

*

No one with homicidal urges should edit an anthology.

*

"The poetry gatecrashers". *Aux armes, citoyens.* Couldn't gatecrash a phonebox.

*

Horrible sense that people want to own poetry in order to build over
it. Claims laid by journalists who never read anything but Ted 'n'
Sylvia and John Hegley; by academics who clearly don't like it but
need to show it who's boss; and by *soi-disant* subversives who wouldn't
know a poem if it bit them on the arse. Anyone who has spent time
trying to advocate that the work be read rather than blethered about,
despised or dismissed or colonised will recognise the soured, weary
feeling produced after the first decade. Refuse the invitation to give up.

*

Simple-minded disavowals of politics by otherwise sophisticated
persons. Englishmen giving the impression of being "a bit thick",
more convincingly than they know.

*

Death to entryist hippies:

HAIKU
First you give me all
Your money, then I give you
All this old rope, free.

*

SERIOUSLY, LIKE
Winter again with the forces of Northern reaction,
Vanguard of the "bitter" ampersand,
The marmoreal slash.
The Modernist incontinence!
Pale scolds with posh addresses,
Still more Socialist than you, like.
The little presses fold away like trousers,
Dead men's trousers with the hanged
Tongues sticking out. *For in my Father's house*
*Are many trousers. All shall be*
*Donated to await the gratitude.*
*Let a filing cabinet be named for this*
*And launched at Monkwearmouth*
*At nightfall with torches.*
The corpse of the erstwhile promoter
Delays in the mouth of the Tyne
That underlined remark that changes everything,
L'esprit d'escalier submarine.
*Shall these bones live? – Not*
*If we can help it, Sonny. Not round here.*

*

WELCOME MAJOR POET!
We have sat here in too many poetry readings
Wearing the liberal rictus and cursing our folly,
Watching the lightbulbs die and the curtains rot
And the last flies departing for Scunthorpe.
Forgive us. We know all about you.
Autumn gives way to midwinter once more,
As states collapse, as hemlines rise, as we miss both,
And just as our teeth fall discreetly into our handkerchiefs,
Slowly the bones of our co-tormentees will emerge
Through their skins. QED and hic jacent.
Except we are seated bolt upright on customised
"Chairs" of the torturers' school. Here it comes,
Any century now, the dread declaration:
And next I shall read something longer. Please
Rip out our nails and accept your applause!
Stretch-limo back to the Ritz and ring home:
Bore the arse off your nearest and dearest instead,
Supposing they haven't divorced you already
Or selfishly put themselves under a train.
Please call them, at length and at public expense.
Send flunkies for cold Stolichnaya, an ox
Or an acre of coke and a thousand quid hooker.
Why not make it three, in a chariot
Flown to your penthouse by eunuchs on leopards?
Whatever you like, only spare us the details of when
You were struck by your kinship with Dante and Virgil.
And don't feel obliged to remind us just now
What it was Robert Lowell appeared to be saying –
You'd read him the poem you mean to read us –
When the doors of the lift he was in and you weren't
Began closing. Just leave us the screams
You could hear as the vehicle descended: Poor Cal.
Up to then he'd been perfectly normal. Ah, well.

*

I want to write poems which are places, in which paraphraseable
meaning has been drawn back into the place itself, so that the
reading of the poem resembles inhabiting or at any rate contem-
plating the place. The original landscapes of my life – Anlaby Road,
Hull, in the mid 50s; the flat behind the butcher's shop, with its
garden of lilacs; Salisbury Street, with its vast, lost orchard; the
tenfoots between the avenues; the riverwide greenmantled drains

before they were filled in the 60s; the goods line at the back of the houses; the bodily stink of purple furnace ash and free milk in the vast yards of St Wilfred's RC Infants: these are not something to use but to enter, though I don't know why. They are sufficient.

Politics is also inscribed in this material whenever I examine it, although I'm sometimes told I'm wrong by the pure in heart. This should ideally have been the sole item in this document. It would also contain railway arches, viaducts, junctions, cuttings, dead stations, torn-up lines, dockside buffers, lock-gates, estuaries, the Ouseburn, statues of De La Pole and Collingwood, lighthouses, sea-lanes, ice-bergs, places which only exist as numbers on an Admiralty chart.

*

In a poetry discussion room on the Internet recently someone claimed that 'form is no longer convincing or necessary'. This is not untypical of the striking level of daftness displayed in these contexts – a condition entertainingly accompanied by Marlovian claims to world-making scope. What we could do with is a relatively disinterested discussion in the light of the reinvigoration of poetic forms in the last 20 years. When we consider form in Muldoon, Paterson, Dunn, Duffy and Harrison, for example, are we talking about the same phenomenon? 'We' could do with? Who's this 'we'? Are 'we' culture? Are 'we' Devo?

*

A Performance Poet, impassioned, at a conference: 'But look, you bastards, the Belgians are laughing at us.' At least it hasn't all been in vain.

# MICHAEL HOFMANN

Michael Hofmann was born in Freiburg, Germany in 1957, the son of the novelist Gert Hofmann. He moved to Britain aged seven, and was educated at Winchester and Cambridge. His first collection *Nights in the Iron Hotel* (1983) marked Hofmann as a skilled, prosaic, ironic poet in the manner of Lowell. His at times bitter relationship with his father anchors his subsequent collections *Acrimony* (1986), *Corona, Corona* (1993) and *Approximately Nowhere* (1999). His criticism appears as *Books and Pictures* (2000). A poem, he writes here, is 'a machine for re-reading'; in its ideal form: endless, inexhaustible, and able to convey both a scene and a trace of itself as an object made of words.

## 'I happen to believe'
### (2000)

I happen to believe (still) that a poem should have some reason to exist, in the same way that something in the clouds is required to *happen*, to produce a flash of lightning, and poems for me resemble lightning more than they do sunshine or showers. Poems are by their nature occasional, contingent, unpredicted and not quite repeatable. One of the great books of the century by my "discovery" of the past five or ten years, Eugenio Montale, is called *Le Occasioni*. 'Yet why not say what happened?' writes Robert Lowell, at his most Mephistophelean.

This is not the same as "confessional". The poem may not get written without its hurt or its drama, but it's not the hurt or the drama that make it a poem. These things are, literally and punningly, a "pre-text". They are what get you to start thinking in images, and improvising and arranging words. Without them, I wouldn't think it was worth my while crossing the room to hunt for a piece of paper; in their absence no book is worth keeping. They are Yeats's 'sword upstairs'. I like the formulation of Bernard Spencer: 'a situation, out of which comes a so-far unformulated excitement.' It's not the situation that matters to the reader, or, once he has it, to the writer. (Akhmatova is saying the same thing when she says that poetry comes from all sorts of rubbish.) In his *Adagia*, Wallace Stevens makes the crucial point that a poem is not *about* an event, it *is* an event. A "confessional poem" is a contradiction in terms: the real action has, by definition, already taken place elsewhere. The reader, quite properly, responds to it exactly as he would to a piece of news or gossip: 'Lovely for you!' or 'Oh, you poor thing!' And that's why he's perhaps a little mulish when it's put to him that he might read such a poem – Olds or Sexton or lesser Berryman – again. Why should he, he's heard it before...

The ideal poem, it seems to me, is one you want to pick up and read right away – the irresistibleness of the "excitement" – and can also endlessly revisit. Montale is like that for me, and Lowell, and the German poet, Gottfried Benn. Some of their poems I have read probably hundreds of times, and still never tire of reconfiguring in my mind's eye and ear. This is the only way that a poem, the short form, the lines not full, the page not full, can take on a novel. A successful poem, in my definition, is 'a machine for re-reading'. The sentences on my own things that have most pleased me saw them in just such terms: 'These poems stuck to me like a burr', or 'kept me up half the night'. Funny accolades, you might think, but their undertone of irritation, accusation and surprise authenticates them for me.

And how does it happen, if it happens? What makes some things exhaustible and others practically not? My own part of the answer – but of course everything to do with this is highly speculative anyway, a mixture of citing authorities (there are none), conjecture and metaphor – is to shift as much as I can into the language. To show the reader a scene, but also to show him *paint*. To engender in him, without distracting him from the realism of a given picture, an awareness that these are words. To give every appearance of straightahead uncomplicatedness, and then have the whole thing full of hooks and barbs, to use misprision, improbability and discord to delay and point and thicken speech. The poem, in hindsight, is the product of an "impossible voice". A common or garden line is actually a mosaic of magnets, charges and repulsions in every word. Translating a score of novels has taught me the futility of routine description – how little is transacted there. Poetry, a much smaller number than prose, must make itself endless by coming up with some recurring decimal or pattern of decimals. All this, of course, is merely an expansion of Gottfried Benn's belief that in writing the ability to fascinate the reader is a primary quality, and that everything else counts for not very much.

Otherwise, there is a process called annealment, the heating to a high temperature and slow cooling of glass or metal, to toughen them. Making a poem feels like that, writing as yourself and reading it back as someone else. Distance, perspective, irony, derision (terribly important!), all come into the picture. The poem acquires independence, the poet, in Montale's comparison, is like the props man who's stumbled upon it, 'unaware that he's / the author'.

# MICHAEL DONAGHY

Michael Donaghy was born in New York, 1954 into an Irish-American background, and educated at Fordham and Chicago University. He was poetry editor for *Chicago Review* and moved to London in 1985, where he is a freelance writer and musician. His first collection, *Shibboleth* (1988), won the Whitbread Prize for Poetry and the Geoffrey Faber Memorial Prize. His subsequent books are *Errata* (1993), *Conjure* (2000) and *Dances Learned Last Night: Poems 1975-1995* (2000). He is a Fellow of the Royal Society of Literature, and writes a kind of high formalism, laced with humour, eroticism, tragedy and allusion. His 'report card' is a witty ridicule of programmatic writing.

# My Report Card
## (2000)

1. '...a fidgety affectation of style after style which suggests that unlike more mature poets of his generation, Donaghy has not yet found his voice'. F. Olsen, 'Noted in Brief', *Hierophant*, Spring 1993.

2. Thales teaches that all things are full of gods. Anaximenes teaches that every stone on the beach has a soul. I'd certainly credit a page of poetry with a mind of its own. In our desire to locate the presence of the poet behind the frame of the words, we tend to animate the poem – the organic analogy – so it seems to be *returning* our attention, or we breathe life into its inanimate imagery – a marble torso of Apollo, London's mighty heart, a wafer lifted and consecrated.

3. Proust recalls his mother at Combray, how gracefully she'd turn a social blunder to her advantage 'like good poets whom the tyranny of rhyme forces into the discovery of their finest lines'. I'm in it for the discovery. If writing poems were merely a matter of bulldozing ahead with what you'd already made up your mind to say I'd have long ago given it up for something more dignified.

4. Must get round to reading 'The Feeling of a Presence and Verbal Meaningfulness in Context of Temporal Lobe Function: Factor Analytic Verification of the Muses?', Persinger, Michael, A.; Makarec, Katherine, *Brain and Cognition*, 1992, November, Vol. 20 (2): 217-26. Persinger and Makarec (to quote from the abstract) hypothesise that the profound sensation of a presence, particularly during periods of profound verbal creativity in reading

or writing prose or poetry, is an endemic cognitive phenomenon. Factor analyses of 12 clusters of phenomenological experiences from 348 men and 520 women (aged 18-65 years), who enrolled in undergraduate psychology courses over a ten-year period, supported the hypothesis. The authors conclude that periods of intense meaningfulness (a likely correlate of enhanced burst-firing in the left hippocampal-amygdaloid complex and temporal lobe) allow access to nonverbal representations that are the right hemispheric equivalents of the sense of self; they are perceived as a presence.

5. One morning in the 60s when I was queuing outside the confessional in church it impressed my adolescent soul that the adults milling about me were guilty of an original sin of arrogance, of assuming it was they and not the massed total of their experience that had sinned. One way to cope with such moments of vertigo is to experiment with different signatures, other voices. (See under 'poetry' and 'confessional', separate entries.)

6. Must look into forming some kind of movement and drafting a manifesto. Also, must try to be more direct. *Poetry's a way of thinking; a clarity between the truth of music and the truth.* See? No sooner are the words out but they turn to lead. It's embarrassing to talk about one's own poetry in prose, which may be why we have to endure so many poems about poetry.

7. Whenever I get the urge to write a poem about poetry I take a cold shower.

8. Which reminds me, MANIFESTOS ARE RIDICULOUS. Key scene: The mountainous silhouette of Charles Foster Kane emerging from behind the editor's desk waving his 'Declaration of Principles', and Jedidiah requesting the draft for a souvenir: 'I have a feeling it's going to be worth something one day,' he grins, 'like my first report card.'

9. 'the horror of the forest, or the silent thunder afloat in the leaves, not the intricate dense wood of the trees' (Mallarmé); 'a wind with a smell of children's spittle, crushed grass, and a jelly-fish veil which announces the constant baptism of newly created things' (Lorca).

10. Must try harder at sport.

# SELIMA HILL

Born in London in 1945, and educated at Cambridge, Selima Hill has lived on the Dorset coast for many years. Her style is idiosyncratic and highly original: humorous, erotic, anti-rational, at once worldly and domestic. She has won many admirers since the publication of her first volume *Saying Hello at the Station* in 1984, and *The Accumulation of Small Acts of Kindness* won first prize in the 1988 Arvon/Observer International Poetry Competition. Her later works – *A Little Book of Meat* (1993), *Trembling Hearts in the Bodies of Dogs: New & Selected Poems* (1994) and *Violet* (1997) – reflect the belief she outlines here, that a poem should be non-judgemental, but nevertheless just.

# Racoons – *or*, Can Art Be Evil?
## (2000)

Can Art be evil?

What can't writers say? Why not?

Does the writer have responsibilities?

Who knows? I will forgo some kind of lofty philosophical enquiry and look instead at what happens in practice. In my own practice as a poet. Not that I want to present my practice as a model, but, on the contrary, I am looking at it only in as much as it is the one that I know best.

Last week then, to give the most recent example, found me working on a poem very provisionally titled 'L.W.Rd.': Long, white road. I had started with a strong visual image, the long white road, and a strong emotional mood, a mood of extreme tenderness. I had a first person singular, 'I', and an old man, 'him', who was wearing a pair of tight uncomfortable shoes. The light was very bright. It was as if I was now walking into the poem and looking around.

On the linguistic level, I had two phrases that felt important: 'I carried him/to somewhere cool the sick like him call home,' with its short simple syllables, the consonants *s*, *c* and *h*, and the varying *o* sounds, and, the second phrase that felt significant, 'what can't be done by floating with the living.' I was engaged in a kind of mental knitting, working on getting the first phrase to reach and join up with the second phrase. It felt like translating a foreign language, of a text which was already there. Like translating Latin, in particular, where the sentences can be long and tortuous, and identifying even the subject and object can be an adventure.

At this stage, the aesthetic considerations seem to override any moral ones that might apply. I seem to be working with some kind of Truth, but one which is aesthetic or even spiritual rather than moral. With an ethic which is inclusive, expansive and celebratory rather than exclusive or proscriptive.

To return to the poem. I was having a problem with 'I' as the subject. I thought I wanted a strong female carrying a weak male but I kept getting stuck. I changed the 'I' to 'she', and, by abandoning the little island of 'me', immediately felt freer. Fiction, ironically, gave me more space in which to keep closer to the authenticity and energy of the original feeling. And the road began to fill up. With pilgrims, nurses, mothers with small children, swimming-pool attendants – all strong and compassionate people, who I called 'them'. Very quickly, 'I carried him' moved, via 'she carried him', which felt too sexual, to suddenly, 'they carried her'.

Aha! This felt like an enormous relief. As if a knot had at last come loose. And then – at the risk of sounding like someone gazing into a crystal ball – I was "getting", I was seeing, not a dark handsome stranger, but water-wings. The vivid orange of the plastic, the jolly buoyancy, the chubby shapes, their shininess, the way you breathe air into them, like someone giving the Kiss of Life, or embarking on some serious meditation, all seemed to give a sense of rising above something, of cherubs; a sense that there is kindness available somewhere in our world. This felt good. And I finished the poem easily and happily.

Analysing the experience later, I became aware of my need to forgive an abusive man, as in 'I carried him'. And it made me aware of a greater need – the need to be forgiven, and feel supported, myself. As in 'they carried her'. Now this may be naive, even dotty, and anyway irrelevant, but certainly the experience of working on the poem, subjectively, for me as the writer, struggling along the long white road to the blue swimming-pool, felt good. Good, I mean, as a moral rather than a literary value.

Let me then return as reader to the poem.

After a poem is finished, usually several weeks after, I will return to it with, as it were, a searchlight, and sweep across it like a guard in a watch-tower. What am I looking for – as, now, the reader, rather than the writer of the piece?

First of all, I am judging it as an integrated and authentic aesthetic whole. I listen to the music without the sense. I see it in terms of colour – in the poem in question, a vibrant Prussian Blue with Burnt Sienna in the middle distance, lit by a bright light. At this level aesthetic considerations, mysterious as they are, certainly seem to override moral or social ones.

But people live, after all, as Lalic has pointed out, 'neither with Beauty nor with Truth but with other people'. If it is not going to be read by anyone else, I am free to put down whatever I want, even though I may not know why I want it. Once it is considered as published material, however, I will look beyond the aesthetic to, secondly, the literal and conceptual – what does it mean? Does it matter? Where are we? What does the reader want? Croatia, Paddington, wildfowling? Why the shoes?

Thirdly, the morals of the thing. Is it libellous? Is anyone's reputation going to suffer? Or their feelings? (I am aware that there is no space for other people to defend themselves.) Is it pornographic, sexist, racist? Will it incite people to violence? Is it plagiarised material? Am I exploiting someone else's work, or life?

Or might it, on the other hand, have a positive (morally "good") effect?

By acting as a witness, for instance. By saying things other people, for whatever reason, cannot say. Acknowledging difficult feelings, secrets and lies, epiphanies. Examining what it means to be alive. By granting the reader, as a friend once put it, 'the luxury of recognising what it's like to accept humanity'. By helping the reader to slow down; take stock; listen. To feel the beauty at the heart of things.

It is not the place of art to draw conclusions or even to understand. On the contrary, isn't the whole point that it is non-judgemental? that it undermines the making of value judgements? And yet, at the same time, is just. It is modest, helpless, useless, but at the same time determined, and just. I think of Heaney's phrase – 'to set the darkness echoing' – where darkness is what it is, and we neither flinch nor sink. Or Harrison's 'lighting a lantern in a hurricane'. And can a lantern be a bad thing?

In as much as I believe, therefore, that art is a kind of witness or honouring produced from a kind of love, I rather naively believe that you can't go wrong. And that it's worth a try. Who knows? 'Since we do float,' as Elizabeth Bishop puts it in a letter to Robert Lowell in the 60s, 'since we do float on an unknown sea I think we should examine the other floating things that come our way very carefully; who knows what might depend on it? So I am enclosing a clipping about racoons.'

# SARAH MAGUIRE

Sarah Maguire was born in 1957 in West London, and educated at the universities of East Anglia and Cambridge. She has published two collections of poems, *Spilt Milk* (1991) and *The Invisible Mender* (1997), and her tone is both confessional and erotically charged in its conveyance of what she describes here as the 'intimacy of experience'. She was the first writer to be sent to both Palestine and Yemen by the British Council and is co-translating the poems of the Palestinian poet, Zakaria Mohammed. A trained gardener, she is editor of *A Garden Inclosed: The Chatto Book of Botanical Verse*, due for publication in 2001.

# Poetry Makes Nothing Happen
## (2000)

Anyone visiting Palestine should be warned that you'll be in for lavish attention from Israeli security at Tel Aviv airport on the way home. The interrogation techniques employed on friends of mine range from tipping all your goods and chattels – including (opened) toiletries – onto the floor five minutes before your flight's due, to threats of your elderly aunt (sick with cancer) being strip-searched if you don't reveal the names of 'local people' attending a dinner party in Ramallah. So you can imagine how much I was looking forward to this parting encounter following my first visit to Palestine in September 1996 (which coincided with the terrible violence that erupted as a result of the Israelis opening the tunnel in Jerusalem under the Al-Aqsa Mosque).

It was four in the morning. I smiled helpfully at the plump student earning extra cash who'd been assigned the happy task of asking me what I'd been up to in 'Judea and Samaria' (we don't mention the P-word here) during the troubles. I showed him my letter from the British Council explaining the purpose of my visit (I was the first writer to be sent to Palestine by the BC). 'So, what is your profession?' he asked me. 'I'm a poet.' 'A poet!', he exclaimed with unprofessional enthusiasm. 'I love poetry, especially English poetry. I really admire your W.H. Auden. Do you like Auden?' 'Yes I do,' I said. 'I particularly admire…' And my mind went blank. Well, almost blank. Standing in Tel Aviv airport in the small hours of the morning undergoing Israeli interrogation, the only line of Auden's I could remember was, 'Poetry makes nothing happen'.

'Poetry makes nothing happen' is the fear that haunts all poets,[1] particularly those of us who live in the West, where poetry so often seems to be some kind of arcane, elitist, exclusive entertainment for the over-educated. What on earth is the point of writing poetry? Especially the kind of post-Romantic lyric poetry endorsed by the literary establishment that I find myself engaged in producing. And particularly if your formative years, like mine, were spent crying over Gramsci's *Prison Notebooks* in the small hours,[2] if exciting weekend outings were anti-fascist demonstrations, and when love blossomed during plenary sessions of bad-tempered conferences scuppered by the Sparticist League (remember them?).

I'm sure you can work out exactly why my unconscious had decided to let that little line of verse pop into my worn-out, strip-lit, anxious brain at that particular moment. Having spent all my working life struggling with Auden's assertion, I now found my-self in a situation where I was rather hoping his statement would be read at face value and treated as gospel, where being engaged in translating Palestinian poetry could be construed merely as an eccentric literary foible – and could I go home now, please?

But what was Auden really saying? Was the man who wrote 'Spain 1937' actually implying that poetry is truly pointless? The troublesome line in question is taken from the second part of Auden's poem 'In Memory of W.B. Yeats (*d. Jan. 1939*)', which continues,

> it survives
> In the valley of its own making where executives
> Would never want to tamper, flows on south
> From ranches of isolation and the busy griefs,
> Raw towns that we believe and die in; it survives,
> A way of happening, a mouth.

Despite the fact that poetry 'makes nothing happen', Auden argues that it still, 'survives' – even though it doesn't seem to have much impact in the public, business world. Instead, poetry occupies the real places we inhabit, the places we believe and die in, places which are solitary and often sad. But more important is the very end of that section: having told us that 'poetry *makes* nothing happen', Auden says that poetry, instead, survives as *a way of happening*, a mouth.

What I think Auden is arguing in 'In Memory of W.B. Yeats' is that we're fundamentally wrong if we expect poetry to have a *function*, to change things in the way that political actions can change things. If we ask poetry to be political in a vulgar sense then we end up with vulgar answers and vulgar poetry – specifically vulgar Marxist answers and Stalinist poetry which, as we know, in practice means lots of hymns to the valiant workers and diatribes about tractors and wheat: the kind of poetry that isn't poetry at all, but propaganda.

But, if poetry doesn't have a political function as such, does this mean that we have to adopt a high-art position about it, one that would argue that it lives in a hermetically-sealed aesthetic realm of its own, immune to history and politics, a form of decoration to get us through the extremes of 21st century anomie? This art-for-art's-sake argument stems from the same philosophical misapprehension, the same paradigm, which clings onto a reductive function for poetry. One says that poetry *must* have a political function. The other that it *can't* have a political function. The problem, of course, is with the notion of *function*. Both of these linked positions view poetry teleologically, examining it from the perspective of what's perceived to be its final ends: entertainment or revolution.

Instead, Auden tells us that poetry is 'a way of happening, a mouth.' A way of being in the world, of speaking in silence. Something far less tangible, more complex and troublesome than executives would want to bother with. But how – and why – does the radical, committed poet write lyric poetry if that poetry doesn't *make* things happen? How could poetry be a *way* of happening? Of course, all the way through I've been talking about lyric poetry, poetry which, as the American critic Helen Vendler points out, 'must start as the self's concentration of itself into words'.[3] Of all literary genres, lyric poetry is the most subjective, personal and private. And if we think of subjectivity as something secret and individual, separated from history and society and politics, then there's every chance for lyric poetry to be conservative, costive, narcissistic and smug. But if we understand that, as Jacqueline Rose puts it, 'There is no history outside its subjective realisation…just as there is no subjectivity uncoloured by the history to which it belongs',[4] this special focus on the self can be lyric poetry's most radical strength. 'The personal,' as that definitive feminist statement has it, 'is political.'

In his wonderful essay, 'The Hour of Poetry', John Berger talks about the 'labour of poetry' being connected with its 'intimacy'. It's precisely because the poem can render the most intimate and elusive of subjective experiences in language that it's able to bear witness to what's excluded from dominant discourses. For example, of all the information I've imbibed since adolescence about the First World War in films, novels, photographs and documentaries, it's still Wilfred Owen's poems about gas in the trenches that haunt me most powerfully, their intimate terror being a more visceral and effective attack on 'the old Lie'[5] than any amount of pacifist pleading, any number of horrifying statistics. It's the sheer, stubborn memorability of Owen's language, the way he draws on so many disparate discourses (from polemical anger to 'unspeakable' pain) in such a small space, which allows him to articulate experience which is at once profoundly subjective and politically resonant in all its gravid, lived reality. Yet although Owen's war poems are responding to a major historical event, thus imbuing his work with a particular urgency (lives are at stake), this fusion of the elusively subjective with the implacably material is not solely confined to this handful of poems: the smallest and most seemingly 'personal' lyric can also be capable of unsettling the given order of the world through speaking of speechless desire or loss.

It's not only lyric poetry's committed exploration of the intimacy of experience which can make it such an effective 'way of happening' but its employment of metaphor – which in Greek means 'to transfer, to carry, to bear' – as its defining methodology. The 'self's *concentration* of itself into words' is achieved through metaphor. Using metaphor, the poet can transfer elements which, in ordinary life, are kept apart, thus melding incidents and details together, ignoring – as Owen does, as all good poets do – the logic of metonymical progression, the logic of separation. As John Berger puts it,

> Every authentic poem contributes to the labour of poetry...to bring together what life has separated or violence has torn apart...Poetry can repair no loss, but it defies the space which separates. And it does this by its continual labour of reassembling what has been scattered.[6]

This, then, is poetry's labour: to bring together, carry, transfer pieces of language that have been torn apart, decontextualised and placed in different categories (subjective/objective; personal/political). And it does this through the figure of the intimate self (the invisible mender). A way of happening. A mouth.

*With thanks to Biyi Bandele, John Berger and Jamie McKendrick*

## NOTES

1. Well, I'd like to think it's the fear that haunts all poets.
2. Tears of frustration, I'm sorry to report.
3. Helen Vendler, *The Music of What Happens: Poems, Poets, Critics* (London and Cambridge, Massachusetts: Harvard University Press, 1988), 378.
4. Jacqueline Rose, *The Haunting of Sylvia Plath* (London: Virago, 1991), 8.
5. 'The old Lie: Dulce et decorum est / Pro patria mori' from 'Dulce Et Decorum Est'.
6. John Berger, 'The Hour of Poetry', in *The Sense of Sight: Writings by John Berger*, edited and introduced by Lloyd Spencer (New York: Vintage, 1993), 249. Think of this definition next to Dr Johnson's famous description of metaphysical imagery consisting of 'heterogeneous ideas...yoked by violence together'.

# SIMON ARMITAGE

Witty, sardonic, tough-talking, matter-of-factly lyrical, Simon Armitage is, in the words of one contemporary, the 'priest of a generation' who more than anyone reflects the spirit and accessibility of contemporary British poetry. He was born in Huddersfield in 1963 and lives in nearby Marsden; he studied Geography at Portsmouth Polytechnic and worked for many years as a probation officer. The publication of *Zoom!* (1989) marked Armitage as an original and distinctive talent, and an unlikely meeting of O'Hara, MacNeice and the M62. His subsequent collections include *Xanadu* (1992), *Kid* (1992), *Book of Matches* (1993), *The Dead Sea Poems* (1995), *CloudCuckooLand* (1997) and his millennium poem, *Killing Time* (1999). He edited *The Penguin Book of Poetry from Britain and Ireland since 1945* (1998) with Robert Crawford, and has also published a poets' memoir of Iceland with Glyn Maxwell (*Moon Country*, 1996), a book of prose writings (*All Points North*, 1998), and a version of Euripides (*Mister Herecles*, 2000).

# Re-Writing the Good Book
## (2000)

There's an old idea still doing the rounds, about how to beat the Christmas card racket. Instead of sending cards to friends and family every December, wouldn't it be better to exchange the same cards each year, thus saving a great deal of trouble and expense. Here's how the scheme would works. In the first instance, party X sends card A to party Y, and party Y sends card B to party X. The following year, X writes a new message in card B and returns it to Y, and Y reciprocates with card A. And so on, and so forth. The card becomes a record of the relationship, its style and design being redolent of the era in which the relationship was formed. The collection of cards held by a person at any one time also serves as a ready-made Christmas card list, and best of all, new messages must be composed, to avoid repetition of the usual Yuletide blandishments and platitudes. Of course the Christmas card companies don't like it very much. In a management brainstorming session at Hallmark, some aspiring executive christens it the Scrooge-system, and the insult is marketed through the lifestyle sections of weekly magazines. Also, charities lose out on shed-loads of easy money, but as we all know, the responsibility for the less fortunate is primarily a matter for government.

Most people who hear of the scheme appear convinced and

impressed by it, and if the idea appeals for several good reasons, three are particularly relevant to this argument. Firstly, humanity is still moved by short, heartfelt messages of a poetic nature, and in the age of language overload, probably more moved by this kind of communication than any other. Secondly, handwriting transmits a raw, primitive charge, providing a direct link with the author otherwise lost through print. And thirdly, the true and original artefact is possessed with an incomparable and undeniable magic that no kind of facsimile can imitate or match.

Poetry seems to be in pretty good shape at the moment. Between generations, it fluctuates between hibernation and hyperactivity, sometimes lying dormant and introspective, and sometimes taking its arguments out onto the streets, trying to engage and persuade ordinary people of its worth and meaning. At the extremes, it risks a state of complete and irreversible coma on the one hand, and the embarrassment and shame of going totally over the top on the other; but between those peaks and troughs it continues to exist. There is, however, a vision of poetry, based on the Christmas card system, that would transform poetry into a front-line art form for the next century, a vision that points the finger at poetry's current underlying problem: the book.

In this new scenario, as well as being a language-based art, poetry would also be a visual art, and instead of hundreds, thousands or even millions of copies of a poem, there would be one only. The original. Of course, the poem might well be appear in books and other media, but only in the way in which, say, *The Angel of the North* has been made familiar to us, through image reproduction and description. In the new order, an original poem would be the artwork itself. A re-printed poem would carry the same creative kudos as the poster of the girl with the tennis ball up her knickers, and the same value as a photocopied fiver.

Most poets think hard about their work already, but from now on, poetic composition would also take into account the actual craft of producing the poem, be it handwritten, typed, painted, carved, installed, recorded, or whatever. There would be no limit to the ways in which a poem could be fashioned or fabricated, and a poem would remain in the public consciousness as a picture containing words, not simply as text. Recitation would be the only other method of transmission or manifestation, and the new emphasis on a poem's unique appearance would certainly assist in the learning of a poem by heart. The new poetry, combining both art and language, could become the single most important cultural signifier of the 21st century.

Of course, I'm describing a vision of the future, but if it were a desirable vision, the process could be accelerated. Poetry publishing would have to be banned, or discredited, or deemed unfashionable so as to avoid the emergence of underground presses. Putting sentiment to one side, the publishing of children's poetry would be particularly prohibited, since a new and uncorrupted breed of audience would be crucial to the success of the project. Audience would replace readership. As for finance, sales and commission would replace royalties and advances. A good poem would be extravagantly rewarded, an ordinary poem would be judged in the same light as a local watercolour. The most revered poets would be those who could work with their hands and their voices, as well as their brains. Millions would pass through the turnstiles of the National Poetry Gallery each year, standing wide-eyed before the latest sonnets. Thousands would attend every important live event – like recitations combined with exhibitions or unveilings – and would look, listen, read, remember, and learn.

So, the notion can be stretched to an absurd conclusion, but there are however, a number of serious points arising and extending from this fantasy. Firstly, bookish people imagine themselves as purists, but are actually perverts, belonging to a deviant culture. The appropriation of poetry by the literati can be quite properly compared with the enclosure of common land in England, the Highland Clearances and the hijacking of ancient medicine by Western science. We should never be surprised by the way in which the privileged minorities eventually take control of every valuable commodity, but how much more exciting it would have been if poetry had been commandeered by people who did more than sit at home with their thumbs up their arses. Poetry continually runs the risk of being unexciting because of its continual attempts to appeal to unexciting people – people who enjoy reading – an essentially passive, silent and solitary activity.

Secondly, print has the effect of standardising and neutralising its subject. Imagine the impact of a poem whose texture was that of a Rothko canvas, or a Henry Moore bronze, or a Hendrix riff. Too many poems are simply one-dimensional descriptions of themselves; we need to think more about the primary aspects of the poetic product, and to equip it with as many of its maker's intentions as physically possible. And thirdly, related to that point, poetry needs to restrict those practitioners who seek to encourage admirers without actually meeting them, preferring to hide behind the barrier of a dust jacket and within the anonymity of print. More shirtiness and less shiftiness, please. Accountability should be the new watchword, with more readings, and more contact and interplay between poet and audience. More bold statements and less whispered asides are required, if poetry is to avoid becoming the preferred medium for those who choose to make snide remarks from behind their hands or under their breath, or from somewhere beyond the covers of a book.

Books, let us remind ourselves, are not the true and everlasting home of poetry. Literature and books are inseparable, but poetry pre-dates the book, pre-dates the alphabet even, and should not be content with its current format. If it was premature to be talking about the death of the book, it is now passé to be talking about the death of the book as premature. Only the most bespectacled antiquarian could seriously envisage a book-reading culture still going strong in 500 years' time, but poetry, in some other guise, will surely persist. Poetry should look to its core and elemental strengths before its next metamorphosis; hopefully any future incarnation will be something more vital and exotic than the dry and humble book.

Merry Christmas, and a happy New Year.

# GLYN MAXWELL

Born in 1962 of Welsh parentage, Glyn Maxwell grew up in Welwyn Garden City, and studied at Oxford and Boston University (the latter under Derek Walcott). His first three collections *Tale of the Mayor's Son* (1990), *Out of the Rain* (1992) and *Rest for the Wicked* (1995) – collected in *The Boys at Twilight: Poems 1990-1995* (2000) – were followed by *The Breakage* (1998) and *Time's Fool* (USA 2000, UK 2001), and his output includes two books of verse drama and a novel, *Blue Burneau* (1994). His poetry has been described by Sean O'Brien as both 'highly elaborated' and 'obtrusive': formal, rhythmic, conspiratorial and Audenesque (with Simon Armitage, he recreated Auden and MacNeice's trip to Iceland in *Moon Country*, 1996). His interruptive use of syntax, in particular, is so sophisticated that, in Joseph Brodsky's description, Maxwell draws 'metaphor from the syntax itself'. 'Strictures' is a powerful defence of formalism in which he writes of poetry as a structured body, whose rhythm should modulate around the monotony of the average heartbeat.

# Strictures
### (2000)

Poetry is an utterance of the body. Not the best utterance – which is pre-linguistic and made of salt water – but the best a body can do, given it has language. It is the language in thrall to the corporeal, to the pump and procession of the blood, the briefly rising spirit of the lung, the nerves' fretwork, strictures of the bone. Poetry is matter that can string itself between the pulse of a life and the silence of its death. The best of it has ends nailed to both: its spaces recall the original and final absence; its marks convey the tremor and burden of the respiring span. To read the true poem, the surviving poem, aloud is to express the very shape of a self, to sound it. Poetry is decoration of the breath with stirrings of the mind.

Those who reject form in poetry reject form in body. What they do is alien to what's human. There is no other reason readers have delighted in form. What a reader perceives in formal poetry is kind, likeness, echo of existing. To make things without echo, evading likeness, or in no spirit of kind, is a lightless quest. To study to do so is perverse, wanton, defeated. Those few poets who have prospered without formal structure of some kind show an atten-tiveness to the space, the whiteness, the loss, the silence that is as keen as that shown by more conventional poets to the language, the beat, the life, and the warmth. No good poet has ever been equipped to marshal the emptiness who has not first mastered the sound. Those we term great – if we still allow ourselves to tell wine from water – are attuned to both.

A good poem is strung upon a version of itself that is mechanical, fixed, monotonous; one that obeys an average heartbeat, clockwork breath, steady blood, measured footfall. Some readers like their actual poems that way: they prefer a lullaby to a story. The sturdiest model in English poetry is the iambic pentameter. (Some deride it, perhaps because they believe it was spoken in previous times and is therefore archaic, like monarchy or castles. Some believe its primacy is a historical accident. But then some write poems that intend no meaning; some write poems that mean to be forgotten.) Merely take the iambic pentameter for an example. Its regularity shadows the poem: something must shadow the poem, and that something must in some way make the sound of the body at rest, so that the body in thought, the body at play, when it is heard can be believed. A poem that plays on nothing plays on unfixed strings, makes nothing because it doesn't seem to be bodily work. It may amuse, may concern, may be challenging to the mind, but if it doesn't in some way replicate or recall the experience of itself being considered, it requires a label other than poetry. And the experience of thought is a rhythmic one, because the experience of consciousness is rhythmic. The most deep-striking thought may pause the breath, but in doing so it can quicken the heart – then the breath that ends it, or divides it in two, is forceful, audible, and demands expression. If it is cut out of the experience, erased, glossed, thought insignificant, then the experience has not survived transmission as language. Poetry should combine the look of the light that hits the mind with the physical feeling of undergoing that contact: should express both what moves and how it moves. If the poem is all about the light itself, we may find it hard to share in the feeling; but if the personal feeling is all, we may wonder at it, shrug, and turn away, knowing nothing about the light. And of course the monotonous figure beneath the poem, the wooden instrument on which it plays, may be all manner of things: iambic pentameter is merely English's 4/4.

The ways of departing from the figure, the metronome, are infinite. They are mathematically calculable only on paper, where syllables, vowels and consonants can be herded into generalised dimensions. But generalised dimensions are not the case. The distances between words are greater in the air than on the page: the difference is akin to that of the two-dimensional and the three-dimensional. King Lear's five consecutive utterances of the word 'never' over the dead Cordelia are five different words, remote as continents. On the tongue, in the voice, at the ear, distances are of infinite number, giddying, incalculable. This means that the master of metrical form is the master of all human voice. Just as the master of line- and stanza-break is the master of all absence. But only four centuries after Shakespeare it feels strange to need to say this. The most positive poetic achievement of the 20th century was not the breaking of the pentameter to serve contemporary discomfort, but the remastering of it to serve contemporary breath. The true revolutionary is Frost, whose lines most closely approximate the meeting of breath and thought, and whose silences are beyond anyone's in kind and depth.

Frost's is a poetry that knows so much, and only so much. Contemporary poets can know little more: the perimeter of what they know must make its presence felt – literally – in the verse, the little gasp at the wood's edge, the wordlessness before starlight. The arrogance of the contemporary poetic theorist is Victorian, the notion of Poetic Understanding as ever-advancing. The word 'poetries' is its oriflamme. The arrogance of obscurity is medieval, is of the cloister. Obscurity cannot be poetry because the body is not obscure. Obscurity in verse is language taking leave of its senses. It may be interesting, it may be exciting, but only until we need oxygen. The body will remember only what it needs. It will reject what doesn't sound like body. It will not care for it, or protect it from time.

# JOHN BURNSIDE

John Burnside was born in Fife in 1955 and returned there in 1996, having worked for many years in the computer industry. From the publication of his first collection, *The hoop* (1989), he has established a lyrical style that is spiritual, mystical and quasi-religious – themes clearly reflected in his statement here, in which he writes that poetry (and in particular, the love lyric) is a form of spiritual anointment, a metaphysical rite-of-passage. Among his subsequent books are five poetry collections, including *The Myth of the Twin* (1994), *A Normal Skin* (1996) and *The Asylum Dance* (2000), and fiction titles including *Angels and Animals* and *Burning Elvis*.

# Strong Words
### (2000)

I was first drawn to poetry as an instrument and a discipline, a means by which I might discover what I knew about myself and the world; thus, from the beginning, I felt that my own work was always and necessarily provisional, and so, philosophical. The subjects which interested me were: what is "real" (as opposed to merely factual, i.e. "true"); what is the relationship between self and other (and why do we feel obliged to make such a distinction); and what do we mean when we talk about the spirit. Having said this, I am dismayed by the common misapprehension that a poet who makes such a choice – the choice of a quest, as it were, as opposed to a settlement – has no political or social interests or usefulness. Does the "message" of a poem have to be crude (rather than subtle) or clever (rather than intelligent) to be taken into account?

From the beginning, I was interested in the spirit. If I am convinced of anything, I am convinced that it is essential to live *as a spirit*. By this, I do not intend anything religious, in the orthodox, or indeed, in any other sense. Clarification might come from saying that, to the extent that we can speak of such things at all, I would say that we are not born *with* a spirit (as we are born with lungs, or a heart), but it is our peculiar gift to live *as* spirits, by an imaginative (or magical, or alchemical) process: an *inventio*, by which we create ourselves from moment to moment, just as the world around us creates itself out of nothing. For myself, poetry is the discipline by which I live, and the means by which I articulate this process. Thus, for me, poetry is a form of alchemy.

In asserting the importance of alchemical thinking, I do not intend to be in any way anti-rational. A reasoned, functional view of the world (Confucianism, as it were) is vital; by itself, however, it is not enough, and can lead to reductive thinking. I would only say that such a view must be moderated by the spiritual, by which I mean a way of thinking both reverent and inventive in its vision of nature (and so, of necessity, of the other). There is no doubt that, as persons, we live in a set place and time (we belong to a culture and a society); as spirits, however, we also live in eternity, and are stateless. As spirits, we have no special interests; we are not interested in winning so much as playing. We belong, as it were, to the game itself. Our response to the world is essentially one of wonder, of confronting the mysterious with a sense, not of being small, or insignificant, but of being part of a rich and complex narrative.

In this sense, the lyrical impulse begins at the point of self-forgetting.

The lyrical experience centres a human being in his or her world in a spiritual way, and this spiritual centring (or its absence) precedes and defines the social and political life of a person and of a social group. The making of a world – of *home* – is determined by the spirit which the participants bring to the process. The right way to dwell is to constantly examine the making of home: where and what are its bounds? how do we belong there? what do we consume, and what do we have the right to consume in this place? The just answer to these questions can arise only from a spiritually rich life, and I believe that the activity of the poet might contribute to this spiritual richness in a number of ways. There are poets who invoke Wittgenstein's famous dictum, 'Of that whereof one cannot speak, one must remain silent', contenting themselves with the social, the descriptive, the partisan-political pronouncement – that closed form of writing, in which the mystery of the world is refused out of a fear of seeming lost for words (or artless). With all due respect to Wittgenstein, however, I would set against his (much misunderstood) remark, an observation made by Heidegger, in his essay, *The Origins of the Work of Art*. Here, he reminds us of the importance of language to the new way of thinking that we must discover in order to dwell meaningfully in the world. And he continues:

> Projective saying is poetry: the saying of world and earth, the saying of the arena of their strife and thus of the place of all nearness and remoteness of the gods. Poetry is the saying of the unconcealment of beings. Actual language at any given moment is the happening of this saying, in which a people's world historically arises for it and the earth

is preserved as that which remains closed. Projective saying is saying which, in preparing the sayable, simultaneously brings the unsayable as such into the world.

Recently, I have come to the conclusion (all conclusions being provisional, it need hardly be said) that the poem in its ideal form, the paradigm poem, as it were, is the love poem – by which I mean, not a specific form of address, but a kind of privileged and entirely disinterested invocation, something almost abstract. For we become most aware of ourselves as spirits when we love. When we love – as when we write – we cease to be conditioned social existences, and emerge into being. So the best love poems are also philosophical, continually reminding us that there is a huge chasm between the ways in which we are identified in our everyday transactions and the ways in which love describes us. At the most fundamental level, love calls us back from the realm of the merely factual to the mystery of the real. This is the true function of the love poem: to remind us of who we are, and who we are capable of being: while our everyday social roles define us as persons, love reminds us that we are also spirits.

Finally, the lyric, and especially the love poem, reminds us that "outward" life is about a certain form of limitation, a defeat of sorts. The lyric says there is a possibility for every sentient being to experience the opposite of that defeat, which is not, of course, victory (defeat and victory being equally illusory) but transcendence of the idea of victory-defeat, in life as a spirit. But in what does this life consist? Simply a quest, a journey, leading away from the social demand for persons and towards the self-renewing continuing invention (*inventio*) of the spirit. For me, poetry is both the account of, and the map by which I navigate my path on this journey and, as such, is an ecological discipline of the richest and subtlest kind. In this sense, writing is thus a political act: one which expresses, not the agendas of special interest groups, but the search for an appropriate manner of dwelling upon the earth.

# ROBERT CRAWFORD

Born in Bellshill 1959 and educated at Glasgow and Oxford, Robert Crawford is Professor of Modern Scottish Literature at St Andrews. His critical work includes studies of Eliot, Alasdair Gray and Edwin Morgan (who has been an inspiration to his own poetry), and he edited *The Penguin Book of Poetry from Britain and Ireland since 1945* (1998) with Simon Armitage. Like MacDiarmid, Crawford's poetry was initially engaged with the assembly of a Scots poetic language (*Sharawaggi*, with W.N. Herbert, 1990), although the bulk of his later work chooses English as its dominant tongue, and frequently explores the clash of emotional and technological worlds (*A Scottish Assembly*, 1990; *Talkies*, 1992; *Masculinity*, 1996; *Spirit Machines*, 1999). This play between 'centrality and marginality', as he dubs it here, is what bonds Crawford's fiercely intelligent verse into such a positive affirmation of life.

# Cosmopolibackofbeyondism
### (2000)

Cosmopolibackofbeyondism is a creed with a wink in it. Poetry's obsessions – love, death, God, sound, silence – travel across times and cultures; nothing could be more cosmopolitan. At the same time, verse is a marginal act, operating way out at the back of beyond, at the limits of what can be said. Its centrality and marginality are bonded.

Every poem is an island. To get to a poem requires sailing out from the mainland of routine language. Some poems are close to shore, others much further away; on every island it is possible to feel remote and at home. A poem is defined by the rugged shore of its right-hand margin, cutting it off from prose. Yet just as any poem-island has the tang of the back of beyond, it has, too, aspects, shared speech-forms, political shapes, faiths, which link it to other places. All poems are connected, most simply through the shared cosmopolis of verse.

'Verse' means 'turning'. Some of the ancients likened verse to the movement of oxen as they ploughed a furrow, then wheeled round to plough the next. In this sense every maker of verse is a plough-man poet, breaking open a field of silence. On its little journey, each verse line leads silence into sound, sound into silence. Unlike prose, verse marks a birth and death between every line and the next. Any line, at its centre, its wee acoustic cosmopolis, is moving from margin to margin, sea to sea. It is alert to the back of beyond.

Line-breaks are the fundamental act of patterning in a poem, the one on which all other patterns depend. To write in two-line stanzas readily heightens this; there's not just a turn from line to line, but every second line there's a bigger intrusion of the margin, a firth flowing into the poem. Poems should be read aloud, their margins heeded, but even in silence the breaking of lines constitutes the life of verse. Borges wrote, 'Beyond the rhythm of a line of verse, its typographical arrangement serves to tell the reader that it's poetic emotion, not information or rationality, that he or she should expect.' The poetic line signals a kind of magical interference with the prose world of daily transactions.

Yet, precisely because poetry involves a playing with expectations, it is a gleeful thing to make the informational part of poetic emotion. Opposites attract. The enduring, backofbeyondish, sacred aspects of verse must be fused with, though not lost in, the available language and textures of the age. The textures of our era's language are informational.

In that sense we have all become cosmopolitan, but unless poets can also dwell at the back of beyond, they cannot respond to the full spectrum of words. Bound up with international, cosmopolitan English lingo are colorations peculiar to local microclimates. Dialect, backofbeyondisms, jargons of science and information must all be heard. Poets should be simultaneously central and marginal, to such a degree that it is no longer clear which is which.

One of the most revealing lines of English poetry is Donne's iambic pentameter

I wonder by my troth, what thou, and I

which places the self, the 'I', at the margins, at the alpha and omega of the line. 'My troth' at the line's heart is not really the central 'troth' of betrothal, but, revealingly, something throwaway. Centre and margins have changed place; the ego, so crucial to this poem, is also peripheral, way out at each end of the line. Less egotistically, and more movingly, Ben Jonson opens a poem

Farewell, thou child of my right hand, and joy;

where, subtly but significantly, the first syllable tolls more loudly than usual in an iambic pentameter. In sound and feeling this line to Jonson's dead young son is weighed down at start and finish. In each case these poets let their line-ends resonate into the margins beyond, so that the extremities are at least as important as the centre. The lines are acoustically devolved.

Patron saints of Cosmopolibackofbeyondism are many. Hugh

MacDiarmid is one of them. Developing the cosmological imagination of his great Scots and English verse while living in Montrose, then on Whalsay in the Shetlands, he fused vernacular and highbrow, galaxy and doorstep. He presented his vision of a new Scottish modernist poetry to the local YMCA. He saw the impossible, then did it.

More and more as the margins and centres of language, politics, and gender are smudged, Cosmopolibackofbeyondism beckons. To sound its music is to love all language, remaining true to our electronic global present at the same time as keeping faith with local, theological, vernacular, and aureate values. The balance between verse's newness and antiquity is as necessary and impossible as its juggling between centre and margin. Ultimately, poetry thrives on impossibilities and takes them as its most urgent language, its way of saying something new or anew. Philosophy, journalism, and "the media" ultimately distrust the unique medium of verse. They want to erode its all-seeing, mediumistic uniqueness, paraphrasing it in terms more packageably familiar. Poetry, so central to human experience, always tends to gravitate beyond the end of the line. The poet winkingly truncates Wittgenstein: 'About which we cannot speak we must.'

# GWYNETH LEWIS

Gwyneth Lewis was born in Cardiff in 1959, studied at Cambridge and Columbia, and after working for many years as a documentary film-maker is now a freelance writer and lecturer. She is bilingual, and has published two collections in English and three in Welsh, *Sonedau Redsa* (1990), *Cyrif Un ac Un yn Dri* (1996) and *Y Llofrudd Iaith* (1999), a detective story in verse. *Parables & Faxes* (1995), her first English-language volume, was much praised for its formalist style and wit; *Zero Gravity* (1998), her second, has confirmed her status as the new flag bearer for Anglo-Welsh poetry. And it is that bilingualism – and in particular the art of translation – that she examines here. Her dilemma as to how to represent a 'dying language' is seen as relating profoundly to poetry as a whole, and its interactions with an indifferent world.

# Whose Coat is that Jacket? Whose Hat is that Cap?
## (THE ART OF DEEP TRANSLATION)
### (1995/2000)

If you're truly bilingual it's not that there are two languages in your world, but that not everybody understands the whole of your own personal speech. Let me explain. Welsh is my first language. I was born to a Welsh-speaking family living in predominantly English-speaking Cardiff. I remember not being able to understand the children I wanted to play with on the street. I know exactly when I acquired English, as my father taught it to me when my mother went into hospital to have my sister. I was two and a quarter.

Let me give you a quick cultural outline. The Welsh language: a Celtic tongue which has, against all the odds, found itself in the modern world, coining words for 'television' and 'fast reactor fuel rods'. Half a million speakers, numbers in decline – it's an "all hands on deck" situation. A beautiful language, and to speak it is to know the sound of a long, unbearable farewell. It's the key to a literature which goes back to the 6th century. One of the noteworthy features of this tradition is a system of strict consonantal alliteration codified into 24 metres and called *cynghanedd*. Basically, the line gets divided in half and the consonants on each side of the break have to be used in the same order. That is, when the line's not divided into three and rhyme added to the cocktail. Have a look at this when you're in crossword-puzzle mode – it's good fun. Gerard Manley Hopkins used it and Dylan Thomas certainly had the sound of the *cynghanedd* ringing in his ears as he wrote in English.

Of course, living in a largely English-speaking city, Welsh was handy as a private language for us. We used it as a family code – to avoid the scrutiny of over-bearing sales ladies in the shops. In school – I was educated till the age of 18 through the medium of the Welsh – we switched languages mid-sentence when teachers appeared, to avoid punishment for speaking English. People have often asked me: am I a different person speaking English and Welsh? I always answer no, but what is different, of course, is the cultural context in which the words are spoken. When these political values clash the cultural sensitivities can be acute. For example, you can buy matches with the slogan 'England's Glory' written on the side of the box. 'Got your matches ready?' is an innocent enough sentence in English. But in Welsh, against the background of an arson campaign run by nationalists who've been burning down second homes owned by the English in the Welsh heartland, the question 'Ydi dy fatsys di'n barod?' takes on a totally different tenor. The words are the same, but the meaning totally different.

I had a sense of the cultural traps involved in being bilingual very early on. But I also knew it could lead to excitements that rarely came the way of my monoglot friends. A primary school teacher I had at about aged six once told us a story about young Tommy who didn't practise his English reading. One day instead of learning his vocabulary he was wandering around and happened across a rocket. Curious, he made his way in. His eye was immediately attracted by a big red button on the control panel. Under it, written in bold letters was an unfamiliar word: DANGER. 'Danger?' he puzzled. 'Danger?' Not a Welsh word. So he pressed the button. The doors closed and before he could count to ten, he was propelled into space. The moral Miss Rees intended is clear: your life depends on your being able to read English. The unconscious moral – and the one by which I'm still fascinated – was that unfamiliar words lead to huge adventures. Little Tommy might have died a lonely death in space, but think of the wonders he must have seen before his oxygen ran out.

Before I had enough confidence to write in English I spent a lot of time translating my own Welsh poems. I must be one of the very few people to have been allowed into the Writing Division at Columbia University in New York on the basis of a batch of Welsh-language poems. I've been thinking about translation for a *long* time and it seems to me that being it's treated, unjustifiably, as a secondary process in literary life. I'm one of those who believes

that not only is translation possible, it's an essential element in
every nation's culture. Poetry isn't only what's lost in translation –
it's what's gained. In a culture the desire to translate is always a
sign of strength. Only rich cultures are hungry for news of the
outside world – paradoxically, voracity is a sign of plenitude. It's
only cultures who want their members to have a limited political
view that resist promiscuous translation and the absorption of out-
side influences. Totalitarian states don't like translators. Here I take
it that the whole point of translation is to introduce a new element
– of rhythm or thought – into a literary tradition. The point isn't
to produce a version so culturally smooth that nobody would ever
guess it was imported. There has to be something strange, novel
and fascinating either about the style or cast of mind of the new
piece.

Wilfred Owen took the Welsh half rhyme, the *proest*, and used
it in English. In this rhyme the consonants of the word stay the
same, while the vowels change, as in 'cat' and 'kit':

> It seemed that out of battle I escaped
> Down some profound dull tunnel, long since scooped
> Through granites which titanic wars had groined.
> Yet also there encumbered sleepers groaned...

Having rediscovered the *proest* in Owen I've now been using this
rhyme both in English and back in its native Welsh. But, filtered
through Owen's sensibility, it's not the same sound, it's been reviv-
ified and made vital again by translation. This is a form of stylistic
translation. But there's more to this question. Poets working in a
tradition are always "translating" the work of their predecessors
and moulding it to their modern-day needs. But what to translate?

One of my English poems takes as its starting point an old Welsh
folksong which is called 'Bugeilio'r Gwenith Gwyn' ('Herding the
White Wheat'). I put my own spin on the subject, of course, mak-
ing my wheat shepherd a reluctant, resentful servant. The rest of
the poem was suggested by a line in the *Oxford English Dictionary*
which happened to catch my eye:

> Cornelius Varro knows his husbandry
> and he maintains a flourishing estate:
> 'My mutes stand guard at the entrance gate.
> Vowels I lodge with my hired men,
> half-vowels sit by the cattle pen.
> Of course, I let the spirants work the field,
> as they're teaching the clover how to yield
> to consonantal chimings from the church'.
> But I'm uncouth and keep lip service back.

For I'm the one who herds his fields of wheat,
speaks softly till the stalks are white,
the ripe ears heavy. Then I sow my spite
and laugh to see how the rows stampede,
as I spread sedition with the highland wind
till they're wrecked and broken. Then he sends men round
and I watch in silence as they slowly reap
his yearly tribute from my grudging ground.

('The Bad Shepherd')

This smuggling of familiar material from one language into another seemed to me, on reflection, too easy a way of exploiting a Welsh subject-matter in English. I wanted to be a full English-language poet when I wrote in English and not just a translator of material which might not work in Welsh.

As with most figures essential to the well-being of a society, translators have always been regarded with suspicion. In diplomatic circles scare stories abound about situations like the mistranslation of 'La France demande que...' into the belligerent and inaccurate 'France demands that...' These testify to the power that traders in linguistic foreign currency are felt to have in our lives. Indeed, in the Judaeo-Christian tradition the very origin of translation is tied up with man's hubris. Genesis recounts the story of the inhabitants of Shinar who decided to build a tower 'with its top in the heavens' in order 'to make a name for ourselves'. This, of course, was the Tower of Babel. God's response to this pride was to 'confuse their language, so that they will not understand what they say to one another'. Australian aboriginal myths of linguistic origin, by contrast, don't have this idea of multiple languages and sin linked together. If linguistic variety is a punishment from God then, by extension, translators, attempting to repair the broken bowl of language, can be seen as priests trying to repair effects of an original linguistic sin. Our ambiguous feelings towards the idea of Esperanto, a universal language, shows how we regard the work of the translator as both deeply virtuous (healing the broken relationships between men of different cultures) but also as potentially blasphemous ('those whom God has pulled apart, let no man put together').

I would argue, however, that the translator – who's always struggling to find the *mot juste*, and fighting with the incompleteness of one language to convey ideas from another – actually knows more about our true condition linguistically than the happy monoglot who would never dream of touching the Danger button in a rocket. In this, bilingualism helps. You know that one language will only take you so far along the route of your experiential journey.

You know that at some time during your journey on the word bus the driver's going to call the last stop and you'll have to walk the rest of the way with your luggage, up the mountain in the growing gloom, towards the one light left on in the farmhouse ahead. We all reach that moment sooner or later, when language will just not take you any further in your experience. But having made frequent changes of vehicle before means that the sight of the bus departing noisily down the hill is nowhere near as shocking or desolating an event as it might be: indeed, it's even to be welcomed.

In this sense, being part of a dying culture is, paradoxically, of great value to a poet, if you're interested in ultimate questions about language and the nature of reality. It was Lenny Bruce who said that comedy's not just a matter of telling jokes: it's about telling the truth. Similarly, poetry isn't about being poetical, it's about telling things as they are. In Wales, we may soon be facing the end of a fertile coal seam of language. Having taken for granted the warmth of prehistoric forests and the patterns of ferns and insects in our buckets, our shovels will soon be hitting against useless shale. Some Welsh poets look to England, with its confident, viable culture – or even to America, which is even more so – with envy. But the truth is that this is always the situation of language in the face of eternity – the prospect of utter annihilation. Cultural success can only serve to disguise this. The challenge in all cases is to sing as true as possible a song out into the dark before that final extinction of shimmering consciousness, before the brightness falls from the air.

# FRED D'AGUIAR

Born in London in 1960 of Guyanese parents, Fred D'Aguiar grew up in Guyana and returned to London in 1972. His poetry collections, *Mama Dot* (1985), *Airy Hall* (1989) and *A Bill of Rights* (1998), reflect his interest in Caribbean folk tales and his matriarchal childhood; his novels include *Dear Future* (1996) and *Bloodlines* (2000), a verse novel. His work – as his poetics – engages critically with race, and he describes here how, for him, the writing of even the most intimate poem became 'the social act of a black male'. But just as there is a communal imperative in writing, poetry is also a place outside all such demands – a bodiless realm without colour or race; a place for the shedding of skin. He teaches at the University of Miami.

# Further Adventures in the Skin Trade
(2000)

All of my adolescence and early adult life my body determined my experience. The fact that I am black and male affected me at every level: social, economic, psychological and even imaginative going by my poems from that time. By contrast, my dreaming, thinking self, my internal life, that nebulous system of thoughts and dreams, thrived in a parallel universe of REM sleep and waking moments of quiet and stillness. Yet it seemed divorced from my daily struggle as a black man in British society and hardly influenced my everyday existence. I know that this disproportionate influence of my skin over my life is partly because of my location, London, and due, in part, to my time, from the mid-70s through the 80s, but the armoury of an analysis does not make it hurt any less. To become a poet in the London of the last quarter of the 20th century meant that my black and male body, rather than any romantic impulse towards love of utterance and the utterances of love, would drive my need to speak and write poems. Poetry, that art of the marvellous, of a simultaneous compression of language and an endless expansion of meaning would be born, not out of love of life, so much as a life without love. The event of the poem could never be predicated on a pretence of my hallowed individuality. Instead, my every word became the social act of a black male in his early 20s in a white majority culture.

To write a word or image, to make sense in sounds (or at least sound as if I was making sense!) I fooled myself into thinking that I was raceless and free. I wrote with the illusion of a privileged individuality, that is, in a spirit of imaginative laissez-faire, but functioned in spatial terms (my movement in and through a British landscape and cityscape) as a black youth. Born in London but not of London, writing in English but not of the English, British but under the rubric of a racial and cultural difference, my tongue forked, my skin bristled with the scales of my unlikeness. I became Hydra-headed, speaking from multiple selves to multiple constituencies. Each poem staged my insider-outsider stance. My romantic impulse locked horns with my social self. Whereas many poems began in the realm of race, and positively delighted in my black and separate status from Englishness (but within English and England) these same poems ended up in quite different territory, quickly shedding their black skins and urban setting, to become raceless and placeless, countrified and rarefied. Each poem, so it seemed, sought to reconcile the dialectic of politics and place with the poetics of mind and space. Each poem aimed for pure expression. I wanted my poems to be songs, to exemplify rhythm, to shed the social self and affirm nothing short of the soul.

Poetry is instruction rather than injunction. It teaches that there is no kernel or centre to race or skin. I literally lost myself in poetry during these times of riots by black youth in cities across England. While I stood shoulder to shoulder with black youths opposite police lines in Brixton, Lewisham and Southall (and, for a short spell, on unemployment lines for blacks as the country prospered) I dreamed up poems and became nothing but pure action in thought, pure energy in language. The words in a poem might be traced back to a particular social milieu or romantic impulse but they reached for far more when they tried to sing off the page. I was nothing during those creative moments strangely elevated out of chronological time, nothing but a chord, a note, a drumbeat, a heartbeat, a hip-swinging, finger-tapping rhythm. A tune, a breath, two unblinking eyes, a pulse in the thigh, blood in my ears, a fine tremor in my hands all seemed to work themselves into these creative moments making it clear to me that whatever was in my head was registered through my body. If each poem had to be honest then it was honesty with the realisation that there could be no single truth so much as the story of a kind of truth. And truth as a kind of story in a world of stories governed by the sensuous or at least a world where the argument is framed by the machinery of things perceived as "out there".

History played as big a role as society in the shaping of my poet's imagination. My first awareness of history was of my place in it as the descendant of slaves. In history, stories of blackness always limited the humanity of blacks to something less than whiteness. Slavery and poetry pulled in opposite directions since poetry could never be enslaved and a slave could never really remain a slave and be a poet, not if poetry meant liberation or at least a freedom of thought unhindered by any material circumstance even if born out of it. At the same time my imagination seemed historically aware. In other words, rather than catapulting my self into zero-gravity space free of history, I functioned best when locked into a particular historical dilemma. My imagination plunged into the history of its environment even as it sought to surface from it and leave it behind for a space not governed by any social or historical predicament. The historically aware imagination then is fostered by history but ultimately free of any loyalty to history. It is as if history were the parent that the imagination had to acknowledge every time as it fled to a place of its own making.

I remind myself that when I fell in love with reading and writing and listening to poetry I was not historically aware, I was flesh and bone and blood. I did not write as a reader nor did I read as a writer until much later in my reading and writing life. But history saved me even as it imprisoned me for a while. History gave me direction whereas before I became conscious of its pushes and pulls I was at the mercy of my impulses (most of them grounded in the romantic tradition). When I discovered that I was black in Britain and at the mercy of a hundred thousand negative images of blackness that I had to counter, an historical imagination gave me a purpose. If history were an engine for the imagination then coupled to it were two cars or twin gifts, the first was the wider community of black people and the second the loose fraternity of poetry (at least as a reading experience).

I am a poet who happens to be black and a black who happens to be a poet. My poetic sensibility may not be predicated on the colour of my skin, but the colour of my skin certainly generates my poetry. My awareness of a history of blackness originated from a set of negative reinforcements of my skin colour but these forces did not drive me to become a poet. Poetry of one sort or another would have happened anyway. What skin did and continues to do (because it is coupled to history I suppose) is shape the nature of the poetry. Skin is one of many registers of my presence in history. I am thankful for the edge and agenda conferred by my skin on my creative endeavours. But I shed my skin during the event of the reading and writing of poetry almost as frequently as I wear its mask or find that poetry filters through the lens or film of skin. Skin becomes colourless during lovemaking even as I delight in touch and sensation. If poetry is worth its salt then it must admit to two contradictory though not mutually exclusive loyalties, the need to be honest and the will towards pure individuality. Poetry is both communal and private. Language is shared but it behaves as if it could live without breathing and the chemistry of the mind. I want that next poem. To get it I'll shed my skin, I'll lose my name, pretend I have no history, be history's fool, become elemental, all of these, none of these.

# LAVINIA GREENLAW

Born in London in 1962, Lavinia Greenlaw has worked in publishing and arts administration and is now a freelance writer. She has published two collections of poems, *Night Photograph* (1993) and *A World Where News Travels Slowly* (1997), and her concerns for science and communication affect a world in flux, at once vulnerable to collapse but wondrous in its resistance. And so her poetry may delight in the bridge that defies gravity, and may equally take horror at the human price of scientific advance; but it is always driven, as she describes here, by 'making sense of how things work'. Lowell and Bishop are presences in her poetry, and it is the latter that Greenlaw turns to here to reflect a little light upon her own writing.

# Interior with Extension Cord
### (2000)

A poem creates an interior – Frost's 'strange barn' with its own laws and geometry, but laws and geometry all the same. What it contains is also interior; that is, fundamental, ordinarily ungraspable things here given shape. However far it may reach, a poem should be arranged so that once inside it, you can see everywhere at once. There should also be a door or window: a hint of the long view.

Elizabeth Bishop described her watercolours (collected in William Benson's *Exchanging Hats*) as 'Not Art, NOT AT ALL'. While skilful and delightful, they are less remarkable as paintings than as a vivid illustration of her poetics. 'Interior with Extension Cord' is a strange barn indeed, and I turn to it as a picture of how a poem might be built.

While 'not art', this picture is ebulliently artful. The white (clapboard?) walls and ceilings that take up most of the space are watery and only faintly striped. This tenuous structure is glued together by hard black lines that delineate the edges of the walls and door and act like arrows, directing the eye into the corner. Showing us how to see as she sees, what it is that interests her here, is more important to the poet than realism.

It's not just the composition that interests Bishop, but what it does to the eye. The ridiculously long extension cord is an even thicker black line tacked from the little lamp it serves, all the way up one wall and across the ceiling in the foreground, skewing the perspective. The lines of the floorboards reflect those of the ceiling, adding to the pull into the corner but stopping abruptly just before meeting the edge of the foreground, arrested by a couple of impatient horizontal strokes that align with the extension cord instead. This creates a frame within the picture like those found in 17th century Dutch interiors, reminding the viewer that what they see has been mediated and limited.

For me, the impulse to write a poem often comes from making sense of how things work. This might be a play of forces or a visual conundrum like that created here by the corner and the cord. Painting is another way to explore pattern, machinery and design, as Bishop did in her poetry all the time, turning the realignments of daybreak into the coupling of trains and switching of tracks. Her patience with exact detail is seen here in the four-legged stool with its twelve struts – the most solid object in the room. Bishop learnt a great deal about observation from Marianne Moore, of whom she said, 'If she speaks of a chair, you can practically sit on it when she has finished.' Moore may have been more elegant, but Bishop's wobbly stool is no mere prop.

Description on its own, however beautiful and precise, is not enough. There must be drama. In a Bishop poem, the landscape and furniture are part of the dramatic action and it is the same in this picture. That stool sits between a table and a doorway, accentuating human absence by indicating the two different directions in which someone who had been sitting on it might have gone. It is as austere and uncomfortable-looking as the room itself, adding to the air of transience created by those diluted walls; the bare floor; and the careless tacking not only of the extension cord but also of a couple of indiscernible paintings and a lopsided sign, to the walls. The table is an adapted ledge on which the lamp is precariously balanced. The sturdiest piece of furniture is a white cupboard which, though firmly outlined, sinks into wall, unsettling the picture's gravity and echoing Bishop's poem 'Love Lies Sleeping': 'As we lie down to sleep the world turns half away / through ninety dark degrees / the bureau lies on the wall'. This is also reminiscent of Vuillard, whom Bishop admired and whose interiors are similarly galvanised, in one case by his sister dissolving into the wallpaper.

The muted colours of the picture are as misleading as Bishop's modulated poetic tone. Beneath the smooth surface are extremes of mood and perspective: the black stool and white walls; the solid warmth of the yellow lamp; and the cord upsetting everything, more like a fuse leading to a bomb. It seems to me that the more coherent the surface, the more intensity it can contain, and that disturbance that takes some discerning is simply more interesting. But the skin of a poem must be taut enough for the reader to be able to trace what lies beneath it or it remains a cool surface. Bishop was expert at this balance, able to sustain excitement while remaining coherent and clear. I am still weighing it up.

Apart from Bishop's sweep across the floor and the things hung on the walls, there are other frames in the picture. A bulky rail on casters is included, but only its very edge. Instead of allowing the lines of the room to wander away, Bishop stops them with this abrupt vertical that directs the gaze up towards the source of the extension cord in the top left-hand corner. The sliver of wall you can see through the rail is almost like glass, making the thing into a mirror. I thought it was a mirror until I made out the boards behind it, a doubletake Bishop would insist on remaining part of the picture, as in 'Shadows, or are they shallows'; 'inverted and distorted. No. I mean / distorted and revealed'; 'It may be solid, may be hollow.'

There is also the doorway, heavily outlined and with no visible door. Beyond it is what might be a bush in flower or a heaped-up wilderness. Either way, this is certainly more than a garden. The faint dark wash behind is given scale by the thin line of sky that tops it. This is a mountain, faraway hills; in any case, the long view.

The excitement of this picture, of Bishop's poems, is in the open door and the extension cord: the distance one can travel and the doubletakes that make the journey so surprising. Above all, it has the dynamic perception Bishop enjoyed in Hopkins, 'the releasing, checking, timing and repeating of the movement of the mind.' Bishop encourages a poet to let slip and then set to, as she said to Miss Pierson, 'There is a mystery & a surprise and after that a great deal of hard work.' And as with the lucky unknown Miss Pierson, it makes a difference if you remember to enclose a stamp.

# KATHLEEN JAMIE

Kathleen Jamie was born in Renfrewshire, 1962 and studied philosophy at Edinburgh University. *Black Spiders* (1982) appeared when she was only 20, and was followed by *The Way We Live* (1987). *The Queen of Sheba* (1994) is a powerful work in which she takes the temperature of a Scotland-before-devolution. She has also collaborated on books with the poet Andrew Greig (*A Flame in Your Heart*, 1986) and photographer Sean Mayne Smith (*The Autonomous Region*, 1993). Her most recent collection, *Jizzen* (1999), is a tender and affecting exploration of motherhood, and confirms Jamie as is one of the most evocative lyrical voices now writing. In poetry we are seeking what she calls 'permission', a gradual accumulation of the authority that carries us from one new subject to another. Poetry is, in this sense, strictly moral; and the poem itself, 'an approach toward a truth'.

# Holding Fast – Truth and Change in Poetry
## (2000)

When we were girls, my friends and I played a game called 'Mother-May-I'. We played it in the lumpy tarmac lane out the back. 'Mother' would turn away, so she couldn't see the players' progress and favour one over another. Her task was to call instructions to the players, one by one. 'Linda!' She'd call over her shoulder, 'take three baby steps! Lorraine, take two giant-steps!' One by one we made our moves. However – and this was the point of the game – before we did so, we had to ask 'mother's' permission, even though we'd already had our instruction. Before moving, we had to call 'Mother-may-I?' If, in the urge to be first to cross the lane and tap 'mother' on the shoulder, we took our giant steps without asking permission, we'd quickly be called to rights by the others, and forbidden move at all. Furthermore, Mother could be capricious, and withhold permission. When we called 'Mother may I?' she might well say, 'No, you may not.'

I suppose our game played out the lurching progress we were making toward adulthood, but I'm reminded of it now because it seems to me that much of writing is about permission. I mean here the long process of becoming a poet of any authority. This process lasts a lifetime and over-arches the writing of individual poems.

Each development in our writing begins when we seek permission to approach it; to approach a new area of experience. We ask permission, that is, to blunder into a delicate place. We ask permission to assume "ownership", and appropriate to ourselves whatever it is our writing is moving toward. How much of history or nationship may we assume to ourselves? May we plunder the past? Reveal the secret histories of our lovers, and families? Be intellectual? Be a poet at all? It's a courtesy, which at times hardens into a moral question, this 'May I?'

Who grants permission? In our game it was 'mother', who was at once an authority figure and, of course, one of ourselves. When we write poetry, an exchange is operating between self and others. It does not feel as hard, as clear-cut as a dialectic; because the distinction between self and "other" is not sharp. If our poetry is engaged with, and received well by others, by readers and critics, their interest and engagement gives us the moral strength to permit ourselves to make further moves. Flattery is lovely, but I mean here something deeper than flattery or praise. I mean an interest which strengthens and reinforces what we are doing. (This, incidentally, makes nonsense of the idea that poetry is "private".) 'May I?' we ask, and grudgingly, perhaps, the answer comes. Yes. You may. A very few people will do, a few peers, a few friends is sufficient for this exchange to happen. We might say that poetry doesn't have mass readership, because it doesn't need it, and to hanker after it is to miss the point. Poetry is a place of engagement, rather than consumption.

In our game, by the accretion of permissions and consequent moves, we made our way toward the authority-figure, Mother, until eventually we tapped her on the shoulder. Symbolically, we became adults ourselves. As poets, something similar pertains. We accrue permissions, and consequently make poems, which in turn grant us permission to extend into new, scary areas. Through that we develop poetic authority.

Each poem individually does not require an inner "permission", but "permission" is required for the bigger breakthroughs which occur maybe once every few years, perhaps once a decade. "Permission" is an overcoming of doubts and fears. Once we feel it's granted, and we are ready to explore the new place, we may write as many poems as are there to be written. It starts off scary, and revelatory. When it becomes easy, the project is done.

Beneath that over-arching process of permission-seeking, there is the sticky business of writing individual poems. The getting-the-hands-dirty. To write a poem is also to undertake a process, but a shorter process, and different to a poet's life-work of growth.

To write a poem is to work with change, to deal with a shape-shifter. When we begin a new poem, we begin to engage with the ideas or material, to build up energy. Then suddenly, we're in there, writing it, bringing it through change, and a poem is what we have left of a process of change which has exhausted itself.

These lines are from the old Scottish ballad, 'Tam Linn':

> They'll turn me in your arms, lady
> Into an esk and adder,
> But hold me fast and fear me not
> I am your bairn's father.

> They'll turn me into a bear sae grim
> And then a lion bold
> But hold me fast and fear me not
> as ye shall love your child.

This ancient ballad tells how Janet won back her lover, Tam Linn, from the fairies, from the Otherworld. She did as she was instructed, and held fast onto Tam Linn as the fairies whipped him through these different forms. This is high shamanism, and I don't believe that writing a poem is shamanic, but we do likewise "win" a poem by bringing it through changes. The changes a poem undergoes are not so magic and wild as were Tam Linn's, of course, but the poem is only done when all its possible changes are complete. In the ballad, when all of the changes were gone through, what remained in Janet's arms was Tam Linn. When all the poem's possible changes are gone through, what remains on the page is the finished poem.

Some versions of 'Tam Linn' include an interesting line:

> But she held him fast, let him not go
> And cried aye 'Young Tamlin'

That is, Janet kept naming Tam Linn as the fairies turned him from newt to snake to lion to bear. Naming him. That is, she *kept applying language*, until the true shape of Tam Linn was attained.

Janet had one advantage over a poet – she knew what Tam Linn looked like. He was, after all, the father of her child. A poet doesn't know, when she starts work, what the finished poem will look like. She knows this much: that the finished poem will be alive, it may be gorgeous, but it will be static. Its changes are worked through. At that point she can let it go. It can go forth, even win praise and prizes. But, because to live in stasis is intolerable (hence the poets' reputation for dalliance, we externalise that inner restlessness) we begin the next process, which may, if we feel we are moving into a whole new area, require a permission which may or may not be granted, at least not for a while.

(Too much metaphor. I used to think poetry was more like religion than I do now. But they are like in this regard, if nothing else: we talk about both through metaphor.)

How does the meta-process, the seeking of permission to move into new and difficult areas, link into the repeated finite process of making poems? I think that they link through truth, but I tread warily, because I feel the word 'sacred' hovering around, and don't know quite what to do with it.

I believe this: just as much as sound and rhythm, what makes a poem is its relationship with truth. A poem is an approach toward a truth. Be it a discovered truth or a constructed one, a poem is an approach toward a truth. Truth is not exclusive to poetry, of course, but there is no poem which does not engage with truth.

Given that, when we ask the overarching 'May I?' perhaps we are seeking not permission, but admission. Admission to a place which cannot admit lies. We seek inner permission because we know that when we are writing in this new place, we will have to seek truths. The answer may come 'No' because we know, deep inside, we're not ready for this particular challenge, this deepening out. More often than not, though, I think that if the question is beginning to formulate itself, the direction is beginning to be mapped, the permission is ready to be granted.

A poem is an approach toward a truth. But poems can be funny, witty, quirky and sly. They can be mischievous, tricksterish. Their truths don't sound like the truths of the court-room or inquest. Does this, then, show us something about the nature of truth? Can we say there are many truths, or, rather, many aspects of Truth? That truth itself is a shape-shifter?

When Tam Linn changed through adder to lion, these things were not untruths, an adder-shape is true for an adder, after all. But an adder-shape is not true for Tam Linn. And to write a poem is to work with the language until, as near as we can get it, the true shape, the truest utterance of that poem, is arrived at. We write until the poem is perfect and worked out. (We say 'worked out' to mean solved, of a sum, and to mean exhausted, of a mine.)

Close to 'truth' lies 'moral'. (And 'sacred' – I still feel *scared* breathing down my neck.) It might be worth taking a look at moral, while we're here, because our idea of the moral needs to be revisited and refreshed. It's awful po-faced and hodden grey.

The overarching 'May I?' question is a surely a moral question. Have I the right? it asks. Have I the strength? Because this may cause hurt. Permission is granted on the understanding that we will seek the truths of the matter. Seeking truths must surely be a moral act. We ask a moral question, and begin then the moral act of making a poem. The poem we end up with may be a joke, a song, a piece of bare-faced cheek, but still our work is moral if we are working toward reaching a truth. (I wonder now, of course, if a poem could tell a lie.)

I want to say that the place we enter when we are writing a poem is a moral place, and furthermore, a democratic place. Open to all, if writing a poem is an attempt to reach a truth, if poetry is a method of approaching truths, and each of us with a human soul and 'a tongue in oor heids' can make an approach toward a truth, poetry is inherently democratic.

So. Poetry is a moral and democratic place where language concerns itself with truth. For sure, we make plenty of poor poetry – clumsy moves toward a banal truth – but that's okay. My father's house is an open house, and it has many mansions.

*I am indebted in this piece to Willa Muir's work on ballads.*

# DON PATERSON

Don Paterson was born in 1963 in Dundee, and left school to work as a musician. He lives in Edinburgh where he leads a double life as a writer and a professional musician in the jazz-folk band Lammas. *Nil Nil* (1993) was a prize-winning engagement with class politics and sexual obsession – an at times confrontational realisation of his comment that there are 'some grudges that have to be renewed annually'. His skilful blend of traditional and post-modern form has seen parallels drawn with the work of Paul Muldoon. But his second collection, *God's Gift to Women* (1997), winner of the T.S. Eliot Prize, saw a more spiritual writer emerging, and clearly marked him as one of the major talents of his generation. His versions of the Spanish poet, Antonio Machado, appeared as *The Eyes* in 1999. He is Poetry Editor at Picador.

# Aphorisms
## (2000)

Our poetic tautologies – those little sonnets and jingles of ours that seem to do no more than bite their tales – only appear redundant to those unpoetried individuals incapable of viewing the vertical axis: they see us return to the same point, but don't see the ascension in *pitch*.

\*

The reader may be witness to the miracle, but can never participate in it; poetry must remain a private transaction between the author and God. The true poem is no more than a spiritual courtesy, the act of returning a borrowed book.

\*

I always find myself drawing a thick black line down the gutter of my notebook...I suppose the presence of the abyss, however vestigial, prepares an excuse for all the absent felicities – as well as those monsters which occasionally claw their way up to the page...

\*

The insane enthusiasm of a nursery gardener who prunes his roses long before they flower, even the very buds...the brutal aesthetic of the bare branch and the thorn...to think what a vicious, perfect bloom this strain would immediately bring forth were we to simply *allow* it!

\*

If we expect our work to survive our death even by a single day, we should stop defending it now, that it might sooner learn its self-sufficiency.

*

To induce a horrific paralysis of boredom in the reader, in the compass of *one sentence*...

*

Every morning the writer should go to the window, look out and remind himself of this fact: aside from his own species, not one thing he sees – not one bird, tree or stone – has in its possession the name he gives it.

*

If I have any ambition as a poet it's to write *precisely* nothing; this can only be achieved by purifying the definition of the act until it becomes utterly distinct from that of not writing anything, or its antithesis, writing *more or less* nothing. To leave the page covered, and the silence intact...and then to *enforce* that silence in the reader's life for the duration of the poem...

*

Sleeping with your own muse is an almost unpardonable breach of male literary protocol; but to sleep with a friend's, and tell him about it, is to do him the greatest favour as an artist. In his blows he is already thanking you in his heart.

*

The tiny oeuvre is a courtesy to the reader and a bribe to posterity. A man or woman that had the modesty to write *these* words and no more might be immortalised for their discretion...

*

In all beautifully expressed tautologies there is a grain of gold that is surplus. This reliable alchemy applies to all arts that obey chryso-metric laws. Those, like philosophy, which obey *isometric* principles, always fall a grain short: they spiral down to a lower octave, not a higher one. The true poem picks up a real thread from the hem of the robe of the departing spirit, the glittering clew in the dark wood that one day will lead us back into the light. The true philosophy delineates the precise nature of its own failure; therefore, knowing the exact form of *deus absconditus*, we might recognise the godless trail when we stumble across it.

*

The language of the angels and of the blessed consists of a single verb, possessing an infinite number of tenses, moods and conjugations. In the language of the demons and the damned, every word is a part of speech entirely unrelated to any other, and this tongue is the subject of enforced study for those wretches who, under the scourges of the infernal grammarians, are condemned forever to the memorisation of vast and endless textbooks. The two languages are, of course, precisely the same – the only difference being that this knowledge is withheld from the latter party.

*

We should always remember that the better part of etymologies lie forever buried from sight. Words are locked coffins in which the corpses still lie breathing.

*

One of the deepest consolations afforded to the poet is the daily – no, continual – reflection that somewhere, right now, there is a man or woman of infinitely greater wit and intelligence making a complete buffoon of themselves as they labour over the composition of a simple couplet.

*

Poetry is the music of consciousness.

*

The first procedure of good style is the inversion of the form in which the idea occurred to the thinker.

*

Of all the arts, music is the most perfect and exacting; it allows no margin for error whatsoever. When we hear a note in our heads and attempt to replicate it with our voice, or at the piano, our nearest miss is the most disastrous choice we could have made; someone else will come along a hit a note a whole fifth out, with far less discordant consequences. In poetry, the near-synonym or the ugly chime jars only with those properly attuned to the medium, who perhaps already perceive it as a form of music, a form of vibration.

*

All critics write their reviews in the sincere belief that the author will read them. What a bliss to deny them this pleasure! Imagine – to write in a style unmoderated by criticism, simply because you had *never bother to read any*...only the badly reviewed, however, could be intoxicated by this idea...

*

All praise or damning only serves to interpolate the author – again – between the work and its source, and can only interfere with the abstract and inscrutable mechanism by which that work is delivered. Those who find praise an aid to their production will produce nothing of value; the source is impure, already turbid with self-hood. Burn your reviews, and warn your friends to give you no word of them.

*

The principal difference between the aphorism and the poem is that the aphorism states its conclusion first. It is a form without tension, and therefore simultaneously perfect and perfectly dispensable. There is no road, no tale, no desire.

*

Why does the reader so often assume that poetry should be written with emotion? Could they imagine anyone essaying a violin concerto or a sculpture, say, if their hands were shaking in fear, or their eyes misting over with love or grief?

*

To the man who has heard nothing but Mozart, everything else he subsequently hears puts him a little in mind of Mozart...Bad poetry critics often conceive of similarities that owe nothing to the work itself and everything to the paucity of examples they have to draw on.

*

As a compositional skill, music is easily superior to poetry in that it can be *exercised at will*; the composer is often detained in nothing more than the business of making a single large and subtle calculation – the emotion consequently registered by the listener having at no point in the process actually been *felt*. This is unthinkable in poetry, where Frost's law of 'no tears in the writer, no tears in the reader' still holds absolute sway; but more often than not – whatever the agonies or raptures of the poet – the reader is left dry-eyed and perfectly indifferent. But to have felt *nothing*, and *still devastate an audience*...that sensation is probably as close to divinity as we will get.

*

Art should always replace a yearning; a poem must take the shape of a woman, a man, a god, or a ghost, or else it's probably no poem at all...

*

The relief I took in reading a bad aphorist! I had begun to wonder if brevity was some kind of unassailable virtue in itself. Though perhaps the one-word poem is always brilliant.

*

A poem is a machine for remembering itself.

*

Poetry is the art of saying things once: or more precisely, understanding what that statement truly implies.

*

Translated verse is usually given away by the strenuous informality of its delivery. As if you had presented your passport and visa before anyone had asked for them: such behaviour only arouses suspicion.

*

The untarnishable brilliance of lost work...I remember a sequence of comic poems I completed when I was ten years old, and thought very highly of...then my horror when, a year later, I realised I had misplaced them. Even now, I still have the feeling they would have secured my reputation.

*

Poetic truth occurs at the point in the steady refinement of a form of words where they cease to be paraphrasable but have not yet become purely oracular. A definition also, perhaps, of the aphorism, the poem's talentless, tone-deaf brother.

# JOHN HARTLEY WILLIAMS

John Hartley Williams has taught English at the Free University of Berlin since 1976. He was born in 1944 in Cheshire, grew up in London, and attended the universities of Nottingham and London. *Hidden Identities* (1982) showed an affinity towards American Modernism, while his second book, *Bright River Yonder* (1987), chose the Wild West frontier for its backdrop, and included the Arvon International Prize-winning 'Ephraim Destiny's Perfectly Utter Darkness'. His subsequent works have a more European focus and are by turns erotic, comic, political and experimental, and include three collections, *Cornerless People* (1990), *Double* (1994) and *Canada* (1997), a prose/poem memoir *Ignoble Sentiments* (1995), and a translation (with Hilde Ottschofski) of the Romanian poet Marin Sorescu, *Censored Poems* (2000).

# A Manifesto

## (2000)

Extrilism is neither a theory nor a conviction. It is a fact. It is derived from the words: exile, extricate, extrapolate, inexplicable and ectoplasm.

You cannot adhere to a creed of extrilism, or profess it or even proselytise for it. You are, or you are not, an extrilist. Extrilism has nothing to do with Literature or Art or any other tumbril on its way to the gallows. Extrilism means being in the crowd watching the tumbrils pass and experiencing a sharp yet unidentifiable pain somewhere in your gut. Extrilism means pointing at the culprit en route for Tyburn and asking a neighbour without the slightest intention of irony: 'Why walk if you can ride?' If the extrilist, in order to express an overpowering sense of extrilism, puts pen or brush to paper or canvas and produces something that to the un-initiated resembles Literature or Art, this is an error. Extrilism's most sacred impulse is error.

The secret of extrilism, to which all extrilists are privy, is that it contains within itself the gleefulness of its own disappearance. As any extrilist can tell you, this is a serious bloody error. However as absence of worldly success is the criterion by which all extrilist productions are measured, the more gloriously this negative goal is attained, the more valued is the result.

Now to the most clearly identifiable characteristics of extrilist works.

Item:

1. Every extrilist poem must have the character of a fact which has been denied.

2. Denied factual character grows in proportion to the imaginary elements which constitute it.

3. Reversing one's horse repeatedly over bus drivers, for example.

4. No language may be used that has not been used before.

5. Extrilist verse will only be discovered on library shelves by bona fide students of oblivion.

6. Extrilists, like shamans, are apt to vanish suddenly. Never fear. They've obviously gone *somewhere*.

7. Extrilism is the science of that borderline area between arriving and disappearing.

8. Extrilist poetry releases an energy which is out of all proportion.

9. Out of all proportion to what, one may ask?

10. Extrilist procedures annihilate babble by reversing common sense.

11. The outcome is thus extremely practical and may be used safely in the home.

12. Only the entirely imagined is completely real.

## ACKNOWLEDGEMENTS
## & FURTHER READING

# I. Individual Authors

The statements by the following authors were written for *Strong Words* and are first published in this book: Simon Armitage, Eavan Boland, John Burnside, Ciaran Carson, David Constantine, Robert Crawford, Fred d'Aguiar, Michael Donaghy, Douglas Dunn, U.A. Fanthorpe, Elaine Feinstein, Lavinia Greenlaw, Selima Hill, Kathleen Jamie, Brendan Kennelly, John Kinsella, Medbh McGuckian, Sarah Maguire, Glyn Maxwell, Andrew Motion, Grace Nichols, Sean O'Brien, Bernard O'Donoghue, Don Paterson, Anne Stevenson, Hugo Williams and John Hartley Williams; and the interview with Derek Walcott is first published here.

The following statements are previously published, or originally published in a different form, as noted:

**Fleur Adcock:** 'Not Quite a Statement' is published here for the first time, but the full text of her 1989 lecture is in C.B. McCully (ed.), *The Poet's Voice and Craft* (Manchester: Carcanet, 1994).

**W.H. Auden:** 'The Virgin and the Dynamo' was first published in 1962. The complete version appears in Auden, *The Dyer's Hand and other essays* (London: Faber & Faber, 1963), 61-71. *See also* 'Reading' (3-12), 'Writing' (13-27), and 'The Poet and the City' (72-89), in Auden, *Dyer's Hand*; *also* Foreword to Auden, *The Collected Shorter Poems 1927-1957* (London: Faber & Faber, 1965), reprinted in Auden, *Collected Poems* (ed. Edward Mendelson), revised edition (London: Faber & Faber, 1991), xxv-xxvii.

**Amiri Baraka** (LeRoi Jones): 'How You Sound??' was first published in Donald Allen (ed.), *The New American Poetry 1945-1960* (New York: Grove, 1960), 424-25. *See also* 'Expressive Language' (373-77) and 'State/Meant' (382-83) in Donald Allen & Warren Tallman (eds.), *The Poetics of the New American Poetry* (New York: Grove, 1973).

**Elizabeth Bishop:** 'Letter to Miss Pierson' was first published in Bishop, *One Art: Selected Letters*, ed. Robert Giroux (London: Chatto & Windus, 1994), 595-96, copyright 1994 by Alice Helen Methfessel, reprinted here by permission of Farrar, Straus & Giroux. *See also* 'It All Depends', in John Ciardi (ed.), *Mid-Century American Poets* (New York: Twayne, 1950), 267. An extended interview with Bishop appears in Plimpton (ed.), *Women Writers at Work: the Paris Review interviews* (London: Harvill, 1999), 152-73; Bishop's prose is published as Bishop, *The Collected Prose*, ed. Robert Giroux (London: Chatto & Windus, 1984).

**Basil Bunting:** 'The Poet's Point of View' was first published in 1966. Reprinted here from *Three Essays*, ed. Richard Caddel (Durham: Basil Bunting Poetry Centre, 1994), 34-35.

**Hart Crane:** 'General Aims and Theories' was written in 1925 and first published in Philip Horton, *Hart Crane: The Life of an American Poet* (New York: W.W. Norton, 1937). Reprinted here from Crane, *The Complete Poems and Selected Letters and Prose*, ed. Brom Weber (New York: Liveright, 1966), 217-23; copyright © 1933, 1958, 1966 by Liveright Publishing Corporation; used by permission of Liveright Publishing Corporation. *See also* 'Modern Poetry', in Crane, *Complete Poems and Selected Letters and Prose*, 260-63.

**Robert Creeley:** 'To Define' was first published in *Nine American Poets* (Liverpool: Artisan, 1953). Reprinted here from Creeley, *Collected Essays* (Berkeley and Los Angeles: University of California, 1989), 473-74, copyright © 1989 the Regents of the University of California. *See also* 'A Note' (477-78), 'A Sense of Measure' (486-88), ' "Poems are a complex" ' (489-90) in Creeley, *Collected Essays*.

**E.E. Cummings:** 'Foreword to *is 5*' was first published in *is 5* (1926). Reprinted here from Cummings, *Complete Poems 1904-1962*, ed. George J. Firmage, by permission of W.W. Norton & Company: copyright © 1991 by the Trustees for the E.E. Cummings Trust and George James Firmage. *See also* 'A Poet's Advice to Students', in Cummings, *A Miscellany Revised*, ed. George J. Firmage (London: Peter Owen, 1966), 335; *also* 'since feeling is first', in Cummings, *Complete Poems*, 291.

**Keith Douglas:** ' "Poetry is like a man" ' was first published in a symposium 'On the Nature of Poetry', in *Augury: An Oxford Miscellany of Verse and Prose* (Oxford: OUP, 1940). Reprinted here from Douglas, *The Complete Poems*, ed. Desmond Graham, reissued with an introduction by Ted Hughes 1987 (Oxford: OUP, 1995; London: Faber & Faber, 2000), 123, by permission of Faber & Faber Ltd. *See also* ' "…Incidentally you say I fail as a poet" ', in Douglas, *Complete Poems*, 123-24.

**T.S. Eliot:** 'Tradition and the Individual Talent' was first published in *Egoist* (September and December 1919). Reprinted here from Eliot, *Selected Essays*, third edition (London: Faber & Faber, 1951), 13-22, by permission of Faber & Faber Ltd. *See also* 'Dante' in *Selected Prose*, 205-30 ('genuine poetry can communicate before it is understood'); *also* 'Conclusion' in Eliot, *The Use of Poetry and the Use of Criticism* (London: Faber & Faber, 1933), 143-56; *also* 'The Music of Poetry', in Eliot, *On Poetry and Poets* (London: Faber & Faber, 1957), 26-38.

**Robert Frost**: 'The Figure a Poem Makes' was first published in the 1939 edition of his *Collected Poems*, and is reprinted here from Frost, *The Poetry of Robert Frost*, ed. Edward Connery Lathem (London: Jonathan Cape, 1949). See also '[Sound of Sense]', Frost to John T. Bartlett, 4 July 1913 (79-81), and '[Sentence Sounds]', Frost to John T. Bartlett, 22 February 1914 (110-14) in Frost, *Selected Letters*, ed. Lawrence Thompson (New York: Holt, Rinehart and Winston, 1964).

**Allen Ginsberg**: ' "When the Mode of the Music Changes the Walls of the City Shake" ' was first published in *Second Coming*, 1/2 (July 1961) and is reprinted here from Ginsberg, *Deliberate Prose: Selected Essays 1952-1995*, ed. Bill Morgan (London: Penguin, 2000), 247-53. *See also* 'Notes to Howl and Other Poems' in Allen (ed.), *The New American Poetry 1945-1960* (New York: Grove, 1960), 414-18; a version of this appears as 'Notes Written on Finally Recording Howl' in Ginsberg, *Deliberate Prose*, 229-32. 'It occurs to me that I am America' from 'America', in Ginsberg, *Collected Poems 1947-1980* (London: Penguin, 1987), 147.

**W.S. Graham**: 'Notes on a Poetry of Release' was first published in *Poetry Scotland*, 3 (July 1946). Reprinted here from Graham, *The Nightfisherman: Selected Letters of W.S. Graham*, eds. Michael and Margaret Snow (Manchester: Carcanet, 1999), 379-83. *See also* Graham, 'A poet's interview with himself' (with Penelope Mortimer), *Observer Magazine*, 19 November 1978, 62-63.

**Robert Graves**: 'Observations on Poetry 1922-1925' was condensed by Graves in 1949 from his critical writings of 1922-26, and first published in Graves, *The Common Asphodel: Collected Essays on Poetry 1922-1949* (London: Hamish Hamilton, 1949). The complete version is available in Graves, *Collected Writings on Poetry*, ed. Paul O'Prey (Manchester: Carcanet, 1995), 3-15, from which the extract here is reprinted by permission of Carcanet Press Ltd. *See also* 'The Inner Ear', in Graves, *Collected Writings*, 548.

**Thom Gunn**: 'Writing a Poem' was first published in Dannie Abse (ed.), *Corgi Modern Poets in Focus: 5* (London: Corgi, 1973). Reprinted here from Gunn, *The Occasions of Poetry: Essays in Criticism and Autobiography* (London: Faber & Faber, 1982), 151-52, by permission of Faber & Faber Ltd. *See also* 'Ben Jonson' in Gunn, *Occasions of Poetry*, 106-17; *also* Gunn, *Shelf-Life* (London: Faber & Faber, 1993).

**Tony Harrison**: 'Poetry is all I write' was first published in Book Trust (in association with the British Council), *Contemporary Writers*, 1987, and reprinted here from Neil Astley (ed.), *Tony Harrison*, Bloodaxe Critical Anthologies: 1 (Newcastle upon Tyne: Bloodaxe, 1991), 9.

**Seamus Heaney**: 'Craft and Technique' is the author's own edit of 'Feeling into Words', first delivered as a lecture at the Royal Society of Literature, October 1974, and collected in Heaney, *Preoccupations: Selected Prose 1968-1978* (London: Faber & Faber, 1980), 41-60, published in this revised version here by permission of Faber & Faber Ltd. See also 'A poet at work' in Robson (ed.), *Corgi Modern Poets in Focus: 2* (London: Corgi, 1971), 101-02.

**Michael Hofmann**: ' "I happen to believe" ' is published in this form for the first time, and is a version of an article that previously appeared in *Poetry Book Society Bulletin*, 181 (Summer 1999), 5-6.

**Langston Hughes**: 'How to be a Bad Writer (In Ten Easy Lessons)' was first published in *Harlem Quarterly* (1949/50), and is reprinted here from Hughes, *The Langston Hughes Reader* (New York: George Braziller, 1958), 491-92. *See also* 'Jazz as Communication' in *Langston Hughes Reader*, 492-94; *also* Hughes, 'The Negro Artist and the Racial Mountain', *The Nation*, 23 June 1926 ('change through the force of his art...'), reprinted at http://www.thenation.com/.

**Ted Hughes**: 'Words and Experience' was first published in Hughes, *Poetry in the Making* (London: Faber & Faber, 1967), 118-24, reprinted here by permission of Faber & Faber Ltd. *See also* 'Context' in Hughes, *Winter Pollen: Occasional Prose*, ed. William Scammell (London: Faber & Faber, 1994), 1-3. (Heaney's comments in Haffenden (ed.), *Viewpoints: Poets in Conversation* (London: Faber & Faber, 1981), 73-74.)

**Randall Jarrell**: 'Answers to Questions' was first published in John Ciardi (ed.), *Mid-Century American Poets* (New York: Twayne, 1950), 182-84, and reprinted in *Jarrell, Kipling, Auden & Co.: Essays and Reviews 1935-1964* (New York: Farrar, Straus and Giroux, 1980), 170-71. *See also* 'The Obscurity of the Poet' in Jarrell, *Poetry and the Age* (New York: Noonday, 1972), 3-27.

**Patrick Kavanagh**: 'Self Portrait', was originally broadcast by Radio Telefis Eireann, 30 October 1962, and published as Kavanagh, *Self Portrait* (Dublin: Dolmen, 1964), second edition 1975, and reprinted in Kavanagh, *Collected Pruse* (London: MacGibbon and Kee, 1967), 13-22; reprinted here by permission of the Trustees of the Estate of the late Katherine B. Kavanagh, and through the Jonathan Williams Literary Agency. *See also* 'Signposts: A selection of aphorisms and observations' in Kavanagh, *Collected Pruse*, 25-30; *also* 'Author's Note' in Kavanagh, *Collected Poems* (London: MacGibbon and Kee, 1964), xiii-xiv.

**Philip Larkin**: 'Statement' was first published in D.J. Enright (ed.), *Poets of the 1950s* (Japan: Kenyusha, 1956). Reprinted here from Larkin, *Required Writing: Miscellaneous Pieces 1955-1982* (London: Faber & Faber, 1983), 79, by permission of Faber & Faber Ltd. *See also* 'The Pleasure Principle' and 'Writing Poems' in Larkin, *Required Writing*, 80-84.

**Tom Leonard**: 'From the Introduction to *Radical Renfrew*' is the author's own edit of his Introduction to Leonard (ed.), *Radical Renfrew* (Edinburgh: Canongate, 1989), xvii-xix.

**Denise Levertov**: ' "I believe poets are instruments" ' was first published in Allen (ed.), *The New American Poetry 1945-1960* (New York: Grove, 1960), 411-12. *See also* 'Some Notes on Organic Form' in Levertov, *The Poet in the World* (New York: New Directions, 1973), 7-13.

**Gwyneth Lewis**: 'Whose Coat is that Jacket? Whose Hat is that Cap? (The Art of Deep Translation)' is based on a talk given at Columbia University, New York, in October 1995. An extended version of this article was previously published in *Poetry Review*, 85/4, Winter 1995/96, 12-17.

**Audre Lorde**: 'Poetry Is Not a Luxury' was first published in *Chrysalis: A Magazine of Female Culture*, 3, 1977. Reprinted here from Lorde, *Sister Outsider: Essays and Speeches* (Freedom, CA.: Crossing, 1984), 36-39, by permission of the Crossing Press, Santa Cruz, CA, copyright 1984.

**Robert Lowell**: 'On "Skunk Hour" ' was first published in Anthony Ostroff (ed.), 'The Poet and His Critics III', *New World Writing*, 21, 1962, 155-59. Reprinted here from Lowell, *Collected Prose*, ed. Robert Giroux (London: Faber & Faber, 1987), 225-29, by permission of Faber & Faber Ltd.

**Hugh MacDiarmid**: 'A Theory of Scots Letters' was first published in C.M. Grieve (ed.), *The Scottish Chapbook*, 1/7-9 (February, March & April 1923). Reprinted here from Alan Riach (ed.), *Hugh MacDiarmid: Selected Prose* (Manchester: Carcanet, 1992), 17-33, by permission of Carcanet Press Ltd. *See also* 'Braid Scots', first published *The Scottish Nation*, 15 May and 23 June 1923 under the name of C.M. Grieve.

**Louis MacNeice**: 'A Statement' was first published in *New Verse*, 31/2 (Autumn 1938), 7. Reprinted here from MacNeice, *Selected Literary Criticism*, ed. Alan Heuser (Oxford: Clarendon, 1987), 98, by permission of David Higham Associates. *See also* 'Preface' (xxi) and 'Conclusion' (197-205) in MacNeice, *Modern Poetry: A Personal Essay* (Oxford: OUP, 1938).

**Marianne Moore:** ' "I tend to write in a patterned arrangement" ' was first published in William Rose Benét and Norman Holmes Pearson (eds.), *The Oxford Anthology of American Literature* (New York: OUP, 1938), 1319. Reprinted here from Moore, *Complete Prose*, ed. Patricia C. Willis (London: Faber & Faber, 1987), 644-45, by permission of Faber & Faber Ltd. *See also* 'Poetry as Expression', in Moore, *Complete Prose*, 657; *also* 'Poetry', in Moore, *Complete Poems* (New York: Macmillan, 1967), 36; *also* 'Some Answers to Questions posed by Howard Nemerov' in Nemerov (ed.), *Poets on Poetry* (New York: Basic Books, 1966), 8-16.

**Edwin Morgan:** 'Roof of Fireflies' first appeared in *Salt*, II (South Fremantle: Fremantle Arts Centre Press, Australia, 1999), 29-32.

**Paul Muldoon:** 'Go Figure' is the author's own edit of 'Getting Round: Notes Towards an Ars Poetica', delivered as the F.W. Bateson Memorial Lecture, February 1998, and first published in *Essays in Criticism*, XLVIII/2, April 1998, 107-28.

**Les Murray:** 'The Instrument' was first published in Murray, *Conscious and Verbal* (Manchester: Carcanet, 1999), 16-17.

**Frank O'Hara:** 'Personism: A Manifesto' was first published in *Yugen*, 7, 1961 (date of composition 3 September 1959). Reprinted here from O'Hara, *Selected Poems*, ed. Donald Allen (New York: Vintage, 1974), xiii-xiv. *See also* ' "I am mainly preoccupied with the world as I experience it" ', in Allen (ed.), *The New American Poetry 1945-1960* (New York: Grove, 1960), 419-20.

**Charles Olson:** 'Projective Verse' was first published in *Poetry New York*, 3, 1950. The complete version is reprinted in Olson, *Collected Prose*, ed. Donald Allen and Benjamin Friedlander (Berkeley & Los Angeles: University of California Press, 1997), 239-49. *See also* 'Letter to Elaine Feinstein', in Olson, *Collected Prose*, 250-52.

**Tom Paulin:** 'Tracking *The Wind Dog*' is the author's own edit of his Introduction to Paulin (ed.) *The Faber Book of Vernacular Verse* (London: Faber & Faber, 1990), 260-62.

**Sylvia Plath:** 'A Comparison' was first broadcast on the BBC's *The World of Books*, July 1962, and first published in *The Listener*, July 1977. Reprinted here from Plath, *Johnny Panic and the Bible of Dreams: and Other Prose Writings*, second edition (London: Faber & Faber, 1979), 56-58, by permission of Faber & Faber Ltd. *See also* 'Context', in Plath, *Johnny Panic and the Bible of Dreams*, 92-93; *also* interview in Orr (ed.), *The Poet Speaks* (London: Routledge and Kegan Paul, 1966), 167-72.

**Ezra Pound**: 'A Retrospect' was a group of statements which first appeared under this title in *Pavannes and Divisions* in 1918; 'A Few Don'ts by an Imagiste', 'Language', and 'Rhythm and Rhyme' were first published from 'Imagisme' in *Poetry*, I (March 1913), 6. The complete version of 'A Retrospect' is published in Pound, *Literary Essays*, ed. T.S. Eliot (London: Faber & Faber, 1954), 3-14; the extract here is reprinted by permission of Faber & Faber Ltd, and the inserted Sappho translation from *Sappho: Poems & Fragments*, translated by Josephine Balmer (1992), by permission of Bloodaxe Books Ltd. *See also* Pound, *ABC of Reading* (New York: New Directions, 1960), especially '...news that stays news' and '...anyone wanting to know about poetry', 29-31; *also* 'Treatise on Metre', in Allen and Tallman (eds.), *Poetics of the New American Poetry* (New York: Grove, 1973), 61-68; *also* Pound, *Selected Letters 1907-1941*, ed. D.D. Paige (London: Faber & Faber, 1950), especially Pound to William Carlos Williams, 21 October 1908, and Pound to Harriet Monroe, January 1915; *also* Pound, *A Critical Anthology*, ed. J.P. Sullivan (Harmondsworth: Penguin, 1970).

**Craig Raine**: 'Babylonish Dialects' was first published in *Poetry Review*, 74/2 (June 1984), 30-32. Reprinted here from *Haydn and the Valve Trumpet* (London: Picador, 2000).

**Adrienne Rich**: 'Poetry and Experience: Statement at a Poetry Reading' was first published in Robert B. Shaw (ed.), *American Poetry Since 1960* (Cheadle: Carcanet, 1973), 132-33. Reprinted here from Rich, *Adrienne Rich's Poetry: Texts of the Poems, The Poet on Her Work, Reviews and Criticism*, ed. Barbara Charlesworth Gelpi & Albert Gelpi (New York: W.W. Norton, 1975), 89. *See also* 'To invent what we desire', in Rich, *What Is Found There: Notebooks on Poetry and Politics* (New York: W.W. Norton, 1993), 214-16.

**Stevie Smith**: 'My Muse' was first published in *X: A Quarterly Review*, March 1960. Reprinted here from Smith, *Me Again: Uncollected Writings*, ed. Jack Barbera & William McBrien (London: Virago, 1981), 125-26, by permission of the James MacGibbon Estate. *See also* 'What Poems are Made Of', in Smith, *Me Again*, 127-29.

**Gertrude Stein**: 'Explaining "a rose is a rose is a rose"' was Stein's response to one of her seminar students at the University of Chicago, 1935, and was first published in Thornton Wilder's Introduction to Stein, *Four in America* (New Haven: Yale UP, 1947). Reprinted here from Stein, *Look at Me Now and Here I Am: Writings and Lectures 1909-1945*, ed. Patricia Meyerowitz

(London: Peter Owen, 1967), 7. *See also* 'Poetry and Grammar', in Stein, *Look at Me Now and Here I Am*, 125-47.

**Wallace Stevens:** 'Adagia', from Stevens's notebooks, is thought to have been written between 1934 and 1940, with different drafts appearing in the 1957 (ed. Morse) and 1990 (ed. Bates) editions of *Opus Posthumous.* The longest complete version appears in Stevens, *Opus Posthumous*, ed. Milton J. Bates, revised edition (London: Faber & Faber, 1990), 184-202; the extract here is reprinted by permission of Faber & Faber Ltd. *See also* 'A Note on Poetry', *Opus Posthumous* (1990), 240; *also* 'The Noble Rider and the Sound of Words', in Stevens, *The Necessary Angel: Essays on Reality and the Imagination* (London: Faber & Faber, 1960), 1-36.

**Dylan Thomas:** 'Notes on the Art of Poetry' was first published in *Texas Quarterly*, 4/4 (Winter 1961), 45-53, as a reply to five questions asked him by a research student in the summer of 1951. The complete version is reprinted in Thomas, *Early Prose Writings*, ed. Walford Davis (London: Dent & Sons, 1971), 154-60.

**C.K. Williams:** 'Contexts: An Essay on Intentions' was first published in William Heyen (ed.), *The Generation of 2000: Contemporary American Poets* (Princeton: Ontario Review Press, 1983); reprinted here from C.K. Williams, *Poetry and Consciousness* (Ann Arbor: University of Michigan Press, 1998).

**William Carlos Williams:** 'On Measure – Statement for Cid Corman' was first published in *Origin* (1954). Reprinted here from *Selected Essays of William Carlos Williams* (New York: Random House, 1954), 337-40, by permission of New Directions Publishing Corporation. *See also* 'The Poem as a Field of Action', *Selected Essays*, 280-91; *also* 'A New Measure', WCW to Richard Eberhart, 23 May 1954, in Williams, *Selected Letters*, ed. John C. Thirlwall (New York: Ivan Obolensky, 1957), 325-27; *also* Stevens, *I Wanted to Write a Poem* (London: Cape, 1967).

**W.B. Yeats:** 'A General Introduction for my Work', written in 1937, was first published in full in Yeats, *Essays and Introductions* (New York: Macmillan, 1961), 509-25. *See also* 'Magic' (28-52), and 'The Symbolism of Poetry' (153-64), in Yeats, *Essays and Introductions.*

**Louis Zukofsky:** 'A Statement for Poetry' was written in 1925 and first collected in Zukofsky, *Prepositions: The Collected Critical Essays of Louis Zukofsky* (London: Rapp and Carroll), 27-31.

Permissions requests relating to individual manifestos should be sent to the copyright holders listed above, and to the authors in the case of statements first published in *Strong Words*.

# II. Anthologies

Dannie Abse (ed.), *Corgi Modern Poets in Focus 1* (London: Corgi, 1971). A five-volume series in which poets offer short introductions to a selection of their work: Volume I features statements by Dunn, (Ted) Hughes, (Herbert) Williams and (David) Wright. *See also* Robson, *Corgi Modern Poets in Focus: 2* and *4*.

—— (ed.), *Corgi Modern Poets in Focus: 3* (London: Corgi, 1971). Statements by Conn, Graves, (Alastair) Reid and Stuart.

—— (ed.), *Corgi Modern Poets in Focus: 5* (London: Corgi, 1973). Statements by Adcock, Gunn, Ormond, Pound and Spencer.

Donald M. Allen (ed.), *The New American Poetry 1945-1960* (New York: Grove, 1960). A landmark anthology of Black Mountain, San Francisco, Beat, and New York writers which offered a radical alternative to the New England canon of poets, and which featured 'Statements on Poetics' from Creeley, Duncan, Ferlinghetti, Ginsberg, Jones, Kerouac, Levertov, McClure, O'Hara, Olson, Schuyler, Snyder, Spicer, Whalen and Wieners.

Donald M. Allen & Warren Tallman (eds.), *Poetics of the New American Poetry* (New York: Grove, 1973). An anthology dedicated to the statement on poetry, featuring Blaser, Crane, Creeley, H.D., Dorn, Duncan, Fenollosa, Ferlinghetti, Ginsberg, Jones, Kandel, Lawrence, Levertov, Lorca, McClure, Mac Low, O'Hara, Olson, Pound, Snyder, Spicer, Stein, Whalen, Whitman, Wieners and (William Carlos) Williams.

Neil Astley (ed.), *New Blood* (Newcastle upon Tyne: Bloodaxe, 1999). Anthology of 38 poets from Britain and Ireland who published their first collections during the 1990s, each selection introduced by the poet, including Dooley, Duhig, Herbert, Kay, Kinsella, Knight, (Gwyneth) Lewis and Stainer.

Jonathan Barker (ed.), *Thirty Years of the Poetry Book Society: 1956-1986* (London: Hutchinson, 1988). An anthology of poems by Poetry Book Society selections, including comments on their own PBS 'Choices' by Barker, Betjeman, Dunn, (Roy) Fuller, Graves, Gunn, Heaney, Larkin, MacNeice, Mahon, Porter, Raine, Redgrove and (R.S.) Thomas. *See also* White, *Poetry Book Society*.

William Rose Benét & Norman Holmes Pearson (eds.), *The Oxford Anthology of American Literature* (New York: OUP, 1938). A vast anthology that includes comments and introductions by a number of writers on their own work.

British Broadcasting Corporation, *Writers on Themselves* (London: BBC, 1964). Includes (Ted) Hughes on 'The Rock' and Plath on 'Ocean 1212-W'.

Sharon Bryan (ed.), *Where We Stand: Women Poets on Literary Tradition* (New York: W.W. Norton, 1993). Anne Stevenson and Eavan Boland contribute to a largely American cast.

Tracy Chevalier (ed.), *Contemporary Poets*, 5th edition (Chicago/London: St James Press, 1991). Huge bibliography of English-language poets, with short essays by the poets on their work, followed by critical comment.

Jeni Couzyn (ed.), *The Bloodaxe Book of Contemporary Women Poets: Eleven British Writers* (Newcastle upon Tyne: Bloodaxe, 1985). A poetry anthology with generous introductions on their own work by Adcock, Couzyn, Fainlight, Feinstein, Jennings, Joseph, Levertov, Plath, Raine, Smith and Stevenson.

Tony Curtis (ed.), *How Poets Work* (Bridgend: Seren, 1996). Nine poets describe how they write, illustrating their essays with poem drafts: Abse, Armitage, Clarke, Dunmore, Feaver, Ferlinghetti, Longley, Paterson and Stevenson.

D.J. Enright (ed.), *Poets of the 1950s: An Anthology of New English Verse* (Tokyo: Kenkyusha, 1955). An anthology which includes an introduction to their own selection from Amis, Conquest, Davie, Enright, Holloway, Jennings, Larkin and Wain.

Gary Geddes (ed.), *Twentieth Century Poetry and Poetics*, 4th edition (Toronto: OUP, 1996). A substantial anthology with a North American slant, which includes statements by Atwood, Auden, Bly, Boland, Creeley, Crozier, Cummings, Eliot, Frost, Ginsberg, Heaney, (Ted) Hughes, Levertov, Levine, Lowell, McKay, Marlatt, Nichol, Olson, Plath, Pound, Purdy, Rich, Roethke, Snyder, Stevens, (Dylan) Thomas, Webb, (William Carlos) Williams and Yeats.

William Heyen (ed.), *The Generation of 2000: Contemporary American Poets* (Princeton: Ontario Review Press, 1983). Poems with prose introductions by 31 American poets including Gluck, Strand, (C.K.) Williams and (Charles) Wright.

Paul Hoover (ed.), *Postmodern American Poetry: A Norton Anthology* (New York: W.W. Norton, 1994). An anthology which attempts to account for Avant Garde since Allen, featuring statements by Andrews, Baraka, Bernstein, Cage, Coolidge, Creeley, Cruz, Duncan, Ginsberg, Hejinian, Howe, Levertov, Mackey, Mayer, O'Hara, Olson, Rothenberg and Silliman.

David Hopkins (ed.), *The Routledge Anthology of Poets on Poets: Poetic Responses to English Poetry from Chaucer to Yeats* (London: Routledge, 1994). A collection of writings by poets on their peers, with a selection of statements on their own work.

Judith Kinsman (ed.), *Six Women Poets* (Oxford: OUP, 1992). An anthology with introductions to their own work by Adcock, Clarke, Hill, Lochhead, Nichols and Rumens.

C.B. McCully (ed.), *The Poet's Voice and Craft* (Manchester: Carcanet, 1994). A collection of papers on poetic technique delivered by Adcock, Brackenbury, Davie, Dunn, Lindop, Morgan, Scupham, Sisson, (Iain Crichton) Smith, Stevenson, Tomlinson, Wainwright and (Robert) Wells.

E.A. Markham (ed.), *Hinterland: Caribbean Poetry from the West Indies and Britain* (Newcastle upon Tyne: Bloodaxe, 1989). An anthology of 14 writers which includes interviews and comments from the poets.

Graham Martin & P.N. Furbank (eds.), *Twentieth Century Poetry: Critical Essays and Documents* (Milton Keynes: Open University, 1975). A collection of statements and commentaries by poets and critics, including Auden, Eliot, Pound, Yeats and others.

Robert Neal (ed.), *Writers on Writing: An Anthology* (Auckland: OUP, 1992). A collection of comments, introductions, excerpts, and poems from Aristotle to Eliot.

Charles Norman (ed.), *Poets on Poetry* (New York: Free Press, 1962). A look at the "theories" of 16 English and American writers from Sidney to Cummings.

Carl R. Proffer (ed.), *Modern Russian Poets on Poetry* (Ann Arbor: Ardis, 1976). Statements by a number of Russian poets including Mayakovsky, Pasternak and Tsvetaeva.

Denise Riley (ed.), *Poets on Writing: Britain 1970-1992* (London: Macmillan, 1992). A collection of essays including contributions by (Douglas) Oliver and (Roy) Fisher.

Jeremy Robson (ed.), *Corgi Modern Poets in Focus: 2* (London: Corgi, 1971). Statements by (Thomas) Blackburn, Heaney, Meredith, Larkin and Owen.

—— (ed.), *Corgi Modern Poets in Focus: 4* (London: Corgi, 1971). Statements by Abse, Harrison, (Daniel) Hoffman and Scannell.

Robert H. Ross & William E. Stafford (eds.), *Poems and Perspectives* (Glenview, Illinois: Scott, Foresman and Company, 1971). A generous selection of critical writings by poets from Plato to the modern American academy.

James Scully (ed.), *Modern Poets on Modern Poetry* (London: Collins, 1966). A collection of statements from the first half of the 20th century, featuring: Auden, Crane, Cummings, Eliot, Frost, Hopkins, (David) Jones, Lowell, Moore, Olson, Pound, Ransom, Stevens, (Dylan) Thomas, (William Carlos) Williams and Yeats.

Geoffrey Summerfield (ed.), *Worlds: Seven Modern Poets* (Harmondsworth: Penguin, 1974). An anthology of poems with introductions to their own work by Causley, Gunn, Heaney, (Ted) Hughes, MacCaig, Mitchell and Morgan.

Eric W. White (ed.), *Poetry Book Society: The First Twenty-Five Years* (London: PBS, 1979). A selection of comments by Poetry Book Society selections, including Dunn, Eliot, Graves, Heaney, (Geoffrey) Hill, Larkin, Raine and Roethke.

## III. Interviews & Miscellaneous Comments

Andy Brown (ed.), *Binary Myths 1: conversations with contemporary poets* (Exeter: Stride, 1998). Interviews conducted by letter with 10 poets, including Bergvall, Burnside, Donaghy and Maguire.

—— (ed.), *Binary Myths 2: correspondences with poet-editors* (Exeter: Stride, 1999). Sequel book of postal interviews with 14 poet-editors, including Allnutt, Astley, France, (John) Kinsella, Morley, Paterson and Rees-Jones.

Robert Crawford, Henry Hart, David Kinloch & Richard Price (eds.), *Talking Verse: Interviews with Poets* (St Andrews & Williamsburg: Verse, 1995). A rich collection of interviews with 26 contemporary poets, including Armitage, Brodsky, Harrison, O'Brien and Paterson.

John Haffenden (ed.), *Viewpoints: Poets in Conversation* (London: Faber & Faber, 1981). Ten poets of the period interviewed.

Peter Orr (ed.), *The Poet Speaks: Interviews with contemporary poets conducted by Hilary Morrish, Peter Orr, John Press & Ian Scott-Kilvert* (London: Routledge and Kegan Paul, 1966). Interviews with 45 poets from the early 1960s.

George Plimpton (ed.), *Writers at Work: the Paris Review Interviews*, various editions – notably, *Women Writers at Work: the Paris Review Interviews* (London: Harvill, 1999). Features Angelou, Beauvoir, Bishop, Didion, Gordimer, McCarthy, Moore, Morrison, Oates, Parker, Porter, Sexton, Sontag, Travers, Welty and West.

Susan Sellers (ed.), *Delighting the Heart: A Notebook by Women Writers* (London: The Women's Press, 1989). Includes contributions from McGuckian.

Claudia Tate (ed.), *Black Women Writers at Work* (Harpenden: Oldcastle, 1985). Including comments by Angelou and Lorde.

Clive Wilmer (ed.), *Poets Talking: 'Poet of the Month' Interviews from BBC Radio 3* (Manchester: Carcanet, 1994). 21 poets, including Fenton, Gunn, Harrison, Heaney and (Ted) Hughes.

Rebecca E. Wilson & Gillean Somerville-Arjat (eds.), *Sleeping with*

*Monsters: Conversations with Scottish and Irish Women Poets* (Edinburgh: Polygon, 1990). Interviews with Boland, Jamie, Kay, Lochhead, McGuckian, Ní Dhomhnaill and Sulter.

# IV. Select Critical Guides (General)

Neil Corcoran, *English Poetry since 1940* (London & New York, Longman, 1993). The best critical guide to postwar British and Irish poetry, although its coverage stops around the 1980s.

Richard Gray, *American Poetry of the Twentieth Century* (London & New York: Longman, 1990). An outstanding account of America's 20th century, beginning with Whitman's legacy and concluding with the Beats.

Ian Hamilton (ed.), *The Oxford Companion to Twentieth-Century Poetry* (Oxford: OUP, 1994). A useful though slightly canon-making reference book, in which over 200 contributors offer a brief account of 1500 20th-century poets.

David Kennedy, *New Relations: The Refashioning of British Poetry 1980-94* (Bridgend: Seren, 1996). An interesting if fashionable account of contemporary poetry, taking-up where Corcoran leaves off albeit with a more cultural studies twist.

Sean O'Brien, *The Deregulated Muse: Essays on Contemporary British & Irish Poetry* (Newcastle upon Tyne: Bloodaxe, 1998). The leading account of contemporary poetry by a contemporary poet, from Larkin up to the 1990s.

Deryn Rees-Jones, *Consorting with Angels: Modern Women Poets* (Tarset: Bloodaxe, 2003). Pioneering study of formal and thematic experimentation through three generations of 20th century British and American women poets.

*With thanks to Sarah and Frances for their help and support.*

# INDEX

Bold face figures indicate writings by the author concerned

# EDNA LONGLEY
# Poetry & Posterity

Edna Longley's latest collection of critical essays marks a move back from Irish culture and politics to poetry itself as the critic's central concern. She considers how poets are read and received at different times and in different contexts, by academics as well as by a wider readership, and from Irish, English and American viewpoints. But her interest in the reception of poetry is still very much influenced by debates about literature and politics in a Northern Ireland context, and in the book's final essay she relates poetry to the "peace process".

In two of these essays, *The Poetics of Celt and Saxon* and *Pastoral Theologies*, she has some fun with mutual stereotypes (the Hughes or Heaney figure), and with English misreadings of Irish poetry and its cultural and intellectual environment, and Irish poets' frequent complicity in this situation. In other essays she discusses Edward Thomas and eco-centrism, the criticism of Louis MacNeice and Tom Paulin, and the poetry of Larkin and Auden. *Poetry & Posterity* follows Edna Longley's recently reissued *Poetry in the Wars*, her classic work on Ireland, poetry and war, and her much celebrated book, *The Living Stream: Literature & Revisionism in Ireland*:

'Unlike many books on modern poetry, this one has a powerful, disruptive case to make and a genuine *raison d'être*... a fiercely unrelenting and implacable critical intelligence at work'
– NEIL CORCORAN, *TLS*

'Combative, rigorously argued, passionate essays aimed at saving poetry from the politicians' – JOHN BANVILLE, *Sunday Independent*

| Paperback: | ISBN 1 85224 435 6 | £10.95 | 352 pages |
| Hardback: | ISBN 1 85224 434 8 | £25.00 | |

## Also available by Edna Longley from Bloodaxe:

*Poetry in the Wars:* A classic work on Ireland, poetry and war, with essays on Yeats, MacNeice, Frost, Edward Thomas, Keith Douglas, Heaney, Larkin, Mahon and Muldoon. 272 pages, £9.95 paper, 0 906427 99 1.

*The Living Stream: Literature & Revisionism in Ireland:* Longley investigates the links between Irish literature, culture and politics. Questioning the fixed purposes of both nationalism and unionism, she shows in particular where Northern Irish writing fits into this process of change. 304 pages, £10.95 paper, 1 85224 217 5; £25 cloth, 1 85224 216 7.

# THE Bloodaxe Book OF
# 20TH CENTURY POETRY

### edited by EDNA LONGLEY

This epoch-marking anthology presents a map of poetry from Britain and Ireland which readers can follow. You will not get lost here as in other anthologies – with their vast lists of poets summoned up to serve a critic's argument or to illustrate a journalistic overview. Instead, Edna Longley shows you the key poets of the century, and through interlinking commentary points up the connections between them as well as their relationship with the continuing poetic traditions of these islands.

Edna Longley draws the poetic line of the century not through culture-defining groups but through the work of the most significant poets of our time. Because her guiding principle is aesthetic precision, the poems themselves answer to their circumstances. Readers will find this book exciting and risk-taking not because her selections are surprising but because of the intensity and critical rigour of her focus, and because the poems themselves are so good.

This is a vital anthology because the selection is so pared down. Edna Longley has omitted showy, noisy, ephemeral writers who drown out their contemporaries but leave later or wiser readers unimpressed. Similarly there is no place here for the poet as entertainer, cultural spokesman, feminist mythmaker or political commentator.

While anthologies survive, the idea of poetic tradition survives. An anthology as rich as Edna Longley's houses intricate conversations between poets and between poems, between the living and the dead, between the present and the future. It is a book which will enrich the reader's experience and understanding of modern poetry.

EDNA LONGLEY is Professor of English at Queen's University, Belfast. Her publications include two editions of Edward Thomas's poetry and prose, and four critical books, *Louis MacNeice: A Study* (1988) from Faber, and *Poetry in the Wars* (1986), *The Living Stream* (1994) and *Poetry & Posterity* (2000) from Bloodaxe.

Paperback:      ISBN 1 85224 514 X      368 pages      £10.95

# THE Bloodaxe Book OF
# POETRY QUOTATIONS

### *edited by* DENNIS O'DRISCOLL

What is a poem? What can it do? How does a poet know when a poem is finished? Can poetry be taught? How can we tell if a poem is any good? What is it like to share the breakfast table with a poet? How political should a poem be? Are there actually "shoulds" and "should nots" in poetry?

Through quotations which are themselves as pithy and memorable as good poetry, hundreds of poetry readers, poetry practitioners and poetry sceptics have their say in this rumbustious and instructive book. Their comments are arranged by subject-matter and juxtaposed to allow sparks to fly – if one poet swears black, another is sure to swear white; and their viewpoints are encapsulated in terse and trenchant language.

Offering fascinating insights into the mindsets and dress codes of poets, their lusts and lives, hates and loves, as well as taking readers to the heart of the creative process itself, *The Bloodaxe Book of Poetry Quotations* is an ideal book for teachers, students, reading groups, workshops and anyone interested in poetry – whether as casual readers, seasoned writers, curious onlookers or aspiring practitioners.

Books about poetry are rarely as entertaining or rewarding as this: an entirely original compilation, drawing exclusively on remarks made over the past 20 years. With its wealth of contemporary maxims, witticisms and jibes, it provides a definitive snapshot of the current state of poetry – the art defined here by Seamus Heaney as 'language in orbit'.

**Dennis O'Driscoll** has published seven books of poetry, including *New & Selected Poems* (Anvil Press, 2004), a Poetry Book Society Special Commendation. A selection of his essays and reviews, *Troubled Thoughts, Majestic Dreams* (Gallery Press), appeared in 2001. Among his awards are a Lannan Literary Award in 1999, the 2005 E.M. Forster Award of the American Academy of Arts and Letters and the 2006 O'Shaughnessy Award for Poetry. He works as a civil servant in Dublin Castle.

Paperback:     ISBN 1 85224 744 4     256 pages     £9.95